I0438569

A Portrait of a School: Coeducation at Andover

By Kathleen M. Dalton

A Report on Research conducted by the
Ten Year Committee on Coeducation,
chaired by Marion Finbury

toExcel
San Jose New York Lincoln Shanghai

**A Portrait of a School
Coeducation at Andover**

All Rights Reserved. Copyright ©1986, 1999
Phillips Academy

No part of this book may be reproduced or transmitted in any form
or by any means, graphic, electronic, or mechanical,
including photocopying, recording, taping,
or by any information storage or retrieval system,
without the permission in writing from the publisher.

Published by toExcel
by arrangement with Phillips Academy

For information address:
toExcel
165 West 95th Street, Suite B-N
New York, NY 10025
www.toExcel.com

ISBN: 1-58348-296-2

LCCN: 99-62695

Printed in the United States of America

Contents

PREFACE

Earthquakes are often followed by aftershocks and tidal waves—the land and the ocean absorb the big jolt at once but the effects of the quake reverberate for some time. After an earthquake has hit, it is hard to tell how long it will take for the plates of earth to settle into a newly stable status quo.

In one sense the earthquake we are studying in this book—the equity earthquake—is still sending aftershocks throughout American education. It began as a series of social changes that gained momentum around the time of the passage of the 1964 Civil Rights Act, which introduced the legal requirement that no sex discrimination should occur in employment, including schools and colleges. The earthquake erupted with the resurgence of the women's movement, continued with the opening of traditionally male professions to women, the diversification of male and female sex roles, and the opening of selective single sex schools and colleges to coeducation in the late sixties and early seventies. The last jolt came from the passage of Title IX of the Education Amendments of 1972 which required the achievement of sex equity in all educational programs receiving federal funds—a stiffer legal requirement of equal treatment than most schools and colleges had ever faced before. American education is still adjusting to the equity earthquake that hit from the mid-sixties to the mid-seventies, for that earthquake had altered the way educational institutions would react to male and female students and faculty and to the issues of gender for some time to come.[1]

What was American education like before the equity earthquake? We often forget that in the early sixties American education in general still treated males and females in different ways. Many institutions excluded women students altogether and had almost no women faculty members. In many coeducational institutions women faculty were often treated as second-class citizens; they were paid less and promoted rarely. Women teachers, though no longer fired when they married, as had been the case in previous decades, were still often paid lower salaries than their male counterparts because their incomes were viewed as "supplemental."

1

Culturally men and women often lived in different educational worlds. Alexander Astin found in his early sixties study of the *College Environment* that men's colleges encouraged competitive educational environments but that women's colleges fostered cooperation, affiliation, and supportive academic environments.[2] Schools and colleges taught men and women how to fulfill traditional roles—boys were encouraged to be the family's sole breadwinner and were often expected to compete athletically at school, while girls were largely excluded from competitive athletics as well as student leadership and were encouraged to choose for their future either a career or a life as a wife and mother, preferably the latter.[3]

The passage of Title IX has helped to break down the separate educational worlds that men and women once inhabited, but legal pressure has been only one of many sources of change. Change within education has also occurred because popularly held attitudes and beliefs about the nature of male and female have been recast. It is not easy to remember how different we were twenty years ago and how different were the possibilities of life for men and women. We forget that a majority of American women, including many who held jobs outside the home, thought of themselves as "housewives" in the fifties.[4] It seems unthinkable to us now that popular writers routinely assumed in the pre-equity era that juvenile delinquency was caused by mothers working outside the home.[5]

Many of the assumptions about women and men that we take for granted today were formerly viewed as radical ideas. American women today are less likely than they were two decades ago to define themselves by the man in their lives: "Once women were trained to marry a doctor, not be one . . . Now, we are becoming the men we wanted to marry."[6] Twenty years ago counseling talented female students toward "men's professions" was rarely done. Likewise generations of students were educated by history texts that ignored half the human race. In those days, too, a student who was raped on campus would typically keep it a shameful secret rather than go through the legal ordeal of bringing the criminal to justice. Because of the profound impact of the idea of equity in American life, today "we have terms like *sexual harassment* and *battered women*. A few years ago, they were just called *life*."[7] Today women's career counseling, 30,000 women's studies courses, and rape crisis centers are closer to the mainstream of American education than any of us thought possible two decades ago.[8] And medical, law, and business schools whose admissions policies were shaken by Title IX are graduating women at unprecedented rates. More equal opportunities in education, as well as a decline in overt sex discrimination, have opened up new business and professional roles to women.

Men have also responded to the idea of equity. Who had heard in 1965 of father-coached childbirth, paternity leave, the divorced fathers' custody movement, shared housework and parenting, or the expectation that masculine strength should be tempered with sensitivity?[9] In 1965 it would have been impossible for *TV Guide* to carry an article by a former National Football League lineman arguing that "violent, macho" men on TV are *not* "real men", but rather that "non-violent, sensitive, modest, and compassionate" men who treat women as equals *are*. But no one laughed when Alex Karras wrote it in 1985.[10] Attitude changes like these are bound to affect all the major institutions of society, including education, sooner or later.

We know that because of the equity earthquake many educational institutions have changed profoundly in the last twenty years. But the full scope of the educational changes and the areas still resistant to change have not yet been studied in a comprehensive way.[11] The most important description of the failure of attitudes and behavior to change at colleges and universities has been written by Roberta M. Hall and Bernice R. Sandler of the Project on the Status and Education of Women of the Association of American Colleges, notably in "The Classroom Climate: A Chilly One for Women?"[12] The Hall and Sandler articles show how official policies of equity have not brought an end to the subtle devaluing of women students' abilities. They also point out that the new era has not stopped the clumsiest forms of sex discrimination in education: the sexual harassment of students and faculty.

One other study stands out as a perceptive yardstick of equity on the college level. A fascinating evaluation of undergraduate education in the late seventies was conducted by Brown University in conjunction with Barnard College, Dartmouth College, Princeton University, the State University of New York at Stony Brook, and Wellesley College, which was distributed in report form as *Men and Women Learning Together: A Study of College Students in the late 70's.*[13] The Brown Project found that by the late seventies the equity earthquake had opened many new doors in the colleges studied:

> In career expectations, academic fields of concentration, and intellectual assertiveness, women conceive of themselves as of equal rank with men. We may have reached a point where such equality is beginning to be taken for granted . . . Other differences, some real and some fancied, persist . . . Some men in their relations to women still can detach sexual attraction from affection. Other men still put down women through aspersions on their intellect or appearance. The newly raised consciousness of women is in some respects fragile. In the intellectual and academic spheres there is still a tendency for women to think themselves as not quite on a par with men. Traditional concerns with family and child-rearing and concerns with the affective life and the responsibilities of people to each other—all of which loom larger for women than for men—make the expansion of roles for women more problematic.[14]

Beyond the Brown Project, the Hall and Sandler articles, and a few other sources, the literature that documents the eventual effects of the equity earthquake on the college level is still waiting to be written.[15]

Even less is known about the earthquake's impact on secondary education. For example, several years ago a study conducted by the State of Massachusetts found that: "girls and women are not given equal educational opportunities with boys and men in Massachusetts' schools, colleges, and universities, both public and private, as students, faculty, and administrators."[16] But the study was conducted before the impact of Title IX was felt. Among the many books written in recent years about the need for reform within American high schools none has focused on the remaining sex discrimination in high schools today, nor do any of the books explore how profoundly gender issues in secondary education have been altered since the mid-sixties.[17] While not presuming to fill the resulting gap in educational research, this book does offer a case study in the effects of the equity earthquake.

In 1973 the oldest boys' boarding school in America, Phillips Academy, and one of the oldest girls' boarding schools, Abbot Academy, joined to become one coeducational institution. The new school resulting from the merger embarked upon an historic experiment in educational transformation, as well as gender politics. Instead of serving the needs of one sex or defining education from the perspective of one sex, the new Andover searched for a revised standard of educational equality which would guide its adaptation to coeducation. After more than a decade of efforts to serve the needs of both sexes, Andover has gained some historical and sociological perspective on its recent coeducational experience by conducting the following Coeducation Study. While we do not assume that Andover's experience has been typical of high schools generally or even of boarding schools, we hope that our attempt to understand the past decade and coeducation as it exists in one school will provide others with useful insights.

What inspired the new Phillips Academy to conduct a study of coeducation a decade after Abbot Academy and Phillips Academy became one school? As the tenth anniversary of coeducation neared, anonymous donors gave P.A. a gift to fund a study of coeducation at Andover. In consultation with the newly appointed Dean of Studies Jeanne Amster, Headmaster Donald W. McNemar in the spring of 1983 called for a faculty committee to celebrate the tenth anniversary of coeducation and to study coeducation.

Though the donors had submitted a proposal for the study, including an outline of possible data to be gathered, they wanted the committee to pursue its research and evaluation in its own way.[18] The Headmaster also gave the committee a free hand in defining and conducting the study, and he and the Dean of Studies aided the committee in gaining access to school records. College Counselor Marion Finbury was appointed to chair the committee, and the committee began defining its research agenda in September 1983. Without any preconceptions about the shape of the final report, without hopes for a condemning or self-congratulatory verdict, the committee launched into its study fueled primarily by curiosity.

4

Conducting a self-study with administration support makes it easier to use school records as a research tool. As we mined such records, we could trace, for example, male and female SAT and grade averages over the years, faculty hiring and attrition rates, and the frequency of visits each sex made to the infirmary and to Graham House, the counseling center. In addition to school records, we built our understanding of the roots of coeducation on Susan M. Lloyd's history of Abbot Academy and Fritz Allis' history of Phillips Academy, as well as sources in the P.A. Archives. Early in the project the committee hired as consultant Brandeis sociologist Janet Zollinger Giele, whose research assistants Mary Gilfus and Peter Dunn also worked on the project. Giele and Finbury wrote the student questionnaire, which after a preliminary trial, was administered to Andover's 1200 students in the spring of 1984 (869 returned their questionnaires). After a preliminary analysis of the student results by the committee, Giele, Gilfus, and Dunn did further studies to find statistically significant patterns in the student responses. In the fall of 1984 the faculty questionnaire was written based on questions faculty members brought to open committee meetings. After the faculty questionnaire was administered and 153 (out of a possible 213) responses were computerized in the spring of 1985, Tony Rotundo and Marion Finbury analyzed the results. Both students and faculty members were offered the chance to write comments at the end of their questionnaires, and Finbury, Rotundo, and I coded those responses to see if any patterns emerged. Two years of careful research yielded rich results : fifty pounds of print-outs, documents, cross-tabs, multiple regression analyses, and more than 5000 "data sets" of information about student and faculty attitudes. Andover's Coeducation Study Project has resulted in the most thoroughly researched study ever published of gender issues and coeducation in an American high school.

As we began to make sense out of our findings we sought to place them in the context of research in educational psychology, the sociology of education, and gender studies. Carol Gilligan's book *In a Different Voice* turned out to be extremely helpful in deepening our understanding of student social life. Due to her research on gender differences in moral development, Gilligan concluded that connectedness with others is much more central to female identity formation than it is to male identity formation. For males, Gilligan sees development occurring through the process of separation-individuation—so much so that she finds that males often view affiliation and intimacy as threats to their autonomous growth. Though we did not use Gilligan's thesis as the basis of our study, her perspective was helpful in highlighting cultural values like affiliation and achievement that have slightly different meanings for each gender at Andover today. Instead of relying heavily upon a theory that emphasized gender differences, we looked for subtle shadings of differences *and* similarities which exist between males and females at Andover and we explored how they changed over time.[19]

In order to measure such differences and similarities in students' descriptions of themselves, Giele adapted Sandra Bem's psychological scale for use as part of the student questionnaire. While in the sixties Bem had classified assertiveness and independence as masculine traits, for our purposes in the Coeducation Study typing students according to masculinity or femininity would be anachronistic. Instead Giele and Gilfus classified personalities according to value-related patterns, as well as Giele's previous research findings on the college level. Therefore, students describing themselves most often as assertive, independent, competitive, and willing to take risks became grouped as having Type I traits, while the group having Type II traits included students who saw themselves as sensitive to needs of others, gentle, sympathetic, and understanding. Students describing themselves as having both Type I and II traits were called Mixed Type. Giele has written an essay which is included in the Appendices to explain the theoretical background of the categories.[20] Our findings confirmed to a certain extent our hypothesis that fewer stark gender differences exist today than did a decade ago, but we also explored the persistent gender differences that concern us as educators.

The Coeducation Committee set the agenda for looking at male and female experiences at Andover by defining a series of questions to be answered about the students and their worlds of learning and about the models of learning provided by the adults educating them. The answers we found to the following questions do not tell us everything about the texture of emotions or the quality of the interactions that may shape students' lives at P.A. Questionnaires and statistics are much too clumsy research tools for that. But dwelling within the questions and answers posed here are the essential issues that Andover and American education in general must address if gender and education are to be fully understood.

1. Do current admissions policies favor one sex or another? Has P.A. successfully attracted qualified applicants of both sexes, and have those males and females been given equivalent financial aid?

2. Has the school encouraged course selection, a classroom atmosphere, and a balanced, up to-date curriculum which offers boys and girls a wide-ranging education and a chance to grow in self-confidence?

3. Does the athletic program serve the needs of boys and girls equally well?

4. Does the school encourage male and female students' urges to lead, to enjoy recreation and social life, to build friendships, and to pursue special extracurricular interests?

5. Has the school recruited and hired faculty and defined their workload expectations so that good teachers of both sexes will gladly build their careers at P.A.?

6. What kind of values does Andover encourage in its students? Has coeducation been successful throughout the school?

What general answers did we find in the Coeducation Study Project? Students in the mid-eighties sometimes surprise us by assuming that full equality of the sexes has already been achieved throughout American education, while feminists on the faculty offer the opposing viewpoint that the fight for equality in education has barely begun. Our study of coeducation has found some truth in both viewpoints at Andover. Tremendous progress has been made in providing equal education to boys and girls at Andover, and in many ways official equity has been achieved. Many people have worked hard to make this school a supportive environment that nurtures the drive to achieve in males and females alike. But a few inequities and problems remain. For instance, female students at Andover hold fewer leadership positions, feel less successful in athletics, and feel less confident generally than male students do. Similarly, women faculty feel less comfortable exerting their influence in the community, and the "triple threat" (coaching, house counseling, and teaching) remains a workload expectation for faculty which suits men better than women.

Our main focus has been on the results rather than all the causes of change at Andover, but we have noted strong catalysts here and there. At Andover legal motivation to achieve sex equity has never made much difference in the form of government enforcement or private suits, but Titles IX and VII have served as legal models of behavior.[21] The leadership of the school has been conscientious about living up to these standards, and that has brought real change. Within the areas of school life we studied—admissions, academics, athletics, student social life, faculty, and community values—we found that many inequities have been eliminated simply by issuing new policies. In the case of locker room space for girls, the Headmaster and the Trustees spent money to bring equity.

Other problems have resisted the policy-making process. Our evidence shows that equity, fairness, and mutual respect between the sexes cannot always be legislated, but legislation in the form of clear-cut school policy certainly has hastened progress. Atmospheric changes—subtle shifts in tone and style—arrived gradually by the late seventies. Andover moved beyond the "token stage" of coeducation when it welcomed more female students and faculty, and after them came a day care center, women's health forums, and a new camaraderie between the sexes. Andover has been blessed since coeducation began with a faculty whose most notable characteristic is its desire to nurture the growth of young people. Coeducation had a solid base of kindness and caring to help it through the adjustment process.

One assumption this study has made from the outset is that the forces that have shaped coeducation at Andover today have affected both sexes. Because much of the literature on gender and education has dealt primarily with discrimination against females, little is known about gender and education from the viewpoint of male students or faculty. Though more of our significant findings relate to females, this study is also devoted to exploring how an Andover education affects *both* boys and girls and how employment at Andover works out for both men and women.

The changes that have occurred within American education because of the equity earthquake have opened doors for many girls and women: for example, competitive athletic opportunities and new administrative roles have been opened to them. At the same time new issues have been raised for boys and men: Would women authority figures be acceptable? Would time-honored values and beliefs change? Would girls and women be seen as interlopers or welcome partners in education? Would job expectations for teachers change as two career marriages and female faculty with children became more common? Thus, ours is a study of coeducation at Andover from the perspective of both sexes. Though original plans included a study of staff and alumnae/ni, finite time and resources forced us regrettably to limit ourselves to studying students and faculty in depth. Many more questions could have been asked, but our task was already monumental.

Gender issues have often been categorized with racial and ethnic issues at Andover, but we have been forced to separate them in this report. The Equity Report written by Jean St. Pierre and Vincent Avery in 1985 used Coeducation Study data and other research to explore how Andover deals with female and minority students academically, and they assumed there were some similarities in the academic experiences of the two groups. Although there are references to minority faculty hiring, minority students' feelings in sex-imbalanced classes, and admissions policies toward minority students in this study, our primary assignment was to look at gender. Since colonial times, gender, race, and ethnicity have had very different histories and provided starkly different American experiences. Yet, we hope the discussions that will follow the release of this report will have the effect of heightening our sensitivity to race and ethnicity, too, as they increase our understanding of gender issues in education.

Among students at Andover today, racial and ethnic minorities are more likely to share a group consciousness than females do, while on the faculty, women as well as racial and ethnic minorities have developed some sense of group identity and support for each other. Due to the persistence of the archaic popular image of Andover as a power elite, rich white male Protestant institution, many students and faculty who are not rich, white, male, or Protestant may still feel like outsiders. They shouldn't. The student body today is made up of more former outsiders than ever before. If we combine all the groups that at one time or another have been outsiders in portions of the private school world (women, Blacks, Hispanics, Asians, Catholics, Jews, and students on scholarship) we find that together they now make up the majority at Andover.

More diversity in terms of class background, gender, ethnicity, race, and religion also exists in the adult community than ever before. The benefits of this diversity in creating a first-rate school environment are evident throughout the Andover community.

When it came time to produce a report, we realized we had enough data for a multi-volumed series on gender and education. The task of writing a useful report out of the massive research findings fell to me. I interpreted the survey data and then conducted research in education, psychology, history, and sociology connected with the specific issues raised by the findings. Though I alone accept responsibility for the scholarship and interpretations in these pages, my final draft was based on the collective efforts of the committee. Marion Finbury has written an Afterword which includes information on our methodology and acknowledgement of the many people who helped us put together this Coeducation Study. I add my thanks to hers.

One measure of any educational institution's intellectual fortitude and range is the degree to which cooperation can be achieved among scholars and teachers grounded in different disciplines. Andover's Coeducation Committee has passed the test of fruitful interdisciplinary collaboration with aplomb. Collectively we brought to our task more than a century of educational experience, as well as Masters degrees and doctorates aplenty. But credentials finally mattered less than the nitty-gritty fact that mathematicians could convince historians about statistical significance, humanists could show social scientists underlying meanings they had overlooked, and sociologists and psychologists could direct us to the latest research. Arguments occurred, and even now differences of opinion about interpretations may persist. But the Coeducation Study engaged us enjoyably in a common academic endeavor, a truly interdisciplinary partnership.

Faculty, students, and administration alike have been supportive of our work. At every stage of the project we were able to count on open-mindedness and encouragement from the Headmaster and the Dean of Studies. The Coeducation Study was fortunate to have as its wise guardian and organizer, Marion Finbury, whose experience as a college counselor at both Abbot and P.A. gave her extra insight into coeducation. The working alliance that evolved between Marion Finbury and me made it possible for the project to strike a balance between centralized efficiency and active committee participation—thanks especially to the committee's willingness to be consulted at odd hours. Tony Rotundo was the committee member who was consulted at the oddest hours, and he generously donated precious sabbatical time to listening to new discoveries, to editing, and to interpreting statistics. He and Barbara Dalton Rotundo deserve special thanks for providing me with abundant moral support during the writing of this study.

In the Coeducation Study Project, "Mother Phillips" once again offered its faculty, students, and administrators an opportunity to expand their workdays to accommodate yet another worthwhile task for the good of the school. And, typically, too, "Mother Phillips" gave us back through the writing of this book more than we ever expected in collegiality, intellectual interest, and a chance to influence a school and a community that matter greatly to us. We hope that our readers can look between the lines of this report enough to see that in its pages tremendous affection for the school and its people is mixed with a sense of urgency about achieving sex equity at Andover and throughout American education. We hope that our readers will share some of the enthusiasm we felt as we learned about coeducation at Andover.

Kathleen M. Dalton
Andover, Massachusetts
October, 1985

Chapter One:
ROOTS OF COEDUCATION AT ANDOVER

BEFORE THE MERGER

In September of 1973 Abbot Academy and Phillips Academy began a coeducational partnership that created a new school. Founded in 1778, Phillips had long offered an educational experience of high quality to boys. The Academy's constitution charged the school with the task of shaping "the Minds and Morals of the Youth" entrusted to its care. Just down the hill in Andover, Abbot Academy had devoted itself to providing girls with an excellent education since 1828. The school pursued its founders' purpose "to regulate the tempers, to improve the taste, to discipline and enlarge the minds, and form the morals" of young women. For much more than a century, each academy was true to its original trust of educating youth of one sex.[22]

In the late sixties and early seventies a wave of coeducation swept up single-sex schools and colleges across the country, in part because students no longer wanted to be cloistered and in part because all of a sudden it seemed old-fashioned and even discriminatory to exclude applicants because of their sex.[23] Coeducation struck Abbot and Phillips finally as too compelling an idea to avoid any longer. The idea of coeducation at Abbot and Phillips Academies predated the women's movement and the equity earthquake in American education, though both set the stage for the final decision to merge.

At Abbot coeducation had cropped up as an idea that faculty and Trustees considered off and on in the nineteenth century.[24] In 1878 Abbot Principal and temperance activist Philena McKeen wrote P.A. principal Reverend Cecil F.P. Bancroft that "Your goodness is incomprehensible, I don't know but it would be the best thing that could be done, to join Abbot to Phillips and put you overall."[25] But no serious negotiations were initiated for the next seven decades, and the two single-sex schools continued to keep a friendly distance from each other while educating young people in the same Andover neighborhood.

Coeducation, or at least coordination, was proposed in 1967 by P.A.'s Steering Committee in order to bring "relevance" to the ivory tower of single-sex academia.[26] Students of that era often reminded educators that the "real world" was coeducational, so education should be, too.[27] But the faculty was not so enthusiastic about embracing every form of "relevance." The P.A. faculty prohibited its male students from attending sex education courses at Abbot even though they allowed them to join Abbot girls in community service projects.[28] Nevertheless, coeducation was an idea whose time had come for the two neighboring single-sex schools.

In 1967 the Abbot Trustees chose a new principal, Donald Gordon. He accepted his post knowing that he might well preside over a merger that could end Abbot's independent existence. Phillips Academy was, at the same time, starting to show more interest in educating girls. Encouraged by three successful coeducational summer sessions, the faculty at Phillips voted in 1967 "to encourage creative cooperation with one or more neighboring girls' schools to develop various kinds of coeducational enterprises."[29]

Throughout the six years that followed, the Phillips and Abbot communities debated coeducation, experimented with many forms of cooperation, and gradually moved closer and closer to one another. But the path to coeducation did not follow a straight line. There were many unexpected twists and turns before boys and girls began taking their education together on Andover Hill. Indeed, there were two different series of events in the late sixties and early seventies that led to coeducation. One was the establishment of a variety of coordinate courses and activities that involved both Abbot and Phillips Academies. The other was an attempt to reach a permanent decision about coeducation at the two schools.

As early as 1968 the academies began to hold joint social activities, and in 1969 each school opened some of its courses to students from both campuses. At first this program of cross-enrollment was limited to courses that lay outside the basic sequence in each subject. In the fall of 1970 the P.A. Trustees voted that the Academy should be involved in the education of women, and that it should do so in close association with Abbot. Rather than commit itself to coordination or merger at this point, the P.A. Trustees opted for study of the various possibilities.[30]

In November of 1970 the faculty of the two schools began planning for some forms of coordination. The two boards had created committees of faculty and staff from both schools to lay the groundwork for coordinated goals and policy in several areas, including curriculum, school organization, and social life. The academic coordination program was broadened in the fall of 1971, when many departments opened their basic sequence of studies to students from either school. A few departments, it should be added, kept such courses closed to cross-enrollment, because—in the words of P.A. Dean of Faculty and later Acting Headmaster Simeon Hyde, Jr.—"the P.A. department heads [involved] are not sufficiently sympathetic with the objectives of coordination to make the necessary compromises."[31]

At one point the P.A. Trustees became convinced that a merger of the two schools was not financially feasible due to Abbot's much weaker financial situation and so committed themselves to pursue long-range coordinate education. They authorized their administration to meet with Abbot counterparts and present a proposal for coordination.[32] After a summer of deliberations with Donald Gordon and other Abbot staff, Phillips Academy Headmaster John Kemper decided that coordination was not practical. It would, he said, lead "inescapably" to some form of merger. Kemper was responding in great measure to what the two schools had learned from their on-going experiment in cross-enrollment. Their daily schedules had not meshed; their academic departments often had different goals, course offerings, and teaching methods; staffing needs at the two schools had been hard to anticipate given the vagaries of cross-enrollment.

Kemper and Gordon felt that, if coeducation were to work, Abbot and Phillips would need one schedule, one faculty, one set of goals, one set of rules—all of which would lead to one administration. In other words, Kemper believed that if P.A. wanted coeducation, it had to merge with Abbot or go it alone in an independent coeducational venture.[33] P.A. watched nearby St. Paul's and Exeter go coed, markedly increasing their applicant pools, while P.A.'s pool, along with most other independent schools, declined.[34] Leaders at both schools realized that clear direction was needed to keep their institutions viable.

Before Kemper brought these thoughts to the Trustees in the fall of 1971, he took the issue to the faculty for a vote. The opponents of coeducation at P.A. were outspoken. One of their leaders asked: "Where are we to find the 300 or 400 qualified girls for a coed school of the quality we want?" A few P.A. faculty opposed any form of coeducation because, as one asserted, they believed society was already "too dominated by women." A few others feared that along with girls would come sexual temptation and "more forced early marriages."[35] For many others in both schools coeducation was feared simply because it promised upheavals of unknown proportions in institutions which they loved as they were. In frustration over the opposition, Donald Gordon contemplated briefly giving up the idea of coeducation with P.A., exploring instead the plan of moving Abbot to New Hampshire to become a coed residential school. The Abbot Trustees resisted his plan, for they were willing to be patient with P.A.'s indecision a while longer.[36]

In the fall of 1971 the P.A. faculty voted in favor of *some* form of coeducation by a four-to-one margin. Then a motion was made from the floor that urged the Trustees to pursue an independent course rather than seek a merger with Abbot. Kemper, whose health was failing, made a dramatic statement in which he laid out his reasons for opposing the motion to pursue coeducation independently of Abbot. Relations between the schools would be seriously damaged if P.A. turned its back on Abbot, he said. Moreover, Abbot had a useful plant and facilities. Most of all, it had experience in educating girls, experience which P.A. lacked.

Kemper also pointed out that the next headmaster should have a voice in any decision about coeducation. The faculty were swayed by Kemper's arguments—the motion was tabled and then withdrawn.[37]

Kemper then set his arguments before the Phillips Academy Trustees. Most of them felt a deep commitment to Abbot and were unwilling to go the independent route. But Kemper's arguments against coordinate education were not enough to allay their fears about the financial dangers of a merger. In the spring of 1972, before John Kemper's untimely death, the P.A. Trustees voted to continue on the road to coordination. Similarly, for a time Abbot's Trustees appeared to prefer continued co-ordination, for it offered their students "the best of both worlds: a secure, relatively small residential community and a host of academic opportunities."[38] It seemed possible, after all the deliberations, that coeducation would never bring Abbot and P.A. together.[39]

On the brink of coeducation, Abbot and P.A. waited for decisions to be made—each school in remarkably different moods. One P.A. teacher described Abbot before the merger as having a "spirit of innovation, informality, and warm personal relations" compared to P.A.'s "competitive, sink-or-swim atmosphere."[40] Still troubled by serious budgetary problems, Abbot nevertheless had launched into a creative revival filled with "a sense of hope, excitement and change," inspired in part by the new opportunities available through coordinated education and in part by the experimental, and some said permissive, spirit of learning encouraged by the Gordon administration.[41]

In stark contrast, at P.A. students and faculty were at odds. After years of heightened political awareness among P.A. students, which included protests against racial segregation, the VietNam War, and Nixon's Cambodian invasion, concern with political causes was accompanied by resistance to nearby authority. P.A. students followed the same patterns of protest that characterized schools and colleges across America between 1967 and 1972: the Anti-war Movement and other mass involvements were often reminders that smaller injustices could be alleviated nearer home. Thus, local conflicts over school rules ensued. As Headmaster Kemper in his last days at P.A. grappled with his own terminal cancer and the seemingly impossible issue of coeducation, "the morale of the community was low" due to incidents like bomb threats at the Bell Tower and student-faculty conflict over compulsory chapel attendance.[42]

One student described P.A. in the early seventies as an institution "in the midst of a struggle between tradition and dissent." Hair length, dress styles, and cut policies inspired heated debate. In the spring of 1971, months before Kemper died, two-thirds of the Senior class signed a petition declaring their "lack of confidence in the administration and faculty of Phillips Academy."[43] When historian and former Dean of the Harvard Graduate School of Education Theodore Sizer took over as Headmaster in 1972, he needed to restore the spirit of educational cooperation and respect between students and faculty. With the healing process came a renewed sense of institutional momentum and even the promise of restored greatness, preconditions to making the big leap toward coeducation with Abbot.

THE MERGER BEGINS

The P.A. Trustees chose Sizer as the new headmaster knowing full well that he was deeply committed to coeducation. He quickly began talks on the subject with Donald Gordon, after receiving encouragement from the P.A. Trustees to work for some tentative agreement, the specifications of which ultimately laid the basis for the final terms of merger. Abbot would end its corporate existence, its assets being transferred to P.A. The new school would be called Phillips Academy, although there would be some attempt to perpetuate the Abbot name (the ultimate result was the Abbot Cluster, the Abbot wing of the gym, and the Abbot Academy Association). All current Abbot students who wished to return would be part of the merged student body and as many Abbot personnel as possible would be placed on the new staff. An Abbot administrator would be named Dean at P.A. A new admissions office would be formed by November of 1972. Finally, the Phillips Academy Trustees would be the governing body of the school, with women and/or Abbot Trustees added as soon as possible. These principles were the grounds on which the two Boards of Trustees agreed to a merger.[44]

That agreement came in September 1972, and the documents of incorporation were signed in February of the following year. The preparations for merger were not accomplished without anger or difficulty. At a time when many P.A. graduates were alarmed about the coming of coeducation, President of the P.A. Board of Trustees Donald H. McLean, Jr. wrote to alumni, insisting that, as Sizer had said, "our culture and our schools are all too full of easy male and female stereotypes. There must be no room for simplistic and insensitive chauvinisms of this kind at our Academy."[45]

Some members of the Abbot family were stung by the decision to end their school's existence. Only half of the full-time Abbot faculty was invited to work at the new school. A few highly regarded teachers were refused jobs because they would not live in dormitories. As it lost its name and as its leaders seemed not to be consulted about all crucial personnel decisions, Abbot became aware that the coeducational "marriage" would not begin as an equal partnership. Don Gordon—who was a P.A. graduate—warned the P.A. Trustees that Abbot in the long run would join in shaping the future of the new coeducational school: "The leap of faith we're making, by extinguishing our school's life, can be made precisely because we believe that with us lodged firmly within your corpus, you will be incapable of remaining the same."[46] One alumna said bluntly that "Phillips Academy ATE Abbot."[47] For many faculty members in their last year at Abbot, anxiety and bitter feelings crowded out hope for the future.[48] How could they have known that after a rocky start the coeducational "marriage" of P.A. and Abbot would work out to be a happy and eventually a fairly equitable partnership?

But despite some bitter feelings, the merger proceeded apace. In the spring of 1973 the final legal complications were untangled, and as the new school opened in September of 1973, Abbot and P.A. began their adventure in coeducation. In the new school boys made up 70.5% of the student body while girls were 29.5%.[49]

Who were the boys and girls who made up this student body? How were they alike and different? Several months before coeducation began, a brief study compared the responses given to a P.A. Office of Research and Evaluation (O.R.E.) questionnaire by entering P.A. and Abbot students in 1971 and 1972. In his analysis of the data O.R.E. Director Frederick A. Peterson found significant differences between boys and girls in background, attitudes, and expectations.

The entering Abbot girls were more likely than the entering P.A. boys to have fathers with graduate degrees, and the girls, more typically than the boys, came from private school backgrounds. Boys entered with a higher proportion of A's from their previous schools, but no marked differences in the aptitudes of P.A. and Abbot students were noted in the study. Other sources, however, show that the mean SAT verbal scores for P.A. boys in the Class of 1973 were 48 points higher than their Abbot counterparts, and the boys' mean SAT math scores were 88 points higher. Observers from Abbot state that, although the majority of Abbot students had scores and capacities similar to P.A. students, Abbot's SAT average was lower because the bottom third of their student body was weaker than the bottom third at P.A.

The O.R.E. study did find that boys seemed more self-confident than girls when questioned about their perceptions of their own abilities. The P.A. study also stated that:

> The boys had a higher opinion of their own abilities than the girls did of theirs in the following seven areas, in descending order of magnitude of difference: science, mechanics, mathematics, persevering in spite of hurt feelings, knowledge of own abilities, physical development, and common sense. Girls had a better opinion of themselves in art and in general imagination.[50]

Entering students from both schools, when asked about their life goals and values, cited personal happiness as their first choice. But 75% of the boys as opposed to 46% of the girls gave a high rating to the life goal of "being important and successful." Similarly, 74% of the boys said making a lot of money was important to them whereas only 50% of the girls said so. Girls put more emphasis instead on seeking creativity in one's career and on avoiding conformity. Boys rated marriage higher as a life goal than did girls (70% to 52%). Perhaps most significant is the fact that girls, when asked about plans after graduation, were less likely than boys to aspire beyond college to graduate work.

ADJUSTMENTS EVERYWHERE

When, in the fall of 1973, former Abbot girls moved up the hill to join boys at P.A., Abbot Academy was absorbed and dissolved. Mary Minard, Abbot alumna, former Abbot teacher and later P.A. teacher remembered that "No matter what it was called, we lost our name, our place, our identity."[51] Yet amidst the feelings of loss of the past and apprehensions about the future was a certain spirit of eagerness to begin the exciting adventure of coeducation, a spirit shared by P.A. and Abbot teachers alike.

No one knew what to expect of the newly "merged" school. There were a few former opponents of coeducation among P.A.'s faculty who doubted girls' ability to handle the rigors of the P.A. curriculum. Some still feared that girls might divert needed resources from the interscholastic athletic competitions, or that their presence might lower the high academic standards that had been the pride of Phillips Academy for so long. To these few it felt at first like the painful end of a great era.

Fortunately, these master teachers from both schools, under the inspiring leadership of Theodore Sizer and his wife Nancy Faust Sizer, rose to the occasion in 1973. The adjustment was a big one for both sides, but the participants proved to be game. Richard Pieters, a staunch former foe of coeducation, spoke for the P.A. spirit of accommodation, if not welcome, when he declared at a faculty meeting, "As you all know, I opposed this action; but the vote has been taken, and now let's make this the best damned coed school in the country."[52]

And the accommodations were many. The P.A. Trustees, once an all-male group, opened its doors to admit both new women Trustees and a group of Abbot Trustees who would serve for an interim period. The administration at P.A. employed 34 Abbot teachers, while they decided to let 15 Abbot teachers go. The year before the merger, only three women worked in the P.A. teaching faculty of 115, but as the new school opened its doors in September 1973, the number of women teachers had grown to 26 in an enlarged faculty of 149. For the first time in P.A. history a woman dean, Carolyn Goodwin, sat in G.W. Hall. No longer was there a need for Abbot to worry about financial solvency: the new school had expanded in student body, faculty, buildings, and program, but the P.A. endowment meant financial stability for the school. It meant, too, that former Abbot faculty would receive better salaries and benefits than they had before the merger and that students would pay lower tuition than they had at Abbot.[53]

The biggest adjustments were made by the Abbot girls who began their educations at one kind of school and then were asked to adapt to the creation of a new school around them. A number of the Abbot girls who moved "up the hill" would later recall feeling "on trial" at the new school, having constantly to prove themselves so that girls would be accepted at P.A.[54] Although many P.A. boys initially claimed intellectual superiority over the newcomer girls, they gradually began to accept the presence of intelligent females.

The traditional P.A. "triple threat"—dorm counseling, coaching, and teaching—was redefined as a "double threat" for some Abbot teachers, (Abbot teachers had not usually supervised dorms) though the "triple threat" lived on as an ideal expected workload. For the first time the new school also faced the need to staff girls' dorms with women house counselors. By hiring new women faculty willing to do dorm duty and by hiring faculty wives to run dorms, the administration provided girls with care and guidance. The flexible spouse hiring policy that evolved in the early years of coeducation enabled the school to benefit from the varied professional and interpersonal skills of faculty families.

In fact, it was generally agreed that the merger marked a turning point after which spouses, especially faculty wives, became a more recognized and appreciated part of the community.[55] Not too many years earlier P.A. faculty wives had been expected to entertain their husband's students and colleagues and to wear proper white gloves while paying social calls. Good works and good ladies' teas had been produced in abundance by "Benevie," the Ladies' Benevolent Society, a genteel social organization founded in 1831 by P.A. and Andover Theological Seminary faculty wives and daughters, many of them Abbot alumnae.[56] A few P.A. and Andover Theological Seminary wives and daughters like Harriet Beecher Stowe and Elizabeth Stuart Phelps had interrupted their domestic duties long enough to write important books like *Uncle Tom's Cabin* and *The Gates Ajar*.[57] But serving as helpmates to the men who made Andover run had been the primary role for women on Andover Hill for almost two centuries—until coeducation arrived.

With coeducation new options for faculty wives opened up. Starting in 1973 the new school offered some wives faculty status as house counselors, and a few faculty wives reported being shocked the first time they were asked for their opinions about school policy.[58] Expresssing her enthusiasm about the new roles besides hostess available for faculty wives after coeducation began, one faculty wife told the *Andover Bulletin* that "Cookie pushing is important, but not when you or the students feel that's all you're good for."[59] Clearly with the merger came increased appreciation for the varied talents that women could bring to the school.

Ted Sizer's partner in stewardship over coeducation was Nancy Sizer, a woman who combined the exceptionally demanding but unheralded and unpaid job of Headmaster's wife and nurturant patron saint to P.A. families with her own strenuous performance as a triple threat faculty member. During those transitional years in women's history, the early seventies, homemakers and career women throughout the nation—women who had taken different paths in life—did not always feel sisterly toward one another. But at Phillips Academy lines of conflict were never sharply drawn because of the Sizers' efforts. The Ladies Benevolent Society also worked hard to be a neutral ground for friendship and support for women of all generations and lifestyles. "Benevie" pulled together the women of the community by opening its membership to women faculty after the merger and a decade later to women staff and staff wives. After several years of coeducation, "Benevie" events calendars combined harmoniously an eclectic mixture of needlework evenings, craft shows, pot luck dinners, decorating lectures, community service, and talks about changing sex roles, women and stress, and women and literature.

Though coeducation had changed many individual lives, its overall effect on the school community was hard to gauge. In order to understand the "impact and implications" of coeducation, the Abbot Academy Association commissioned O.R.E. (with help from the Center for Field Research and School Services at Boston College) to study the results of the merger, using longitudinal data and surveys conducted in 1973-74. The Merger Study written by Fred Peterson found that faculty, administrators, and students were enthusiastic in their praise for the positive effects of coeducation, including making P.A. "a more friendly, comfortable, and natural environment."[60] In fact, boys' overall happiness at P.A. improved 24% the year of the merger. No negative effects on grades, drug use, or relationships were found. But the study also concluded that "the negative effects (insecurity, anxiety, problems of status and role) were visited almost exclusively upon the females of the new community." Former Abbot students showed "a significantly stronger dissatisfaction with the flexibility of teachers and the unfairness of the length of assignments" than boys did. The faculty response to O.R.E.'s questionnaire showed that many viewed the merger and the workings of coeducation as "tense."[61] Fortunately, the understandable tension of 1973-74 and 1974-75 passed and the school turned to making long-range adaptations to coeducation.

Not all of the necessary adjustments to coeducation were made quickly. By 1978, the proportion of girls in the student body had risen to 39%, but the proportion of full-time women teachers had not exceeded 23%. Coeducation in athletics progressed more slowly than many desired. One Abbot alumna declared that "The merger has occurred everywhere except in the Athletic Program." Girls' locker facilities were inadequate, and, according to the *Phillipian*, girls were treated as "second-class citizens in the athletic program." At times girls were allowed to use equipment only if the boys did not need it, and much more school-wide attention was paid to boys' interscholastic competitions than the girls'.[62]

On the other hand, Athletic Director Ted Harrison and P.E. instructor and later Associate Director of Athletics Shirley Ritchie worked extremely hard to provide a wide variety of sports options to girls. Ritchie insisted that "the girls have profited 100% from the merger," possibly because of better facilities, more varied activities, and new encouragement to excel in the competitive athletics that had been P.A.'s hallmark.[63] When Joe Wennik was appointed Athletic Director in 1977, he called for a new building program. He urged the school to build an athletic complex which would be "specifically conceived to represent our philosophy toward co-education" including "a minimum of separate-but-equal, a maximum of shared unity."[64] With funds from the Bicentennial Campaign the new Abbot wing of the gym was added, complete with girls' and women's locker rooms and expansive space for a large and varied athletic program. Coeducation appeared to be truly completed.

The "completion" of coeducation looked very bright to many observers by the late seventies. Gone were the memories of the debates over the merger and the uneasy days of 1973. P.A. Charter Trustee and Abbot alumna Betsy Parker Powell spoke optimistically to the assembled student body and faculty in her Convocation address in 1977, praising the wide-ranging accomplishments of girls at P.A. and the fine uses of Abbot's assets within the post-merger school.[65]

She pointed out that 60% of the academic prizes awarded in '76-'77 school year were given to girls, and that girls had distinguished themselves in many leadership positions on campus, including Editor of the *Phillipian*, Co-Chairman of Blue Key, and Cluster President. Athletically girls had made school history with undefeated squash and tennis teams and an outstanding girls' crew team which won the division title for high schools at the National Invitational Regatta.

Powell added that in 1977, women—including many former Abbot teachers —made up about a quarter of the entire faculty, and women served as Dean of Studies and as deans in two out of six residential clusters. Abbot alumnae had contributed significantly to the Bicentennial Campaign, including providing a teaching foundation. The Elizabeth Rogers Fund, made available in part through the efforts of former Abbot principal Marguerite Hearsey, also provided funds for teaching fellows and for Rogers Fellows, guest speakers chosen from among prominent women in business, literature, and public affairs. The Abbot Academy Association Fund, created in 1973 from $1 million of unrestricted Abbot funds, acted as an "internal foundation" providing financial support for creative ideas, especially those that would improve teaching or the quality of life at P.A. Major Abbot Academy buildings had not been sold, and a residential cluster centered in the Abbot campus was named Abbot Cluster. The Abbot flag was on display at the time in the Headmaster's office, and a dormitory was renamed for Bertha Bailey, a former Headmistress at Abbot.[66]

She might also have added that dynamic theatre, music, and dance programs had grown up in the Sizer years at the same time P.A. adjusted to coeducation, and an expanded counselling service at Graham House had been created. The disciplinary system and the parietal system had been revised as well. In sum, Phillips Academy was a changed institution after its merger with Abbot: Don Gordon's prediction to the P.A. Trustees had been prophetic. Not only had girls and women made a certain place for themselves in the formerly male institution, but the spirit and energy of Abbot lived on in the new school.

In opposition to Powell's upbeat outlook on the progress of coeducation came an unexpected critical view from outside the institution. When the New England Association of Schools and Colleges studied P.A. in order to evaluate it for reaccreditation in 1979, the Association's Visiting Committee issued a report including the following remarks about coeducation at Andover:

> Surprisingly, we found no reference in the current statement of Philosophy and Objectives to a thoughtful assessment of what coeducation is all about. There is, in fact, neither mention of coeducation nor concern expressed for the possibility that thoughtful and deep assessment of differing needs of boys and girls might well be rewarding for the long run future of the Academy . . . The committee recommends that the Trustees and faculty look again at the matter of coeducation with a view towards developing specific and substantial philosophical underpinnings for educational practices which might well be different according to whether boys or girls are involved. Presumed androgyny does not necessarily provide a firm foundation for a coeducational school program . . . In general, we felt that Andover is still a boy's school with girls who are students. As we have already remarked in our comments about purposes and objectives, we have not found a broad sense of looking towards the new roles which are emerging for girls and for women. To put it another way, girls are certainly experiencing the same kind of education which has been traditional and which continues at Andover. In a broader sense, however, we wonder about the philosophical questions: Are boys and girls different in nature and are society's challenges different so that they need at some points different programs and different support systems? What are the implications for the appointment of administrative officers and for the makeup of the Board of Trustees?[67]

The school's immediate reaction was one of surprise and irritation, especially at the Visiting Committee's choice of the words "presumed androgyny." In fact, the lack of a self-conscious philosophy of coeducation and lack of assumptions about each gender's educational needs had seemed to be a virtue. Being gender-blind had seemed as important as being color-blind in the new Andover's welcoming openness to women and minorities. Even faculty members who were feminists had reason to be uneasy about what the school should do with the Visiting Committee's insistence upon a "thoughtful and deep assessment of differing needs of boys and girls." What exactly did the Visiting Committee want us to do?

In response to the Visiting Committee's "androgyny report," the P.A. administration put together in 1981 a response, an "Interim Report to the New England Association of Schools and Colleges" which served in part as a defense of coeducation at Andover. Confessing surprise at the suggestion that the school should "reexamine the premises of its coeducational enterprise," the Interim Report responded with short essays on coeducation written by members of the community. The first female to be elected President of the Student Body, Hadley H. Soutter asserted in her essay that "Female students at this school have very few complaints about what they generally consider to be a very healthy coeducational environment at this school." Coeducation, to her mind, was a "non-issue."[68]

Faculty members' responses which were included in the Interim Report were quite varied. Flagstaff Cluster Dean, Sylvia Thayer, Abbot '54, stated that "this is a fairly healthy environment for teenagers away from home, regardless of their sex, and that most of us adults do a remarkable job of parenting and educating them all!" West Quad South Cluster Dean Jon Stableford, P.A. '63, agreed that coeducation was being handled well at Andover, but he also pointed to areas of needed change. Because students enter P.A. with preconceptions about sex roles and appropriate roles for men and women, sexism, said Stableford, had crept into student life at Andover. He asserted that this was especially true in student politics where boys were hesitant to vote for female candidates even when they were better qualified. In addition, he said that an adequate range of role models was not visible to the young women on campus. Stableford noted further that discussion of the issues related to combining parenthood and careers was needed.

Of all the responses included in the Interim Report, perhaps the most complex and critical was written by Alexandra Kubler-Merrill, Abbot '56, Head of the Graham House Counseling Service. In her view it was unfortunate that the Academy was committed to a 60% boys and 40% girls ratio in the student body. Though she thought the Visiting Committee's use of the word androgyny seemed like jargon, she believed that Andover had a "gender identity problem." To explore these issues in such a community, she wrote, "touches many raw nerves, raises questions of an intimate, often threatening nature. When we look at matters of sex, sexuality, race and class we are at the most elusive and incendiary edges of our lives." She remembered being at Abbot in the fifties, where she was surrounded by "remarkable older women," "well-defined presences who talked to me about being a woman, about being an educated woman and sharing what I was learning." At P.A. such discussions were rare, but Kubler-Merrill insisted that boys and girls needed to talk about who they were and what they may become as men and women. She urged the school to conduct a study that would not just look at the number of buildings remodeled for use by women, but that would probe deeply beneath the surface facts into many of the more profound and less obvious aspects of coeducation.

The administration in the Interim Report questioned the validity of the Visiting Committee's suggestion that P.A. needed an explicit statement of coeducational Philosophy and Objectives. The Interim Report pointed out that the school's deep commitment to promoting the individual development of both sexes was implicit in the school's official statement of purpose: "helping students develop the skills and values necessary for personal fulfillment" and "welcoming qualified and promising students from a wide range of ethnic, economic, and geographic backgrounds, in the belief that diversity itself can be an enriching component of education." Such a response made it apparent that, although the school was committed to supporting coeducation, many at P.A. did not believe any explicit coeducational philosophy or specific goals were needed.

Furthermore, the Interim Report objected to the charge of "presumed androgyny." The Interim Report pointed out that just because typical P.A. female and male students may exhibit, on the surface, the same characteristics of intellectual confidence and athletic competitiveness, that did not necessarily mean that the school remained "a boy's school with girls who are students." According to Admissions Office data, Andover students were telling their friends to come to P.A. only if they were "brainy," "independent," "self-confident," and "sports-loving." Thus, the report proposed that self-selection may produce girls who "to a stereotypical eye" may "resemble male students." Though no conclusions were drawn and few concessions were granted to the Visiting Committee, the Interim Report's response stated that further discussion, especially among students, might be useful.[69]

RECENT COEDUCATIONAL DEVELOPMENTS

Of course, even if the "androgyny report" was, for the most part, ignored, in the early eighties discussion did continue on and off campus. Dean of Studies Phyllis Powell formed a group of girls to discuss women, careers, and life choices, and various women's and/or girls' discussion groups sprang up spontaneously. Even earlier a group of women on campus had written a letter to the Quality of Life Committee noting that the triple threat expected of faculty made it virtually impossible for women faculty members with small children to be hired. They questioned whether a faculty schedule which sometimes required work morning, afternoon, and evening was a reasonable expectation now that the faculty included so many women and men with two-career marriages.[70]

In addition to the informal discussions of gender issues at P.A., women's studies and gender studies courses, like "Images of Women" in the English Department and "Men, Women and American Culture" in the History Department, were added to the curriculum, and for two years a Women's Film Festival was held. The Women's Center had not survived past the early years of coeducation, but networks of support for women lived on.

When in 1981 the Trustees searched for a successor to Ted Sizer, who resigned to write his book on educational reform, they sought more than a competent administrator and teacher. They wanted to hire a couple able to reach out to all the past and present members of the extended P.A. and Abbot communities. In Don and Britta McNemar they found two professionals whose previous experience respectively as Dean of Faculty for the Social Sciences and Director of the Career Counseling Center at Dartmouth was supplemented by the work they had done facilitating Dartmouth's and Connecticut College's transitions to coeducation. At Andover, like the Sizers, they combined a two-career marriage, children, and intellectual interests, with tireless energy and indefatigable work devoted to the sustenance and further uniting of the new Phillips Academy.

Shortly after the McNemars arrived in 1981, a potentially divisive issue arose: how coeducational should the school be? The Faculty Committee on the Composition of the Student Body, chaired by Math teacher Frank Eccles, P.A. '43, recommended that the Admissions Office change its policy of admitting roughly the same percentage of girls that had appeared in the previous year's applicant pool. In 1981, that meant a student body of 39% girls and 61% boys. Though the ultimate authority to decide the issue rested with the Trustees, the Eccles Committee proposed that the faculty go on record as recommending that the percentage of girls be increased to 50% of the student body within ten years.

Thus, as the faculty was asked to debate and vote on the 50-50 proposal, it was presented with an opportunity to discuss coeducation again. Before the November 24, 1981 faculty meeting many feared that old hostilities toward coeducation would resurface. In one of his first major speeches to the faculty, Don McNemar strongly supported the compelling and equal importance of educating boys and girls. After his speech the faculty debated for a short time and then endorsed the eventual 50-50% goal without much dissension. When the Trustees were presented with the 50-50 proposal, they opposed ratifying any fixed quotas. Instead, they adopted a resolution firmly committing the Academy to the equal education of girls and boys and asking that the proportion of students be set annually based on both the educational environment and the applicant pool.

Later that same academic year, McNemar, at the request of an Ad Hoc Day Care Committee, offered space in Draper Hall on the Abbot campus to provide a Day Care Center to be operated by the Lawrence Community Child Care Center, Inc.[71] Priority and flexible schedules would be available to the children of P.A. faculty and staff, but making child care facilities available to the local community served an urgent public need, as well. The child care center, which eventually included an infant program, a toddler room, a playgroup, a pre-school, and after-school care, opened in 1982 in the second year of McNemar's leadership at Andover, and it has been in full and enthusiastic use ever since.

Other changes that also reflected a new era for women at P.A. followed the faculty vote for a 50-50 ratio and the opening of the day care center: rape prevention and safety education sessions were held in every dorm in the '83-84 academic year; Associate Dean of of Residence for Health Issues 'Cilla Bonney-Smith was hired, and soon afterwards discussion groups on sexuality and human relationships were being held and women's health issues such as anorexia were being discussed publicly; and the P.A. administration issued a landmark policy to prevent sexual harassment. McNemar also appointed the first female Dean of Admissions ever to serve at Phillips Academy. Though no explicit philosophy of coeducation had been articulated, profound decisions with long-ranging consequences had been made.

THE YEAR OF CELEBRATION AND EDUCATION AND THE COEDUCATION STUDY PROJECT

Just as coeducation at Andover entered its second decade, with ten years of adjustment as well as progress behind it, the Headmaster and the Dean of Studies Jeanne Amster set in motion the work of the Ten Year Committee on Coeducation. In addition to being the beginning of the Coeducation Committee's reassessment of coeducation at Andover, the '83-84 school year was designated as a year of celebration and education about issues related to coeducation.

The Coeducation Committee planned a series of speakers throughout the '83-84 school year to provide the community with a framework for the discussion of gender issues. Among the speakers were Estelle Ramey, an endocrinologist at Georgetown University Medical School who spoke on male and female responses to stress and "Is Anatomy Destiny?" In the winter term, Tom Cottle, a social psychologist, talked to the community about recent research on sex roles and how people experience gender. The Headmaster's Symposium on race relations also brought to campus Carlotta Miles, a noted psychiatrist who spoke on the psychology of racism and sexism, and coeducation itself was discussed by Edith Phelps from the Center for Gender Education and Human Development at the Harvard School of Education. In conjunction with the Speakers Series, Marion Finbury and the Coeducation Committee organized a special Celebration Weekend, May 4-6, 1984, to recognize the tenth anniversary of coeducation at Andover. A one-woman show by actress Tulis McCall dramatized the struggles of unique women in history. Susan Lloyd, member of the P.A. History Department, led an open discussion of "Curriculum for a Non-Sexist World" based on her work with the Dodge Foundation Seminar, and philosopher Elizabeth Minnich spoke to the assembled student body about the narrowness of any curriculum that excludes half the human race.

Also, the Coeducation Committee presented to the community a few preliminary findings from its ongoing study of coeducation. A panel on "Andover Then and Now" recalled the history of the merger as well as the experiences of the first generations of students and teachers in the new school. At a community-wide dinner and celebration a troup of faculty entertainers recapped for the audience the fears that abounded at the time of the merger, portraying, with lyrics written by Nancy Sizer, the humorous side of male-female relations at P.A. Finally, as the birthday cakes with Abbot and P.A. insignia were rolled out and Rev. Philip Zaeder offered a Celebratory Toast to Ted and Nancy Sizer and Don and Britta McNemar, the entire audience sang Happy Birthday to coeducation. By 1984 Phillips Academy offered boys and girls an educational experience worthy of celebration.

Because Andover recognized that it had already turned a corner in its coeducational journey, the secure moment for taking stock had come. Phillips Academy in the mid-eighties, everyone knew, was quite different from the "tense" school it had been in 1973, but no one would know for sure until the Coeducation Study was done *how* different it had become.

Chapter Two:
ADMISSIONS AFTER A DECADE OF CHANGE

Do current admissions policies favor one sex or another? Has P.A. successfully attracted qualified applicants of both sexes, and have those males and females been given equivalent financial aid?

ADMISSIONS POLICIES

Historians once viewed Andover as "an upper-class institution" where an exclusive group prepared themselves to become America's ruling elite.[72] Whether or not this was ever completely true of Phillips Academy in the past, it is certainly an inaccurate image now. Central to the educational philosophy of Andover since its founding has been its desire to educate "youth from every quarter."[73] Following the P.A.-Abbot merger the school redoubled its efforts to attract a diverse student body, seeking in particular racial, ethnic, and economic diversity. The Andover *Catalogue* states quite clearly, "Andover is no single group's sanctuary. In a day when many Americans, by their actions, are rejecting even the ideology of the melting pot, we assert it."[74] As a result of recruiting efforts, in the 1985-86 academic year many ethnic, racial, and economic backgrounds were represented within the student body, which came from 47 states and included 41 foreign nationals from 19 countries. In addition, 8% of the student body was Black or Hispanic.

Don McNemar has worked with the Board of Trustees to expand available financial aid so that an Andover education could be made available to qualified students regardless of their ability to pay. The scholarship budget for 1984-85 and 1985-86 was sufficient to meet the needs of all students selected for admissions, so all decisions to admit were made without reference to an applicant's financial situation. In 1984-85, 5% of the student body was on full scholarship, and 37% would receive some form of financial aid from the school. Thus, a primary goal of the Admissions Office has been recruiting qualified students who might not otherwise apply to Andover.

Though recruiting to increase the ethnic, racial, and economic diversity of the student body has been a high priority at Andover, the most dramatic new form of diversity the school has sought in the last fifteen years has been female students. But the issue of gender diversity has presented the school with more subtle problems than other sorts of diversity. Racial and ethnic diversity, for instance, present problems of scarcity, so the Academy has simply committed itself to recruiting as many qualified minority students as possible. Accomplishing gender diversity, on the other hand, is a matter of finding an appropriate balance where an oversupply of qualified girls and boys already present themselves for admission. While the community seemed in agreement about racial, ethnic, and economic diversity, it was not in agreement about how much gender diversity was desirable when composing its student body.

How, then, was the school to find the right gender balance? During the first eight years of coeducation, Andover's official admissions policy toward females was a "pool-dependent" policy. A "pool-dependent" policy meant that the number of females admitted would create a student body whose percentage of females would be equal to the percentage of females in the previous year's final applicant pool. Thus, using the "pool-dependent" policy, if 38% of the total applicants in a given year were girls, then the Admissions Office would accept for the following year enough girls to make the entire student body 38% female. In 1973 when coeducation began, 31% of the total applicants for admission to P.A. were female. By 1984 that number had increased to 40%. While female admissions were limited, no official "female quota" was ever set. But neither did the school agree upon the goal of gender equality in the student body. Because of the "pool-dependent" female ratio, females have never exceeded 43% of the student body.

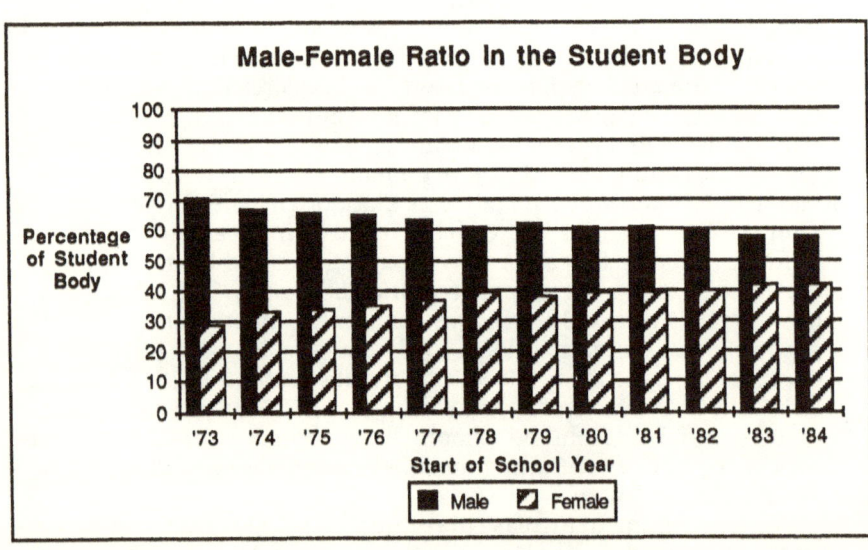

The question of what ratio of girls to admit to the school each year has been discussed ever since the merger. One of the reasons given for maintaining the "pool-dependent" policy is that males and females should have equal chances of being admitted to Andover from their respective pools. For instance, with the exception of 1973, an average of about 28-29% of the male and female applicant pools has been admitted. Therefore, those who favor a "pool-dependent" female ratio argue that it would be unfair to males to admit a higher percentage of the female applicant pool.

However, to some faculty members it seemed odd that the ratio of females in the student body was tied to the apparently accidental number of females who applied, particularly since no other group of applicants had ever been subject to the same limitations. Furthermore, they pointed out that while the school allotted special funds for recruiting racial minorities and thereby increased the number of minorities in the applicant pool, the Admissions Office had never made an explicit goal of increasing the female applicant pool. On the contrary, other faculty pointed out that, in fact, the "pool dependent" policy was a way of setting limits on both sexes: after all, regardless of the quality of the male applicants, they would not be admitted past the 58% male ratio. While many objected to the "pool-dependent" policy, the community has not yet agreed upon a better way to determine the ratio of males and females to be admitted.

Some admissions officers have suggested that an alternative admissions policy such as a sex-blind or strictly merit-based policy would increase the number of female students admitted. But could a boarding school accommodate fluctuating male and female ratios when it had to know in advance how many girls' and boys' dorms and house counselors to have ready each fall? Was the assumption that more girls would be admitted under a sex-blind or merit-based policy based on real evidence?

In the admissisons field the crucial question is which factors to weigh most heavily in the decision to admit: test scores, grades, recommendations, the interview, a student's maturity, his or her future potential, past success, or particular talents or qualities sought by the school. In the past many admissions readers viewed the female applicant pool as slightly stronger on the basis of maturity, past success, and teacher recommendations. Because of these strengths, the female applicant pool has been perceived by some as being likely to be admitted at a higher rate than males in a sex-blind or merit-based system. But others, who would weigh "objective" standards more heavily, state that boys would do better under a merit system because the male applicant pool has in recent years had somewhat higher entering SSAT and SAT scores than their female counterparts (except for 12th grade and PG male admittees who have lower scores than 12th grade girls). Many others, who prefer to weigh all the factors together, say that the male and female applicant pools at Andover are about equal in quality. Therefore, they claim, if a merit-based policy were used, roughly equal numbers of equally quali-fied boys and girls would be admitted. Without set male/female ratios, the Admissions Office would have to sort out which factors mattered most.

The issue of admissions has been complicated since the beginning of the equity earthquake by federal law and inconsistently enforced gov-ernment attempts to set admissions guidelines. For a number of years affirmative action "goals" affected public admissions policies, but after the Bakke case, fixed affirmative action quotas were sometimes viewed as reverse discrimination. Nondiscrimination standards, however, have continued to exert a major influence on public university and graduate and professional school admissions.

Less attention has been paid to private institutions' admissions poli-cies by lawmakers and enforcement agencies.[75] For example, receiving IRS tax exempt status means that even a private institution cannot have racial, Jewish or Asian admissions quotas, but this rule is rarely enforced by the IRS.[76] Under Title IX admission standards, "proportional and/or numerical limitations on the number of students admitted by sex are prohibited," but private secondary schools were exempted from Title IX admissions coverage. The equal protection clause of the Fourteenth Amendment was used in the Berkelman case to stop a college preparato-ry public high school with a larger pool of qualified female applicants from setting "higher admissions criteria" for females by using a ceiling on the percentage of females admitted, but such cases are much more likely to be brought against public institutions than private ones.[77]

Title IX does not cover private independent schools admissions poli-cies at all, but, if Andover were to look to Title IX federal sex equity admissions regulations as a model, the abandonment of sex-separated pools and the elimination of sex as a factor in admissions would have to occur. Title IX regulations prohibit public institutions from giving:

> Preference to one person over another on the basis of sex, by rank-ing applicants separately on such basis, applying numerical limita-tions upon the number or proportion of persons of either sex who may be admitted, or in any other way treating one individual differ-ently from another on the basis of sex.[78]

Federal standards for admissions, therefore, require that admission deci-sions be based upon an applicant's merit judged in the context of one gender-integrated pool. However, private institutions have not, in gen-eral, used Title IX as a model for admissions policies.

The dilemma Andover faces over deciding a proper gender balance in admissions policy is a familiar one for coeducational independent schools and private colleges. In the past most set limits on the ratio of females admitted, and many limited the percent of females in the stu-dent body to the percent in the applicant pool. Since the seventies some of the most selective colleges in America, though they have officially gender-blind admissions policies, persist in keeping a 60-40% male/fe-male ratio, even in cases where the female applicant pool exceeds 40%.

However, recently many Ivy League colleges have started to increase slightly their percentage of females admitted each year, although few have abandoned altogether the idea of letting the applicant pool approximately guide their ratio. Other colleges have rejected the idea of a "pool-dependent" ratio. Brown, for example, has gone to a gender-blind policy which has resulted in a 50-50% student body without significant initial problems, and their experience will be watched carefully by other institutions struggling with the issue of gender balance.[79]

The 1981 Eccles Committee on the Composition of the Student Body reconsidered the "pool-dependent" policy, and recommended that the faculty vote to reaffirm its long-standing commitment to racial, ethnic and economic diversity and at the same time to establish a 50-50% male-female student body ratio within ten years. As noted in Chapter One, the faculty voted to abandon a "pool-dependent" female ratio, though they recognized that it was within their power to make only an advisory recommendation to the Board of Trustees.

When they received the faculty recommendation, the Trustees emphasized the equal importance of educating boys and girls, but did not want to involve the school with fixed quotas. Instead, the Trustees decided to set the ratio of females in the student body on a year-by-year basis, by "taking into account both the applicant pool and whether from an educational perspective the Academy would be a better place for both boys and girls if additional girls were added to the student body."[80] The P.A. administration increased the ratio from 40% at the time of the faculty vote to 42% in 1982, despite an applicant pool which was 39% female. The ratio has been raised to 43% for 1985-86, with decisions made annually. Currently, while the female ratio is being set on a year-by-year basis, the ratio of females in the applicant pool can still influence the eventual percentage of females admitted. Thus, over the years the ratio in the student body has increased. What is not clear yet is where the ratio will go eventually. Admissions policy remains an open question for the future.

In its search for a fair admissions policy, Andover until recently has had little data on the effect of having a greater number of boys than girls in the student body: from a 1973 high of 40% more boys than girls on campus to 14% more boys in 1985. The Coeducation Study research uncovered evidence that suggests that the educational environment can be affected significantly when sex-imbalance pervades students' daily lives. Educational researchers have found that being outnumbered by the opposite sex affects the self-confidence of both sexes.[81] The problem has been documented thoroughly because of Matina Horner's discovery of females' "fear of success" and because of other research done on bright females' anxiety about achievement. These studies have shown that women's "motive to avoid success" is most likely to appear in competitive classroom situations and in settings in which females are in a distinct minority.[82]

Psychologists using projective tests and sociologists observing small group behavior have come to the same conclusion: being outnumbered in class undermines women's self-confidence. According to one of the Brown Project's consultants Constantina Safilios-Rothschild, when a girl finds she is the only female in class, she "is usually handicapped in her ability to learn. She is psychologically and structurally marginal, and this marginality creates learning problems for her."[83] In addition to the effect that being outnumbered has on female self-confidence, males who are in the majority in most classes can be affected negatively by the sex-ratio. Researchers, while exploring cross-sex peer interaction in the classroom, discovered that boys are most often comfortable interacting with their own sex, as if no girls were there.[84] This tendency toward self-segregation is easier to counter if more females are present to encourage positive interactions. The Brown Project also reported that sex-ratios affected male students' attitudes toward females:

> They also found that men's perceptions of women's competence also change drastically with different sex ratios. Men in a group of six men and one woman evaluate the woman in terms of stereotypes. In more balanced sex ratios, men tend to evaluate women in terms of their actual performance, of what they do and how good they are in what they are doing rather than relying on stereotypes. This performance-based evaluation of women helps them overcome marginality and become integrated.[85]

Therefore, males' attitudes toward females can be improved by increased contact and a more equal sex ratio. If Andover reconsiders its admissions policies, the effect of imbalanced classes and an unequal sex ratio on the learning experiences of both sexes will have to be considered.

IMPLEMENTING ADMISSIONS POLICIES

No matter what theory or what eventual goals are set for Andover's admissions, in practice it has been nearly impossible to admit according to any precise formulas. Although the Admissions Office works with an ideal ratio approved by the Trustees, it cannot predict exactly its yield of admitted students who will actually matriculate, nor can the Office know ahead of time how many returning students will withdraw or be dismissed. As a result each year's admissions statistics vary according to these factors. Except for the anomaly of the high female admission rate of 46% in 1983, the percentage of females admitted in 1982 and 1984 was 39%, no different from the 1981 rate of 39% which was set before the faculty vote. In general, before or after the 1981 faculty vote, the ratio of females admitted to acheive the desired ratio has never coincided perfectly with the percentage of the girls in the applicant pool.

One factor influencing the percentage of females admitted each year is the speed at which the Academy converts boys' dorms to girls' dorms. The Admissions Office cannot set its ideal number of female boarding applicants each year until being notified by the Dean of Residence about the number of beds and the number of dorms that will be available to girls. Although it would appear to be a fairly simple process to switch a boys' dorm to a girls' dorm, both the housing preferences of the boys who have squatters' rights in the dorm and the housing preferences of the house counselor have to be considered.

Day Students

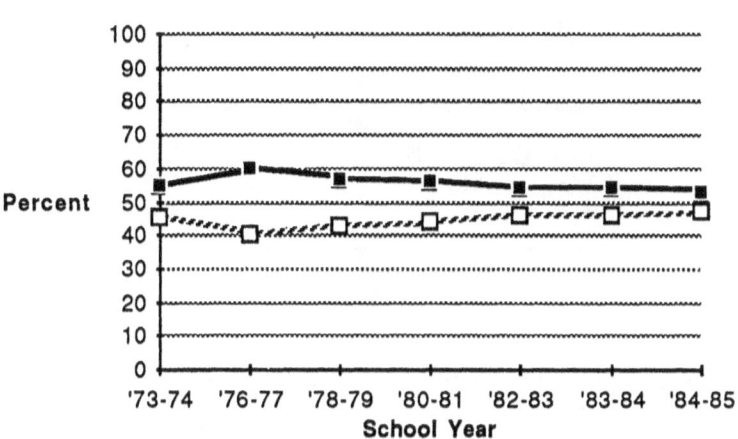

Boarding Students

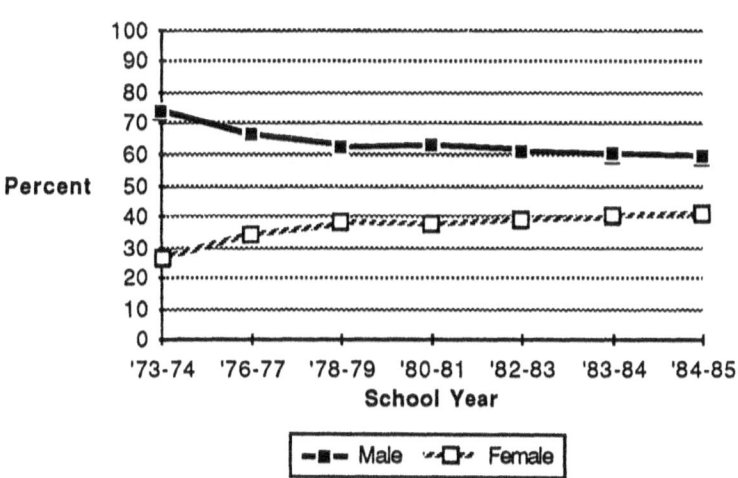

Because the P.A. administration and the 1985 Faculty Ad Hoc Housing Committee have endorsed the idea of gender-agreement between house counselors and dorm inhabitants, a boys' dorm cannot be changed to a girls' dorm until its male house counselor has found alternate housing and a female house counselor has been assigned to live in the dorm. Many colleges can change their male/female student ratios easily: an increase in female students does not require the building or conversion of dormitory space because they can be assigned to coed dorms. But Andover has to consider its housing points system which permits faculty to select their own dorm housing, as well as the necessity of maintaining single sex dorms. Regardless of such problems, Andover dorms have been and could be altered to suit changing admissions patterns. Today there are 27 girls' dorms and 33 boys' dorms, and the school still accepts more male than female boarding students.

	1983-84			
	TOTAL APPLICANTS		STUDENT BODY	
	BOYS	GIRLS	BOYS	GIRLS
Boarding	61%	39%	60%	40%
Day	51%	49%	54%	46%
Total	60%	40%	58%	42%

A larger disparity between male and female admissions exists in boarding admissions than in day student admissions. Roughly the same number of males and females apply to Andover each year as day students, and the school usually admits about the same number of male and female day students. Andover receives many more applications from male than female prospective boarding students, and it accordingly admits a higher number of boarding boys each year. Many more boarding than day students apply each year, but a higher percentage of the day student applicants are admitted each year.

No data is available to explain why fewer females than males apply to board at P.A. This disparity may occur because many families are more willing to send their sons than their daughters to live away from home during high school. Or it may be related to the fact that in some families investment in sons' educations is a higher financial priority than daughters' educations. Possibly the overrepresentation of prospective male boarders in the applicant pool is due to Andover's traditional fame as a boys' boarding school. For both day and boarding students the admissions process is highly competitive. For example, out of 3106 total applicants in 1984 only 626 were admitted.

	FINANCIAL AID		
	1982-83	1983-84	1984-85
Scholarship Funds			
Females	$ 712,465	$ 823,510	$ 980,177
Males	1,090,910	1,219,315	1,281,824
% Females	40%	40%	43%
Scholarship Students			
Females	147	145	165
Males	231	235	229
% Females	39%	38%	42%
Full Scholarship			
Females	13	16	31
Males	20	25	27
% Females	39%	39%	53%
Average Grant			
Females	$ 4,847	$ 5,679	$ 5,940
Males	4,722	5,188	5,597
Ratio in Student Body	41% female	42% female	42% female
	59% male	58% male	58% male

FINANCIAL AID

Financial aid has been distributed according to needs standards established by the School Scholarship Service in Princeton, New Jersey. In 1984-85 43% of the financial aid budget went to females and 57% went to males, which was fairly comparable to the male/female ratio in the student body. For most recent years females received similar portions of the financial aid budget. The average financial aid grant in 1984 was $5940 for females and $5597 for males, and 31 females and 27 males received full scholarships. Of the 394 students in 1984 who received some form of financial aid from the school, 42% were girls. Without a doubt, the school's financial aid program has benefited both males and females extensively and equally.

EQUITY IN ADMISSIONS

As we review the answers to our original question we see that some issues are more complex than others: "Do current admissions policies favor one sex or another? Has P.A. successfully attracted qualified applicants of both sexes, and have those males and females been given equivalent financial aid?" The second set of questions we can answer simply and affirmatively: that general equality and fairness characterize the financial aid program, and that Andover has had tremendous success attracting qualified applicants of both sexes. The answer to the question about admissions policies favoring one sex or the other is more complicated because there is disagreement within the community about the fairness of maintaining a student body with unequal numbers of males and females. Certainly the intent of continuing a modified version of the former "pool-dependent" policy is not to favor one sex over the other, but to give applicants in both pools equal chances of admission and to seek a similar high quality of admittees from both pools. Even so, flexible sex ratios may look to some observers like a lack of commitment to full coeducation.

Current P.A. admissions policies created a student body with a 43-57% ratio in 1985-86, or 14% more males than females. If the faculty vote for a ten year increase to an eventual female ratio of 50% had been followed as the school's admissions policy, the 1985-86 female ratio presumably would have been approximately the same. Both the Trustees' plan and the faculty vote envision a gradual increase in the female ratio in the student body. However, the Trustees' plan does not provide details for the timing of the increase, and it remains unclear whether the Academy will continue over the years to move to a 50-50% ratio.

Further complexity is added to the issue when we examine faculty opinion on the ratio question today. In April 1985 the faculty questionnaire asked whether faculty approved of the current male/female ratio in the student body. Fifty percent of the male faculty and 45% of the female faculty who answered the question replied that they approved of the current ratio. Forty-nine percent of the male faculty and 55% of the female faculty indicated that they thought there were too many males in the current student body. Only 1% of the male faculty responded that there were too many female students. Apparently, either some faculty members were unaware that the ratio at the time they were polled was 42-58% or the faculty has lost the shared concern that inspired its 1981 vote for a 50-50% ratio.

Certainly, the male/female ratio in the student body will be a continuing subject for discussion since it concerns the entire Andover community. For the ratio not only determines how many males and females will have access to an Andover education each year, but it also affects the tone of the school in a number of other ways that are subtle but important. The male-female ratio which has been close to 60-40 for some time has influenced male and female classroom experiences by increasing the likelihood of sex-imbalanced classes. It has contributed to the tendency for females to play a less prominent role in student elections and in the leadership of student organizations, and it has increased the likelihood that female students will be outnumbered in a variety of school activities, an experience which has been shown to undermine self-esteem and achievement motivation. Admissions policies create the basic gender balance or imbalance which permeates every part of Andover's educational environment.

Chapter Three:
ACADEMIC ATMOSPHERE AND ACADEMIC CHOICES

Has the school encouraged course selection, a classroom atmosphere, and a balanced, up-to-date curriculum which offers boys and girls alike a wide-ranging education and a chance to grow in self-confidence?

THE ANDOVER LEARNING ENVIRONMENT

Dropping in on several Andover classrooms, a visitor can see an array of gifted teachers discussing new ideas with highly motivated students. With an average class size of 14, faculty can often draw much of the class into daily discussions. A close working relationship between faculty and students is valued at P.A., and teachers report using class discussion more often than any other teaching technique to encourage classroom give and take.

A student's classroom experience encompasses much more than the ingesting of knowledge. Students learn from the trial and error of class participation, the peer relationships that emerge from shared classroom experiences, and from the quality of the guiding relationships that teachers have with them. Grades alone can never measure a successful classroom experience. Teachers and students often remember years later if a class was remarkable for its electric teacher-student rapport or for its surliness.

The intangible classroom magic that makes the same teaching technique bore certain combinations of personalities and inspire others is sometimes called "good chemistry" by teachers, for they know that interpersonal explosions can come from the "chemistry" just as easily as it can create a magical formula for learning. Therefore, collective classroom experiences are interactive, never determined solely by the way a teacher teaches. Classroom atmosphere evolves out of the combination of the personalities of students and teachers, their values, beliefs, stereotypes, and their feelings about themselves and their attitudes towards others. Not every factor that shapes a classroom atmosphere is obvious; nor do students and teachers always have a conscious awareness of the most crucial classroom dynamics.

Classroom atmosphere, as a result, is hard to quantify. A mixture of excitement, pressure, achievement-orientation, nurturance, creativity, high expectations, cooperation, competition, intimidation, affection, and enjoyment can be found within the classroom atmosphere at P.A. Probably the same could be said of any other school that prides itself on a close faculty-student learning partnership as well as academic excellence and high standards.

But what else can we say about the classroom atmosphere at P.A.? Opinions stated at the end of the student questionnaires covered a wide range. One boy exclaimed that "P.A. has the best damn faculty members - they're loose, intelligent, communicative, very easy to talk to and get to know . . . I like the atmosphere in the classroom." Other students remarked that academic pressure seemed to interfere with their ability to learn; for example, a girl wrote that:

> What I like least about Phillips Academy is the high pressure to succeed, by parents and by faculty. There are subjects that one can't grasp and that person should not be condemned for that. That's another thing, sensitivity to students. Teachers can be so unfeeling you just want to scream.

Only a few students complained of teachers who "make no effort to help you if you're failing," for at P.A. almost every student in academic trouble can gain access to help if s/he asks for it: from tutors, extra sessions with teachers, and Graham House study skills experts. However, not all students feel equally comfortable asking for help at P.A.

High academic expectations are a central part of the classroom experience at Andover, but often students' internal pressure to achieve is more urgent than the pressure put on them by teachers. One student complained that:

> Sometimes the competitiveness of people here bothers me—why can't we just have fun working at our studies? Kids seem to think 'I *have* to pass this test to get into Harvard or Yale etc.' But I don't think that is the reason I came to Andover. I came here for Andover, not what I am doing afterwards! . . . I had Andover which gave me experiences that I couldn't have gotten anywhere else . . .

Many students see getting good grades at Andover as vital to their future success, but good grades are not always easy to come by in a school filled with very bright, motivated students.

While two-thirds of the students surveyed believed that a "good" grade is an honors grade of 5 or 6, 84% of the faculty viewed a 4 as a "good" grade. This apparent disparity in defining a "good" grade suggests that students may be less satisfied with a 4 as a reward for good learning than the faculty thinks they should be. Certainly students prefer honors grades. In fact, though the faculty views a 4 as a good grade, it may be better defined as an average grade. The median grade point average earned at P.A. is slightly above a 4.

Andover's high academic expectations, coupled with the wide array of extracurricular, sports, and social options available to students, have sometimes created a "pace of life" problem, especially for students who try to excel at everything. Many students blame their "pace of life" problem on the amount of homework assigned, for though the faculty voted years ago to limit homework to an hour and fifteen minutes per class, it is widely acknowledged that many courses violate the rule by requiring more homework. Over two-thirds of the students rate the academic workload as "much too heavy" or "a bit too heavy." Again we find a discrepancy between student and faculty perceptions: 92% of the faculty when surveyed indicated that they typically assigned 75 minutes or less per day, indicating that most faculty believe their homework requirements fit into the reasonable time limits.

Student Perception of the Academic Workload

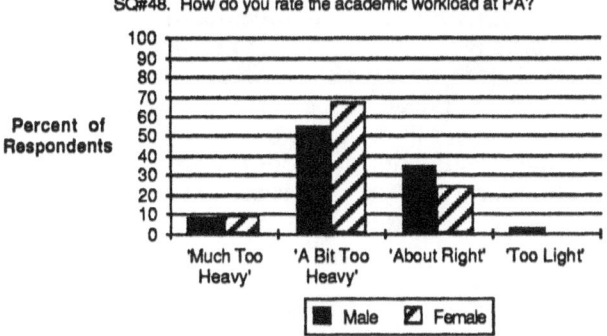

SQ#48. How do you rate the academic workload at PA?

Those males who answered 'Too Light' are in every class. Senior males reported the lowest rate of perceiving the workload as 'Much' or 'A Bit' too heavy.

In fact, many faculty would like to improve the quality of students' academic work, rather than decrease the amount. In general, the faculty was much more satisfied (88%) with students' ability at P.A. than with their academic performance (60% satisfied). Despite the pressure and the discrepancy between faculty and students' perceptions of the academic workload, a large number of students thrive on the P.A. academic atmosphere. When students were asked what they liked most about Andover they listed the quality of the education, the course variety, and excellent teaching by the faculty; these factors ranked in third and fifth place among the top seven things students liked best. Many students recognize that their academic experience at P.A. is a special one.

WHAT STUDENTS LIKE *MOST* ABOUT P.A.: VOLUNTARY RESPONSES TO OPEN-ENDED QUESTIONS

M	F	
129	117	1. Freedom/Opportunity for Personal Growth and Independence
112	130	2. The People, Friendship and Social Relationships in the Community
88	94	3. Quality of Education, Challenge, Course Variety, and Flexibility
42	69	4. Diversity of People
41	58	5. Faculty/Excellent Teaching/Relationship with Teachers
36	32	6. Facilities/Campus/Physical Plant/Location
28	23	7. Athletics

But not everyone thrives equally well in Andover's academic setting. Some students shrink from the pressure of high standards, while other students report they can easily "get by" in their classes, sports, and extracurriculars without excessive work or worry. Why are some students and not others intimidated and sometimes terrified by the intensity of the academic environment? Can we assume that responding to pressure negatively is due strictly to idiosyncratic or personal factors? No, because in every racial and ethnic group studied, females were more likely than males to rate the workload as too heavy. Blacks and Hispanics also rated the workload heavier than other groups, but gender more than race or ethnicity affects students' attitudes toward the academic workload. Although boys and girls earn the same grade point averages and perform equally well academically, girls in every ethnic and racial group were more likely than boys to judge the academic workload as too heavy.

Why should boys and girls have different attitudes about the academic demands of Andover? Boys may be socialized to be more stoic than girls about academic demands, or girls may be socialized to feel less confident of their ability to do well under pressure. Even if this were true, could anything exist within the academic environment at Andover to undermine female self-confidence or to bolster male confidence? Could Andover's special kind of classroom atmosphere work better for some students than others?

IS ANDOVER'S CLASSROOM ATMOSHPERE COMPLETELY "GENDER-BLIND"?

Officially, it is Andover's policy to be "gender-blind" inside the classroom, to treat both sexes with equal fairness, to evaluate them by the same objective criteria, and to help both sexes to fulfill their potentials as learners. There is massive data to prove that the school policy of sex equity in the classroom is carried out very well and that the ideal of fairness is put into practice successfully every day. However, we also have evidence that indicates that teachers do not always treat boys and girls in the same way, and that not all members of the community perceive them in a "gender-blind" way.

How do we know to what extent teacher-student interactions are "gender-blind"? Without intruding into the classrooms as observers, we must rely on faculty and student reports about what goes on, as well as written documents that teachers use to evaluate students' behavior in class. It is safe to assume that if "gender-blind" or "gender-biased" perceptions were recorded on evaluations they would also occur in classroom interactions.

"Gender-blind" evaluations of students would, presumably, mean that in an academic setting both sexes would be judged solely in terms of their performance in class discussions and on tests, papers, or other educational exercises. Attitude and effort, certainly, would be taken into account as well. When a random sample of 1400 evaluative descriptions of students (instructor reports, house counselor letters, college counselor letters, and coaches' comments) was done for the senior classes of 1974 and 1985, the vast majority of the evaluations of students were found to be "gender neutral" or to indicate a common "gender-blind" standard of judgment for both sexes.[86] Only two blatantly sexist items were found out of the 1400: one house counselor letter referred in a demeaning way to females as possessions and another reference in an inappropriate way to a young boy's masculinity. On the whole, the incidents of overt sexism in evaluation are extremely rare at Andover.

The only gender differences in evaluating students showed up in the areas of appearance and competitiveness. In both the '74 and '85 samples, females were evaluated in terms of their appearance much more often than males. An adult's comment about a student was coded in the appearance category only if it seemed to be out of context, that is, if the reference to appearance had nothing to do with the student's classroom, athletic, or extracurricular performance. Comments coded due to unusual remarks about students' appearance included references to beauty, hair, or dress styles, to a minority student's complexion, or to bodies in terms of thinness or thickness. In the Class of '74 sample comments were made about females' appearance four times as often as they were made about males' appearance, and in the Class of '85 sample there were eight times more comments made about females' appearance than about males'. Thus, the habit of evaluating female students more often than males on the basis of their appearance has not declined over the years.

Of course, it must be emphasized that out of the total sample of 1400, only 2% of the evaluations included any references to appearance. Evidently, the norm at P.A. is to evaluate students based upon their attitude and performance, without regard to their external appearance. Evaluation of students is a good example of the vast majority of teachers carrying out the school policy of sex equity by judging students of both sexes fairly using the same neutral criteria.[87] But the 2% exceptions are worthy of notice. Because adolescents are sometimes self-conscious about their appearance to begin with, a teacher's comment about their appearance may make them feel even more self-conscious in the classroom.[88] In addition, students with weak academic self-confidence, especially females, may have trouble taking themselves seriously as scholars if they believe that their teachers see them in terms of their height, weight, beauty, or complexion, rather than in terms of their ability to learn.[89]

In addition, faculty evaluations are crucial to building or eroding self-esteem. The Brown Project found strong links between student self-confidence and teacher supportiveness.[90] Research compiled by the Association of American Colleges' Project on the Status and Education of Women shows that even well-meaning complimentary remarks about a female student's appearance may undermine her confidence in class: such remarks "often make women uncomfortable because essentially private matters related primarily to the sex of the student are made to take precedence over the exchange of ideas and information."[91] If female students (or minorities or students who may already feel like "outsiders") are to be taken seriously in the classroom, research indicates that they should not be made uncomfortable by being evaluated in terms of their clothing or looks.

Just as appearance was more often mentioned in the Andover sample of evaluations of female students, competitiveness or aggressiveness was mentioned more often in evaluations of male students.[92] Competitiveness or aggressiveness were noted as valued traits in the evaluations for the Class of '85 twice as often for males as for females, and boys were judged more often than girls by the teacher's belief that competitiveness or aggressiveness were positive traits to be cultivated in student behavior.

When asked on the student questionnaire to rate whether teachers at P.A. valued competitiveness in students, 42% of the boys and 25% of the girls replied that competitiveness was "highly valued" or "valued" by teachers. Why should such a gender difference exist in students' views about how highly the faculty values competitiveness? Two explanations arise out of the data. Boys are more likely than girls to see competitiveness as valued by teachers because: 1) teachers are more likely to value competitiveness in boys than in girls, and 2) boys are socialized to value it more than girls are. When students were surveyed about which personality traits were characteristic of them, about half of both sexes rated themselves as assertive, but about two-thirds of the boys, compared to less than half of the girls, rated themselves as competitive. Competitiveness is a student trait which is also valued by more male than female teachers: competitiveness was rated as not valued at all by only 24% of the male faculty but almost half of the female faculty indicated they do not value it in students. Certainly, competitiveness is valued by enough faculty and students at Andover to be an influence on the classroom environment. Yet it is a trait which is admired and possessed more often by one sex, males.

Is it a problem for competitiveness to be valued by some teachers and students but not others in the P.A. classroom environment? Competition is synonymous in some teachers' and students' minds with high achievement motivation, yet *Webster's Dictionary* definition also implies that competitive self-assertion may affect interpersonal relationships: "1. a striving or vying with another or others for profit, prize, position, or the necessities of life; rivalry. 2. A contest, match, or other trial of skill or ability." [93]

Competitiveness may become a problem in the classroom if "rivalry" among students gets out of hand, if learning is viewed too often as a "trial of skill", or if educational success is viewed as a scarce "prize" available only to the competitors whose "striving against" or "vying" with their peers yields ultimate victory. Competition in the classroom can also be a problem for the 13% of the boys and 18% of the girls who do not see competitiveness as part of their personalities at all. For example, boys who want to achieve in the academic arena without adopting a competitive style may find it difficult to work with a teacher who values competition highly and who expects all boys to be competitive. Peer pressure to be competitive about academic success is also more likely to exist for boys than girls, but in the classroom it may spill over to affect both sexes. As we will see in the chapter on community values, because of the prevalence of competitiveness in the values of the community, the students of both sexes who do not see themselves as fitting into the competitive value system are the most likely to have low self-concept.

GENDER DIFFERENCES IN STUDENT CLASSROOM BEHAVIOR

In general, when students and faculty were asked about typical classroom behavior, students noticed more gender differences than faculty did. The majority of the faculty rated seven of the ten behaviors listed as being "about the same" for both sexes. Evidently, most teachers do not perceive boys and girls behaving in different ways in the classroom. Students see more behaviors as typical of one sex or the other. It is possible that students may see classroom behavior in more polarized and gender-typed ways than faculty simply because they may have stronger preconceptions about sex-appropriate behavior. However, the faculty may notice fewer gender differences than actually exist in the classroom in part because they may believe that the "gender-blind" school policy requires them to see boys and girls as basically the same. Many teachers have lived through previous eras when discussions of sex differences meant talking about alleged feminine intellectual inferiority. Thus denial of gender differences and official "gender-blindness" signified progress beyond the earlier unfavorable gender typings.

Despite the faculty's disinclination to note sex differences, some of them did agree with a larger portion of students who showed a marked tendency to view boys as more prone to aggressive or uncooperative classroom behaviors. For example, they rated behavior categories "often disruptive", "has a need to speak at every point", "often challenges teachers" as characteristic of boys more often than girls.

There was a parallel tendency to view girls more often than boys as prone to conscientious behaviors and eagerness to please. A majority of the students and male faculty (and a near majority of female faculty) viewed taking careful notes as characteristic of girls. In addition, all groups rated girls more often than boys as careful observers in the classroom. The faculty also viewed taking risks as a male classroom trait more often than a female trait. To what degree are the student and faculty responses to this question useful as descriptions of what actually happens in class? In fact, their answers represent perceptions about classroom behavior, rather than an exact description of daily behavior. Most people reply to such questions according to their beliefs about what ought to be, as well as what they have actually seen. But, obviously, such perceptions have some relationship to actual behavior. In cases where males and females, faculty and students agree at significant rates, we can assume they have told us something about what really happens in class.

One might assume that female faculty would rate girls higher and male faculty would rate boys higher on "positive" classroom behaviors, such as "contributes and moves class discussions along." But our data reveals no consistent pattern of same sex loyalty between faculty and students. For example, while high percentages of the faculty viewed the behavior "contributes and moves class discussions along" as the same for both sexes, women were more likely to see this positive trait as char-

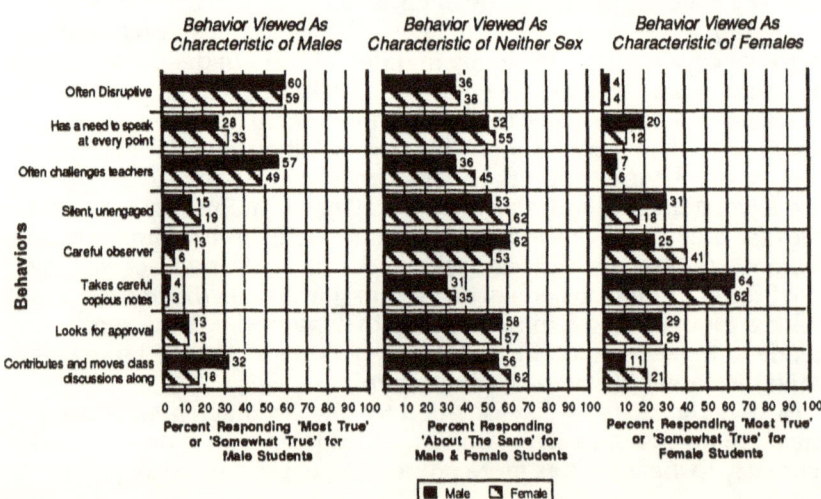

Student View of Male and Female Classroom Behavior

SQ#30 In your opinion, is there much difference in classroom behavior between male and female students?

Faculty View of Male and Female Classroom Behavior

FQ#7. From your experience, can you identify differences in classroom behavior between male and female students?

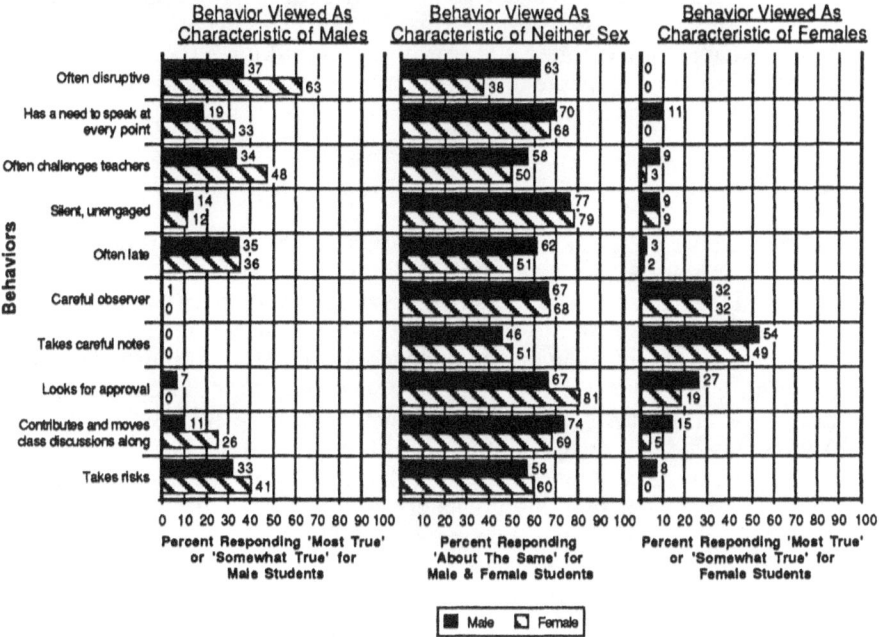

■ Male □ Female

acteristic of boys in the classroom. Men, on the other hand, were more likely to see it as characteristic of girls.

In addition, more than a third of the faculty viewed lateness to class as more characteristic of boys. Being "often disruptive" was seen as more characteristic of boys in class. Sixty percent of the boys, 59% of the girls, 63% of the women faculty, and 37% of the male faculty answered that it was characteristic of boys. Educational researchers elsewhere, in fact, have reported that boys generally are more disruptive in class than girls.[94]

Why were male teachers at Andover less likely than any other group to perceive boys as disruptive? We can only speculate, based on our data and research in educational psychology, that their perception is based on the fact that boys are actually less likely to be disruptive in front of male teachers. This speculation is given further credence by the fact that P.A. boys reported in the survey that they found male teachers more intimidating than female teachers. Other research indicates that boys may behave in more disruptive ways in classes taught by women because they respect men more highly and are used to being "controlled" by male authority figures. How many students shrink in fear when a woman teacher walks into class the first day of school? Studies show very few do.[95]

47

Though other studies show that girls talk less in class, none of our survey data conclusively supports or refutes that conclusion.[96] However, P.A. instructor reports on occasion describe less female classroom participation: a girl never said anything in one class because, according to her teacher, "she claimed she was afraid of making a fool of herself." No information is available to suggest that girls are more likely to talk in class if they have a female teacher.

STUDENTS' VIEWS OF MALE AND FEMALE TEACHERS

When students were asked on the Coeducation Study questionnaire whether "in their experience" "much difference" existed between male and female teachers, they were given a series of statements about teachers which they were to rate as "about the same" or "somewhat true" or "most often true" of male or female teachers. The majority of both sexes responding to all but one of the statements thought the statements were "about the same" for male and female teachers. However, significant percentages did see gender differences among teachers. For example, 42% of the boys and 39% of the girls rated the statement "Some teachers intimidate me" as true of men teachers. Younger students were more likely than older students to see male teachers as intimidating. Students were also more likely to see male rather than female teachers fitting the statements "Some teachers challenge me" and "Some teachers expect too much."

In spite of their tendency to see male teachers as more intimidating, many students do not necessarily like them less because of it. In one study which included high school students' evaluations of teachers, both boys and girls "rated teachers with 'masculine' teaching styles more positively than those with 'feminine' teaching styles on all measures except warmth."[97] Psychologists have found that on the college level some male students in particular may have trouble working with female authority figures such as professors. In one study students showed sex-bias in their less positive classroome valuations of women professors. Female professors were viewed more critically because, according to researchers, they may have been viewed by male students as "participating in a sex-inappropriate profession."[98] Still other studies show that male and female college teachers are treated and evaluated differently by students because of stereotypical expectations that women should be more nurturant. "Greater demands for student contact and support are placed on female professors than on male professors . . . ," but students evaluating teachers are more impressed by historically "masculine" teaching styles of dramatic lecturing and classroom dominance than they are by historically "feminine" styles of nurturance in the classroom.[99] Evidently, some students approach their classroom partnership with male and female teachers with certain preconceptions, and those preconceptions may even hinder their ability to learn.

When students were asked to rate classroom behaviors as being more typical of one sex or another, they were more likely to view male teach-ers as gender-biased. For example, they were more likely to see men teachers fitting the descriptions "some teachers use sex stereotypes in class," "some teachers show favoritism to girls", "some teachers grade boys differently from girls," "some teachers call on boys more than girls." It is crucial to note that we have no data to clarify where P.A. students' preconceptions or stereotypes about male teachers leave off and where actual male teachers' behavior begins. Perceiving maly au-thority figures as authoritative, demanding, intimidating, and sex-bi-ased may be as stereotypical as viewing female teachers as instinctively nurturant. Yet these answers reveal—at the very least—a lot about the

Student Perception of Differences Between Male and Female Teachers

SQ#29. In your experience, is there very much difference between male and female teachers?

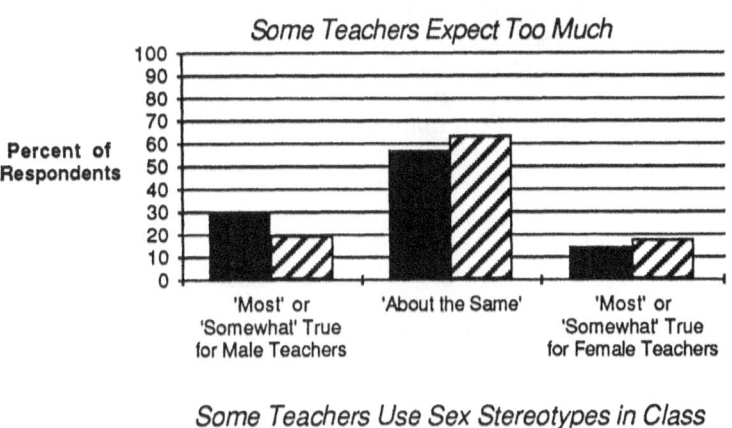

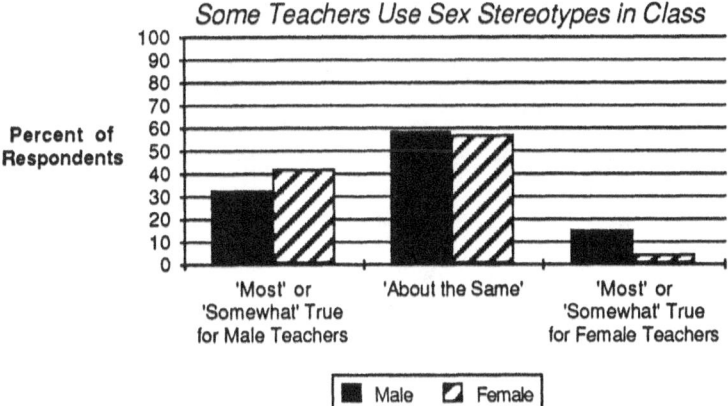

49

preconceptions that some students sometimes bring to class each day. In many students' minds women teachers appear not to have any unique characteristics, either positive or negative ones. Women teachers did not rate higher than men on any of these statements, including the evenly rated statement "some teachers make me feel free to talk in class." Because women did not rank higher than men in any category, it is legitimate to ask whether some of the students' tendency to rate behaviors as characteristic of men was related to the fact they have more experience with male teachers: 75% of the full-time teachers are male. The majority of students and teachers see most classroom behavior as typical of neither sex, but the attitudes and possible behavior revealed in this data suggest at least some sex-bias may exist in the P.A. classroom.

GENDER DIFFERENCES IN TEACHING STYLES

Beyond students' perceptions do we know for sure that male and female teachers behave in the same way in the classroom? Just as students see boys and girls behaving in different ways in the classroom, male and female teachers describe their own teaching styles in divergent manners. Male faculty report using slightly different teaching techniques from female faculty: men are less likely to use socially cooperative or group teaching techniques than are females. Men report using lecturing to convey material more often than women do, and they are more likely than women to indicate that they never use group projects, small groups, assignments structured to enable students to work together, or team teaching as teaching devices. Women are more likely to use films and research assignments, but very few gender differences appeared in the amount of homework given. Most teachers of both sexes report using reading assignments and homework exercises frequently.

The gender differences that show up in teaching techniques could be explained in terms of a Carol Gilligan–Nancy Chodorow theory which views affiliative behavior or special interest in relationships as more central to female identity formation than it is to male.[100] From their theoretical perspective one might expect males to teach in individualized ways, lecturing more, and using techniques that assumed students learned best as separate individuals, without group work. Females, according to the Gilligan–Chodorow perspective, would be more likely to use small group activity, group projects, and team teaching to bring the positive value of relationships to bear on the learning process.

Certainly, much of our data supports the Gilligan-Chodorow theory that women tend to favor learning methods that include affiliation and group cooperation rather than the separate, individual learner model.[101] However, not all responses fit this pattern so neatly. For example, few gender differences crop up in other aspects of teaching style, such as the use of individual student presentations as a teaching technique.

OVERT GENDER BIAS

In studies of other educational environments scholars have found that, far from being truly "gender-blind," teachers often treat boys and girls quite differently. For example, stereotypes about male and female intellectual capacities or the assumption that boys may "do more" with their education may encourage teachers to invest more energy in teaching boys than girls.[102] In addition to praising girls less than boys when they get the correct answer, teachers in the other schools studied also were found to:

> devalue the work of female students relative to males and encourage female helplessness by solving a problem posed by girls, while explaining to boys how to solve the problems . . . teachers call on or make eye contact with male students more frequently than with female students, and . . . female students are more frequently victims of sexual harassment. [103]

While these characteristics have been documented in classroom environments elsewhere, our data does not prove or disprove that any of these findings are true at Andover, except in one case.

In the rare occurrences of sexual harassment at P.A., teachers show overt gender bias and unprofessional conduct. Students and faculty would agree that sexual harassment is absolutely antithetical to academic excellence. While sexual harassment typically is committed by very few teachers, it is nonetheless a problem that disrupts the precious partnership and trust between teachers and students that is at the heart of a fine educational experience. Studies on the college level have shown that, although about a third of the female students surveyed at several colleges and universities have been victims of professors' sexual harassment, many victims never report such incidents for fear of reprisal, or because they consider it a personal problem they must endure alone. Others do not report sexual harassment simply because they do not know where to go.[104] Despite the lack of reporting of such incidents, schools and colleges have a legal obligation to prevent sexual harassment. Ever since the *Alexander v. Yale* precedent was set, sexual harassment of students in educational institutions covered by Title IX has been illegal.[105]

What is the legal definition of sexual harassment? The Equal Employment Opportunity Commission defined it as "unwelcome sexual advances, requests for sexual favors, and other verbal or physical conduct of a sexual nature" which may affect the conditions of employment or which may produce "an intimidating, hostile, or offensive working environment."[106] But sexual harassment has been defined in other ways as well. During the recent Harvard sexual harassment controversy an extensive university-wide survey revealed that males and females view the issue from drastically different viewpoints. Unlike their male counterparts, half of the female faculty and female grad students at Harvard perceived sex role stereotypes, sexual jokes, or sexual questions coming from a person in authority as examples of sexual harassment.[107] While male faculty and students at Harvard typically viewed sexual harassment as a sexual problem, female faculty and students were "more likely to see the problem of harassment to be an expression of masculine power over women."[108]

There have been very few reported harassment cases at P.A., but the school has made it clear that even one instance of sexual harassment is intolerable. Outside of physical and overt sexual harassment, of course, exists verbal harassment. Unthinking sexist remarks, name-calling, patronizing treatment, or "put-downs" are not what we usually think of as sexual harassment. Yet such behavior does harass or bother many women, and it is behavior that is gender-biased in that it is directed toward a female because of her sex. Thirty-two percent of the female faculty reported witnessing or experiencing some kind of overt gender bias or harassment at Andover.

Many females see both physical and verbal harassment and other forms of discriminatory treatment as humiliating, and educational researchers view such behavior as having a "chilling effect" on students' classroom experiences and their ability to gain an education.[108] In order to put an end to physical forms of harassment, Andover issued a new policy which prohibits any P.A. employee from making unwelcome or welcome sexual advances toward a student.[109] P.A. employees have been fired on occasion when charges of sexual harassment have been reported and substantiated against them, but no public efforts have been made to inform students of grievance procedures. The P.A. policy recommends writing the sexual harasser a memo asking him/her to stop specific behaviors as the first step in the grievance procedure. But, because of the power differential and the student's being intimidated in most cases by the harasser, it is unlikely that this procedure would work as well for student victims as for faculty victims. In their open-ended responses to the questionnaires, a few faculty and students referred to the problem of having nowhere to go to stop harassment. In most instances, however, house counselors, cluster deans, or other faculty would help and defend any student who had been physically or verbally harassed, and since the policy was announced no harassment grievance procedures have been initiated, which may be a sign that the policy has stifled harassing behavior.

Beyond sexual harassment and gender differences in evaluations, teaching styles, and perceptions of student and teacher classroom behavior, gender-biased classroom behavior by faculty or students was not studied by the Coeducation Committee. However, the Brown Project found that female students in six colleges and universities were more likely than males to notice sexually-biased faculty behavior, which their study categorized as "sexual jokes by a professor," "intellectual 'put-down' by a professor," "sexual advance by a professor," "professor's comment on appearance," and "course readings biased against own sex." Almost six times as many women as men reported experiencing an "intellectual 'put-down' by a professor." [110]

SEX-IMBALANCED CLASSES

Classroom atmosphere can also be affected by gender in a much more obvious way: students and teachers sometimes feel less comfortable in classes in which one sex greatly outnumbers the other. When faculty members were asked whether they found predominantly male or female classes more, less, or equally difficult to teach than balanced classes, the majority of the men and women viewed the two situations as about the same. However, 35% of the men and 23% of the women indicated that a predominantly male class was more difficult to teach than a balanced class. About 70% of both sexes viewed predominantly female classes as about the same to teach as balanced classes, but 20% of the men and 13% of the women answered that a predominantly female class was more difficult to teach than a balanced class. Eighteen percent of the women and 9% of the men viewed predominantly female classes as less difficult. The majority of teachers do not report sex-imbalanced classes being more difficult to teach, yet some faculty, especially men, indicate that sex-imbalanced classes can be more difficult to teach.

How do students at P.A. feel when they find themselves greatly outnumbered by the opposite sex in class? In general, a majority of students report feeling comfortable most of the time, talking less only some of the time, never feeling ignored, and never feeling they have to work harder for a good grade in such classes. Girls are more likely than boys to indicate each form of discomfort in sex-imbalanced classes. If the girls who reported that they talk less when outnumbered in class "all of the time," "most of the time," or "occasionally" are combined, 72% of the females indicated that their class participation could be affected by being in a predominantly male class.

Among Asian, Black and Hispanic students, a notable level of uneasiness with sex-imbalanced classes shows up. More than any other group, Asian males report feeling uncomfortable being outnumbered by females in class, and about a third of the Asian males indicate significant discomfort in such classes. Black and Hispanic males and females are more likely than overall averages to report feeling ignored and as if they have to work harder for a good grade occasionally or some of the time in classes in which their sex is outnumbered.

While the majority of students at Andover appear not to be bothered greatly on a conscious level when they find themselves in sex-imbalanced classes, the survey data shows that the experience of being outnumbered in class may interfere with female class participation and Asian males' comfort in the classroom, and may contribute to Black and Hispanic students' feelings of being ignored and needing to work harder for good grades in class.

How many classes at P.A. are sex-imbalanced? Thirty-six percent of the total male enrollments in the fall of 1982 (4-5 enrollments or courses are typically taken by each student each term) were in sections where boys made up 70-100% of the class, but only 13% of the total female enrollments were in such predominantly male classes. In courses which boys elect at higher rates than girls, such as advanced math, computer, or science courses, girls may find themselves outnumbered 10 to 1. The same ratio often confronts boys who elect gender studies courses, and on occasion the outnumbered boy or girl will drop the class. Only 1% of the male and 9% of the female enrollments in the fall of 1982 were in sections where females made up 70-100% of the class. Boys are most likely to be greatly outnumbered in classes that girls elect more often: advanced French, women's studies, and psychology courses. Because of the unequal ratio of boys to girls in the student body, girls are more

Student Reaction to Sex-Imbalanced Classes

SQ#28. Some classes at PA have many more girls than boys while others have many more boys than girls. How do you feel in those classes in which your sex has been greatly outnumbered?

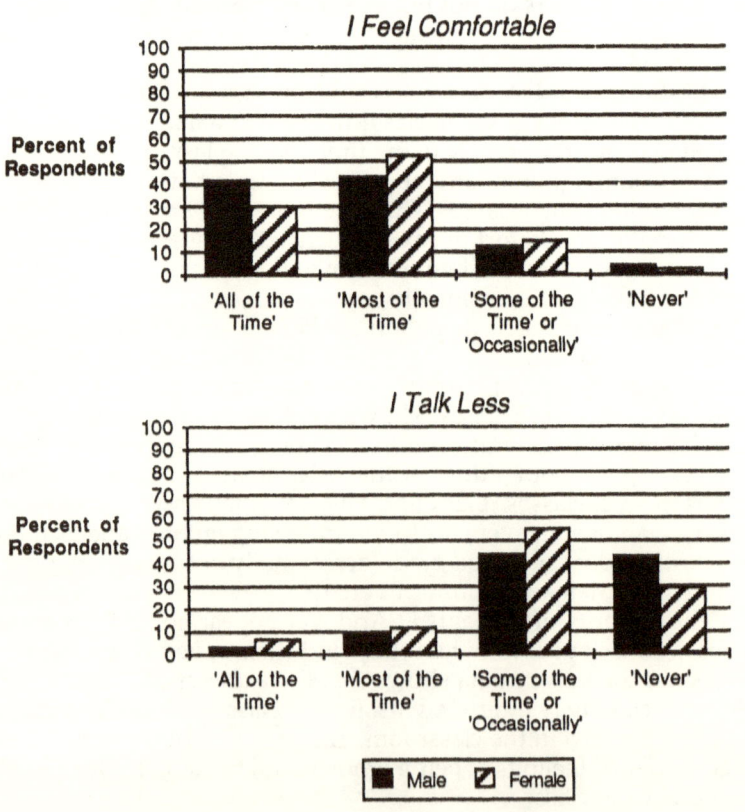

likely than boys to be greatly and mildly outnumbered by the opposite sex in class. In fact, 41% of all female enrollments were in classes in which females were outnumbered, i.e. in which males made up 51-70% of the class.

The research on the effect sex-ratios have on female self-confidence, which was summarized in the Admissions chapter, demonstrates that sex-imbalanced classes may not be the optimal educational experience for either sex. Title IX explicitly calls on educational institutions to study why sex-imbalanced classes occur in their schools and colleges to make sure that the disproportion does not result from discrimination or sex-biased academic advising.[111] At P.A. sex-imbalanced classes are not usually caused by advisors telling girls not to take "male subjects." Instead the unequal sex-ratio in the student body, random distribution processes, and students' own course preferences create the sex-imbalanced class problem.

GENDER AND THE CURRICULUM

How has Andover met the educational needs of its students since the beginning of coeducation? The New England Association of Schools and Colleges' Visiting Committee reported that Andover lacked "substantial philosophical underpinnings for educational practices which might well be different according to whether boys or girls are involved." This statement is still true today, but Andover has just started to revise its curriculum to reflect the presence of women, to integrate new scholarship in gender studies into traditional course content, and to reexamine styles of pedagogy for their impact on each sex.

Though most departments have not yet discussed ways to change course content or pedagogical styles in order to include more awareness of gender issues, a few departments have updated their curricula and explored the implications of teaching in a coeducational classroom. Under the leadership of former Abbot teacher Jean St. Pierre, chair of the English Department, and former chair Kelly Wise, the curriculum of all required English courses has been changed to include "core texts" by important women and minority writers. So in English 10, Competence, and Lit. B students read women writers and they learn about the life experiences and perceptions of women. In addition, "Images of Women" and other English electives are offered to students who are especially interested in the topic. With the aid of an Abbot Academy Association Grant, the chair of the French Department, Abbot graduate Natalie Schorr, initiated a review of the "cultural content" of the department's curriculum and the way that curriculum was conveyed. One of the stated goals of the curriculum review was to "check that the achievements of women are included in the curriculum."[112]

In addition, other areas of the school did the same. The integration of women and gender issues into the Psychology curriculum happened as the department kept apace with the changes in their discipline and in new gender research being conducted by psychologists. Almost every psychology course includes some updated material on sex roles and personality, and the Human Sexuality class is largely focused on gender identity, male and female developmental growth, and male-female relationships. The Addison Gallery has held showings of art by women artists, and ethical issues related to gender have been explored in some Religion and Philosophy courses.

Other departments are on the brink of change. Until 1981, in the History 300 survey required of students for graduation, women did not appear as a subject of study at all, nor were suffrage, birth control, temperance, or women's labor movements mentioned in more than a passing way. In 1982, due to lobbying by recently hired women faculty, one day of women's history was added to the year-long course. P.A. students received a very strong and thorough preparation in U.S. History, but the year that the American History Advanced Placement exam asked a major essay question about women's history they were educationally disadvantaged compared to students from other schools.

While only one gender-related history and social science course which could meet a student's four-term History requirement, Susan Clark's European social history, is offered, two advanced elective seminars, one on Family History and another on Men, Women and American Culture, are offered for seniors who have already completed their history requirement. However, because these electives and the social history course are not offered every year, it is usual for less than thirty students out of more than 1200 to be taking any gender-related history or social science courses in a given year. Course material on gender and/or women's experience has been integrated into the new 9th grade Change and Continuity course, Russian History and literature, African history, and the Courts and Constitutional Development seminar.

Unless they elect one of these courses, the average P.A. student would study women's history only one day in History 300 and then never again. Because the traditional strengths of the department have been political and constitutional history, the integration of social history, especially women's history, into the curriculum has only recently been proposed. Discussions of the future of the History curriculum, especially History 300, were slated for the 1985-86 academic year, and History chair Derek Williams expressed eagerness to include more material on women and minorities in the upcoming revision of History 300.

Out of almost 300 courses listed in the 1985-86 course offerings, two or three focused primarily on gender or women's studies. Andover, perhaps because it is a secondary school, offers less coverage in its curriculum of gender and women's issues than many other institutions. The Brown Project found that 40% of the female and 24% of the male students in the six colleges studied had taken courses that included gender studies or "specialized coverage on women." Is it reasonable to expect more gender or women's studies courses or more inclusion of gender issues in a high school curriculum? Yes, because many other schools like Andover have already done so. Portions of the P.A. community responded favorably when, during the Coeducation Celebration weekend, Susan Lloyd presented a variety of models of curriculum change which Marilyn Schuster and Susan Van Dyne of Smith College had constructed to show several stages of integrating women and gender issues into the curriculum.[113]

But despite these discussions, the process of intellectual integration has only recently gained momentum at Andover. When the faculty was asked "Should we design specific courses to deal directly with gender issues?" only 9% of the male faculty and 25% of the female faculty approved of courses related to male issues. Only 11% of the males and 35% of the females approved of courses related to female issues. Seventy-five percent of the females said gender courses about men and women should be offered as compared to 54% of the male faculty who thought so. In general, the faculty responded most favorably to handling all gender issues within the existing courses.

In 1985 both the Faculty Advisory Committee and the Curriculum Committee discussed the need for integrating more awareness of women and minorities into the curriculum. Because curriculum initiatives are normally taken on the departmental level by the people who know their discipline best, it remains unclear whether any initiatives for change coming from outside of the departments will be fruitful.

Furthermore, was it reasonable, as the "androgyny report" proposed, to expect the school to change its teaching styles and the way it presented course material in response to coeducation? Pedagogical styles are an even more elusive matter than curriculum content, for the strong tradition of individual teacher autonomy in the classroom at Andover is guarded as a cherished prerogative.

Teaching that is sensitive to gender differences in students' learning styles may sound mysterious, yet other schools have started to implement the idea. For example, the Emma Willard school, where Carol Gilligan was hired as a consultant, discovered that too much autonomous decision-making had the potential of "frightening" some adolescent girls, for choice-making without appropriate support systems appeared to be too isolating for many young girls. Thus, while Emma Willard continues to insist that adolescent girls make independent choices about course selection and other matters, they have given more attention to creating supportiveness within their advising system.[114]

The Emma Willard School has also required that every teacher offer students opportunities to work cooperatively in class. The school's Academic Dean Jack L. Easterling says that girls' "sense of responsibility to co-workers," which has been documented in Gilligan's research, can help girls learn better through collaborative learning arrangements. According to an article in *Education Week* about these attempts to restructure classroom learning, the assumption that interdependent learning works better "runs counter to the traditional male-oriented view that competition between individuals leads to better performance."[115]

Another argument has been made for encouraging collaborative learning: research shows that in coeducational classrooms the tendency to avoid interacting with the opposite sex can be countered by cooperation which encourages boys and girls to mix as equals. In the recent *Handbook for Achieving Sex Equity through Education* educational researchers recommend that "to reduce sex segregation, teachers should restructure their classrooms to utilize cooperative cross-sex learning and discussion groups."[116] Thus, the cooperative approach has been recommended as a way of encouraging female confidence and for establishing a pattern of male and female partnership in the classroom.

During the discussion about a coeducational curriculum which Sue Lloyd chaired during the Coeducation Celebration Weekend in 1984, teaching attitudes and styles at P.A. were discussed. Participants asserted that in many classrooms, P.A. teachers still assumed their students were a male audience and that it was common to teach supposedly gender-neutral subject matter with the use of male-oriented examples and assumptions. Military examples used in chemistry and construction-based math problems have been a daily part of classroom presentations without anyone asking whether they were oriented toward traditionally male experience. It was suggested that examples from everyday life experienced by both sexes, e.g. consumer, environmental, or household situations could serve as a useful counterbalance to the male-oriented examples that had predominated for so long.

At the end of Sue Lloyd's forum during the Coeducation Weekend, many participants expressed enthusiasm for exploring issues of gender and the curriculum further. As yet, no coordinated effort to systematically revise the curriculum has been launched, and no comprehensive plans have been made to review sex bias or racial stereotyping in textbooks and other teaching materials.[117] But ideas about curriculum revision and coeducational teaching methods have started to percolate within the faculty. Fortunately, compared with many other sex equity issues, revising curriculum to include women and gender issues, choosing unbiased teaching materials, and experimenting with cooperative teaching techniques were straightforward solutions to straightforward problems. Ultimately, they were much more manageable than the more complicated issues of students' stereotyped course selection and lower female academic self-confidence.

CHOOSING COURSES: MALE AND FEMALE PATTERNS

Students at Andover choose their academic programs with their academic advisors, and in addition to basic requirements in English, Math, Science, History, Foreign Languages, Art and/or Music, Religion/Philosophy, and Physical Education, the average student will have several trimester slots open for free elective choices. Academic advisors encourage students to move on to advanced courses in at least one area, and they encourage students to take a wide variety of courses. Advisors frequently allow the student to pursue elective choices based on the student's own subject preferences.

When students make their own elective choices, however, they do not decide in a vacuum. They may be influenced, not only by their advisor's preferences, but by opinions expressed by their house counselors, parents, and peers. More elusive still are the multitude of cultural influences on students choosing their courses—from negative portrayals of "artsy" men in movies to TV dramas with unflattering caricatures of women scientists.[118] In American culture at large math and science have often been considered "masculine" subjects, and literature, art, and languages have been viewed since before the Victorian Era as subjects which "cultured" ladies should study.[119] Today these stereotypes would be considered laughable and old-fashioned by almost all of the people who formally advise students in choosing their courses. Yet our research indicates that, to a surprising degree, a minority of Andover students still makes elective course choices which are consistent with those old stereotypes. Boys elect more advanced math and science than girls do, and girls take more advanced language study.

Stopping math after meeting the diploma requirement is more characteristic of girls than boys. While less than a quarter of the boys stop math

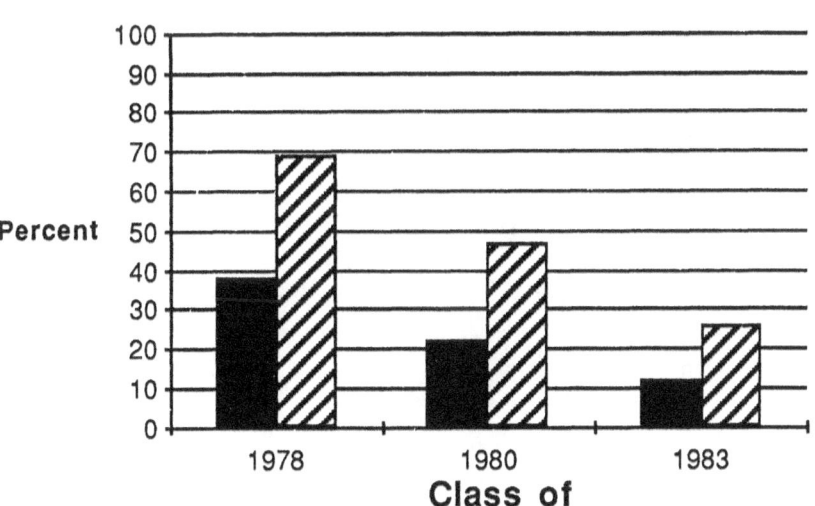

Percent of Students Stopping Math After Meeting the Diploma Requirement in Math*

(*three and four-year students in these classes)

(or take one term after pre-calculus), 38% of the girls stopped math. The higher the grade in their last math course, the more likely both boys and girls were to take further math courses, but a grade of 4 earned in their last math course was more likely to discourage girls than boys from pursuing math further.

But grades were clearly not the only reason that so many girls dropped math after meeting their requirement; even girls who earned honors grades in their required math course were more likely than boys with honors to drop math. According to the results of the student questionnaire, fewer girls (23%) than boys (33%) defined math as their strongest subject, and it is probable that among these 23% are the girls most likely to take advanced math classes. In addition, a larger proportion of girls, 35% (as opposed to 23% of the boys), reported that math was their weakest subject.

Why should more girls than boys perceive math as their weakest subject, and why should girls avoid advanced math more than boys do? Do girls avoid math because of weaker math aptitudes? At the beginning of coeducation, Andover boys had much higher Math SAT scores than the girls, but the gap has been closing over the years. In 1985 there is still a difference in the average Math SAT scores with boys overrepresented (i.e., represented in proportions greater than their percentage in the student body) in the highest SAT ranges (745-800). Yet very few Andover girls have Math SATs low enough to keep them from pursuing any advanced math courses.[120] When the P.A. Math SAT scores are compared with national averages it is clear that math aptitude is not what is holding Andover girls back from advanced math study.

PA Distribution of Math SAT Scores 1983

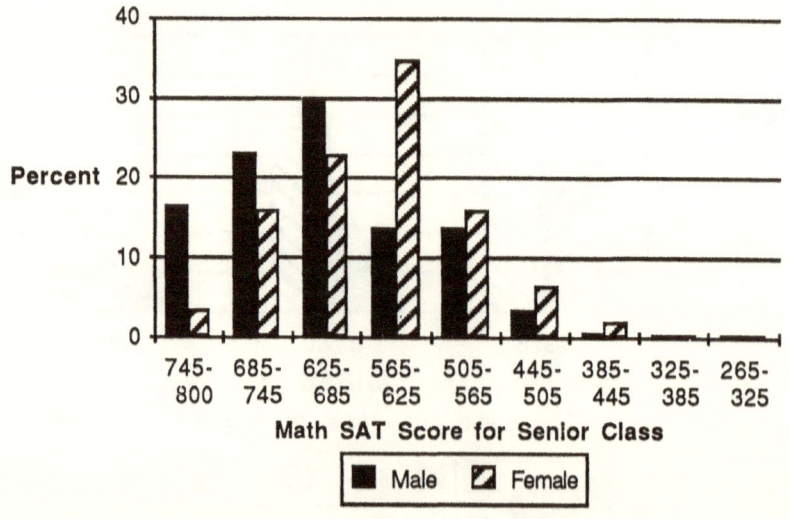

National Distribution of Math SAT Scores 1984

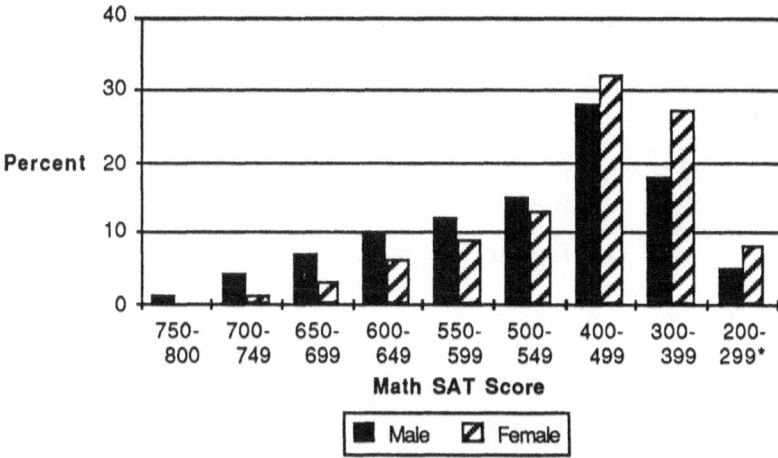

* Note categories of scores differ slightly from PA scores.

Rather than aptitude, social factors are to blame for female avoidance of advanced math at P.A. If girls believe that their peers view advanced math as a "masculine" endeavor and if girls fear being the only female in a class filled with male "math brains," they may avoid advanced math altogether. What effect does the considerable likelihood of being taught by a male math teacher have on girls' avoidance of advanced math? In the winter term of 1985, 25 sections of advanced Math were taught by men and only two were taught by women. Since coeducation began the 26 member math department has never had more than three female teachers at a time. However, in our survey most girls do not report in significant percentages being influenced by the sex of the teacher. On the other hand, a few girls mentioned in a *Phillipian* article being put off by the "overall male atmosphere" and patronizing attitudes in the math classroom.[121] It is possible that more girls would take advanced math if more female teachers taught it, because it might help change perceptions of math as solely a "masculine" subject and it might change the department's image as an all "male atmosphere." But having few female teachers is only part of a complex nationwide problem, for girls all over the country avoid advanced math as Andover girls do.[122]

Encouragement appears to be vitally important to girls' decisions to pursue advanced math at Andover. Girls rated higher than boys their academic advisors' advice, parental suggestion, and teacher encouragement as factors leading them to take advanced math. As studies of female math anxiety show, many talented females underrate their abilities in math, assuming that their intimidation by or discomfort with the subject is equivalent to lack of competence.[123]

Though it is impossible to predict future trends in P.A. girls' avoidance of advanced math, evidence suggests that it is becoming more common for some girls to define themselves as specializing in math. For instance, more girls have been taking Advanced Placement exams in Math recently. In the '77-'78 academic year only 11% of those taking Math APs were girls, whereas in '82-'83 the proportion had risen to 38%. That sharp rise in female students' AP participation suggests that a minority of the girls have specialized comfortably in Math, and that they are getting departmental support for doing so. In fact, taking APs is not always a sign of specialization in a particular subject, but it often seems to be more related to a department's encouragement of the student to take the exam.

Because girls' tendency to avoid advanced math electives was recognized as a problem, steps were taken to make math more welcoming to girls. The chair of the Math Department Doug Crabtree sent "letters of encouragement to girls who had done well in intermediate level Math courses, urging them to consider taking Math 55 or other advanced Math courses." In order to prevent the computer room from becoming a "boys club," efforts were made to encourage student computer supervisors to be "sensitive to behavior that might push girls away." In addition to sponsoring departmental discussions of the problem, Crabtree has worked actively to recruit new female math teachers. He told the *Phillipian* that "There's a lot of what you might call Affirmative Action going on now in the Mathematics and Science programs."[124]

As is the pattern in math, boys are more likely to take science than girls. Girls are more likely than boys to avoid science that is not required. Thirty-four percent of the female students, compared to 26% of the boys,

Average Number of Terms Taken

by Four-Year Students in the Class of 1983

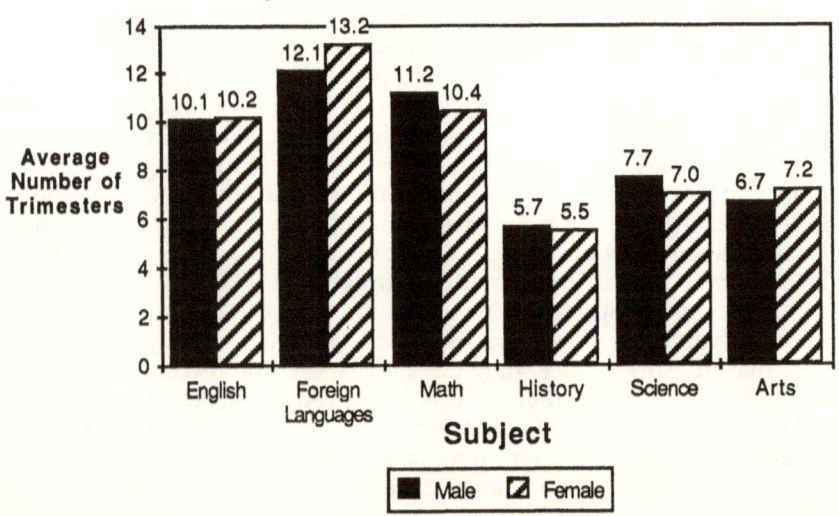

take no science after completing their science requirement. Thirty-two percent of the girls take no science in the ninth grade while only 18% of the boys avoid science that year. When they do take a year long lab science to fulfill the requirement, girls are much more likely to enroll in Biology than Chemistry or Physics. Among three or four-year students who often have time to take science beyond the required level, 34% of the females and 58% of the males will take a second lab science. However, when girls do take extra science they generally take the same amounts as boys. Girls who do elect post-requirement science courses take on the average 4.3 trimesters while boys take 4.5.

While a third of the boys and nearly a quarter of the girls reported that Math was their strongest subject, only 11% of the boys and 7% of the girls viewed Science as their strongest subject. But both sexes also judged science to be their weakest subject less often than they did Math. It should be noted that students were somewhat more likely to note that Math, English, and Language were their strongest *or* weakest subject (than other subjects) probably because of more extensive exposure to these subjects during their P.A. career. They are required to take more terms in these subjects than in the other areas.

Diploma Requirements for Four-Year Students

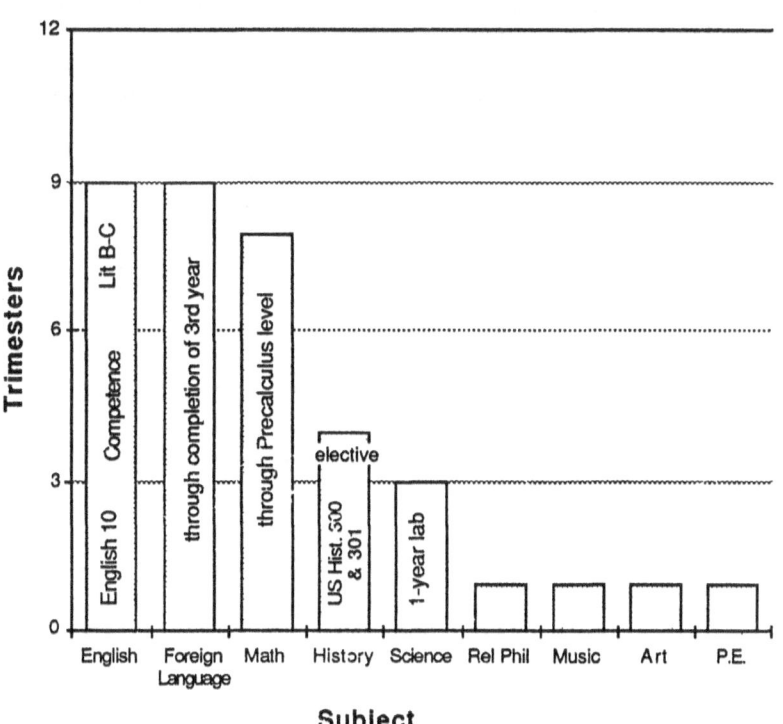

The disparity in the rate of males versus females electing advanced science is not as great as in Math but the trend toward increasing female specialization in Math seems not to be paralleled in science. In contrast to the trend toward more girls taking Math Advanced Placement Exams, the number of girls taking science APs is decreasing. While 77 boys and 10 girls took science APs in 1978, by 1983 only 9 girls and 64 boys took the tests. Boys who had not earned honors grades in Science were more likely to take APs than girls were, and many girls with honors in Science did not choose to take the APs.

Just as the Math department took the initiative to support girls' interest in Math, Chemistry teacher Leslie Ballard, later appointed Chemistry Department Chair, wrote letters to girls who had earned honors grades in required science courses urging them to take more advanced sciences. The Science Division has tried to augment this form of encouragement with occasional women speakers on scientific subjects, and recruiting women faculty has become an increasing priority in the sciences.

Just as boys took advanced Math and Science courses more readily than girls, girls were almost twice as likely as boys to continue studying their "first" foreign language beyond the basic requirement. Among four year students in the class of '83, boys were twice as likely as girls to do the absolute minimum in foreign languages. Instead of choosing advanced study of their "first" language, boys were three times as likely as girls to try a second foreign language. The average number of trimesters of the "first" foreign language taken beyond requirement differs significantly by sex, for males take an average of 1.7 terms, while females take 2.9 terms. French is the language most likely to attract a larger percentage of girls than boys, and Latin does the opposite.

What Students See As Their Strongest Subjects

SQ #31. What is your STRONGEST subject area?

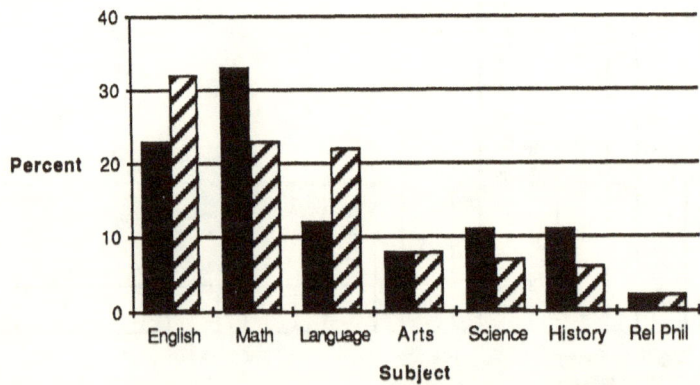

Girls were more likely than boys to see language as their strongest subject, at a rate of 22% compared to 12% of the boys. Conversely, 22% of the boys judged language to be their weakest subject in contrast to 13% of the girls. The trend toward girls specializing in foreign languages more often than boys is also evident in the rate at which girls take APs. Between '77-'78 and '82-'83 the proportion of AP tests in foreign languages taken by girls increased from 47% to 59%, and girls tended to earn 20% more 4 or 5 grades than boys on the language APs. Could aptitude be a factor in boys' more frequent tendency to stop studying their "first" foreign language after completing the requirement? Probably not, because male and female verbal average SAT scores have been roughly similar for the past several years.

When students indicated on the questionnaire which advanced electives they had or planned to pursue, girls more often than boys said they would take English, Arts, Languages, and Religion/Philosophy. Boys more often than girls said they had taken or planned to take advanced electives in Math, Sciences, and History. When asked which subjects they had not pursued or did not plan to pursue, the same pattern of preference emerged. The pattern of course selection noted by students on the questionnaire is also consistent with the pattern of courses they actually take. In a study of gender distribution in courses beyond the requirement in '77-'78, '79-'80, and '82-'83, girls were found to be overrepresented in foreign languages (except Russian, Greek and Latin which have high percentages of males enrolled), English, Art, and Rel/Phil. Boys were overrepresented in Math, Science, and to a lesser degree History.

What Students See As Their Weakest Subjects

SQ #32. What is your WEAKEST subject area?

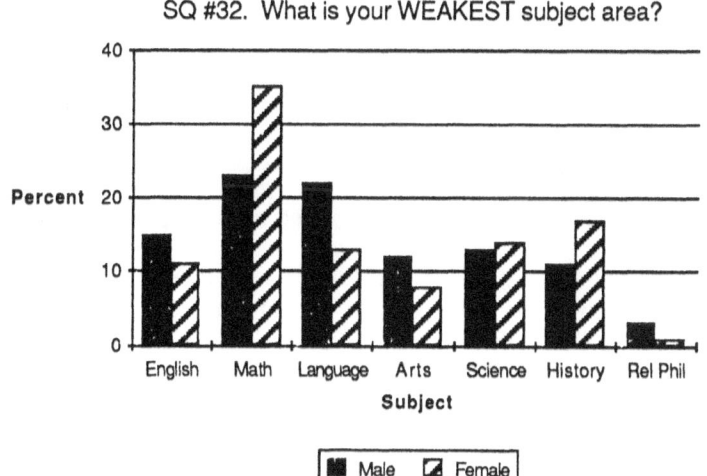

Stopping a Subject After Meeting the Diploma Requirement

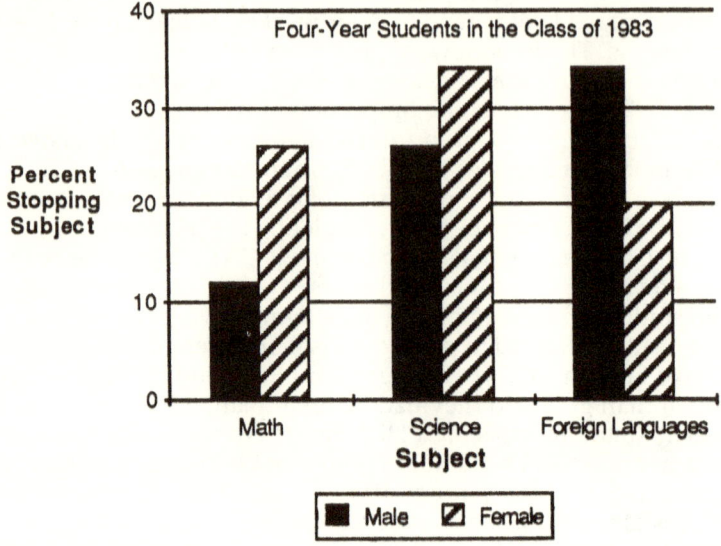

The trends in these gender distributions suggest that female overrepresentation in some foreign language, English, Art and Rel/Phil is increasing slightly, but that a higher proportion of girls are taking advanced History and Social Science courses than before. Girls are now somewhat less likely to be underrepresented in Math and in Chemistry than they used to be, but boys seem to be choosing Physics even faster than before. Biology has shown an increasing tendency to be the girls' "science of first choice."

These patterns of subject avoidance and gender-related specialization point up an overall problem at Andover: girls' avoidance of advanced Math and Science and boys' avoidance of advanced foreign language. We need to keep in mind that typically 66% of the girls do go beyond the requirement in science, and, 62% of the girls do go beyond pre-calculus in math. A genuine educational problem connected with gender-related curricular specialization, however, does exist, especially for girls. Boys' tendency to avoid foreign language creates much less of an educational handicap than girls' avoidance of advanced math and science because rarely does a boy's choice close off future career options. Because Andover's one year science requirement is less than many high schools and less than many selective colleges expect students to take, girls' avoidance of post-requirement science often leaves a serious deficiency in their high school education. The faculty has voted new academic advisors' guidelines to discourage the avoidance of science, and the Science Division has recently revised their course offerings to make them more appealing as electives.

PA Distribution of Verbal SAT Scores 1983

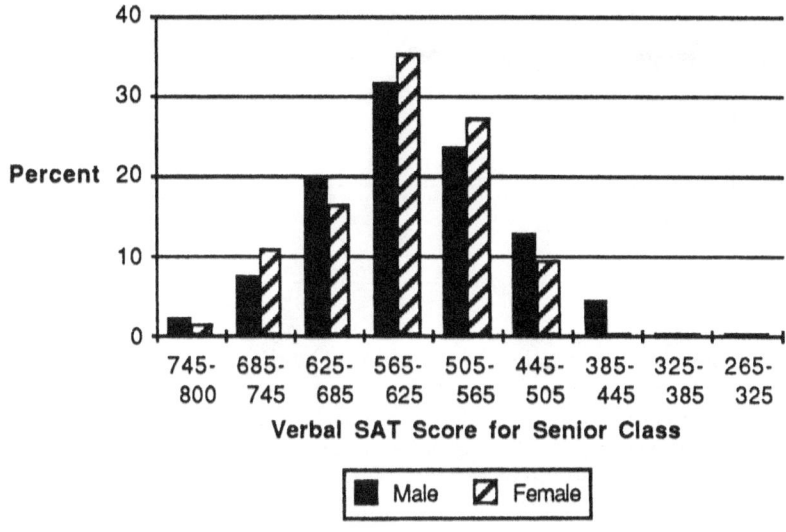

Unwillingness to explore unfamiliar territory and hesitancy to take academic risks does not necessarily make for an unsuccessful or incomplete education, but by closing out certain academic options for themselves girls may be limiting their own horizons. Girls may be eliminating certain college majors and diminishing their chances to have careers in quantitative and scientific fields by avoiding advanced science and math in high school. Many barriers of discrimination that once blocked girls' career paths have been removed. But culturally-encouraged barriers to full educational and professional self-fulfillment, i.e. being socialized to have less confidence in their math and science abilities still stand in their way.[125] Ultimately, education is designed to encourage each individual to reach his or her greatest potential, but boys and girls do not have the same attitudes toward the greatness of their own potentials.

ACADEMIC ABILITIES, PERFORMANCE, AND REWARDS

P.A. students have shown themselves to be an exceptionally able group of young people. High standardized test scores and excellent academic performance are the norm for both sexes. At the beginning of coeducation the gap between male and female SAT scores at Andover was larger than it is today. In the early years of coeducation male math SAT averages in some years exceeded female math averages by 88 points. Female SAT scores have been improving relative to male SATs in the past decade. The overall SAT math average for P.A. males in 1985 was 664, while the

SAT Averages

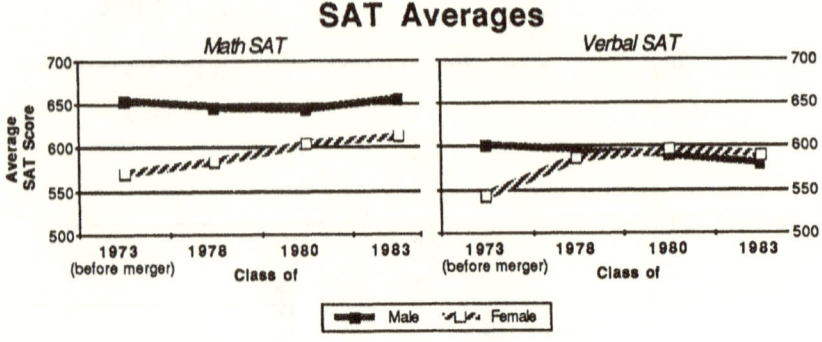

comparable average female score was 632. The disparity is caused in part by the fact that boys more often than girls earned math SAT scores in the very highest ranges (745 to 800). Since coeducation began, girls have been equal to or have surpassed boys in verbal SATs. In the class of 1985 girls' overall verbal SAT average was 592, compared to 594 for the boys. In general, the overall abilities of male and female P.A. students as measured by SAT aptitude tests are approximately the same.

Andover's male and female students are more likely to earn similar grade point averages than they were a few years ago. The Merger Study found that in the first coeducational graduating class boys had higher overall grade point averages.[126] In fact, close to a third of the senior boys had honors averages of 5.0 or above, compared to 19% of the girls earning a Phillips diploma and 11% earning an Abbot diploma. By 1983 girls and boys were earning almost the same grade point averages. However, male and female grade earning patterns often differ in their overall distributions. For instance, males are more likely to earn very high and very low grades. In addition, exceptional success in math and science contribute to boys' more frequent very high grades. Thus, boys' grades are

Grade Averages by Term for Senior Class During Senior Year

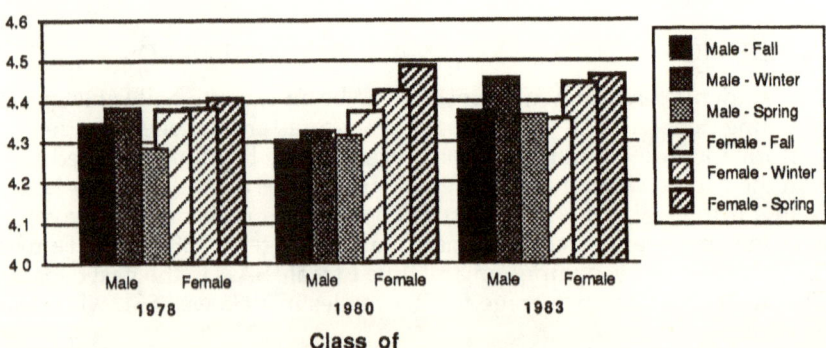

Distribution of Grades

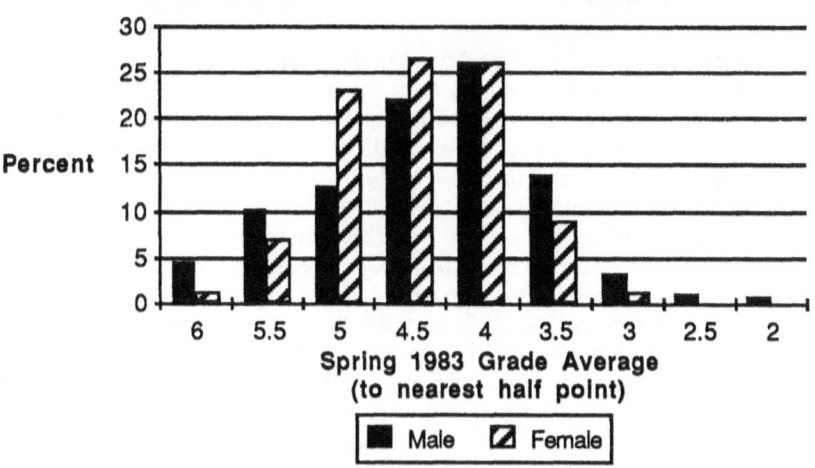

Percent

Spring 1983 Grade Average
(to nearest half point)

■ Male ▨ Female

more likely to be spread out than girls are, and girls' grades are less likely to stray far from the middle ranges.

In keeping with the male pattern of more extreme grade performances, males get into academic trouble by earning low grades more often than do females at Phillips Academy. When students earn consistently low or failing grades for a certain number of terms, the faculty has the option to vote intermediate steps to signal danger, such as "no excuse" or "general warning." After that the faculty may vote to dismiss a student for poor academic performance. Boys are more likely than girls to earn no excuse or general warning votes from the faculty, and they are almost twice as likely as girls to be required to withdraw for academic

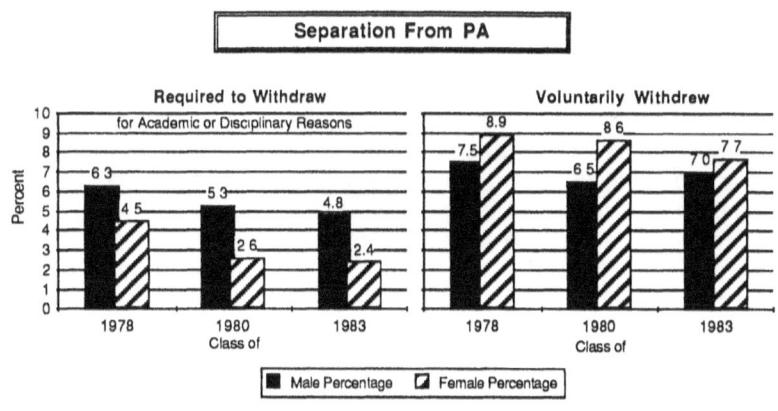

Separation From PA

Required to Withdraw
for Academic or Disciplinary Reasons

Voluntarily Withdrew

■ Male Percentage ▨ Female Percentage

reasons. However, girls are more likely than boys to voluntarily with-draw, to decide that P.A. is the wrong school, or to leave for personal reasons.[127]

In general, boys and girls at Andover are equally able, and they per-form equally well academically. Given their equivalent abilities and per-formances, it would seem reasonable for them to receive equivalent re-wards in terms of prizes and other kinds of recognition. But rewards have not always been distributed evenly. In a three year period almost a hundred National Merit finalists were given recognition at P.A., but boys predominated in this group, possibly because of the greater fre-quency of very exceptional math aptitudes among them. In department-al prizes boys were again overrepresented. In a total count of depart-mental prizes given in 1982, '83, and '84, boys earned 256 compared to 125 earned by girls. In the Math department a total of 58 prizes were given to boys compared to five for girls in those years. Similarly, in Sci-ence 23 boys were awarded prizes compared to 3 girls. Somewhat similar prize patterns appear in Classics, History, and Music where girls earned significantly fewer honors. The only disciplines which awarded females more prizes than males were English (20 female, 19 male) and Art (35 female, 26 male).

While departmental prizes are certainly distributed unequally, it is worth noting that departments usually award prizes to students who have distinguished themselves in advanced courses in that subject. Therefore, if group A chooses to take more advanced electives in a par-ticular subject than group B, then group A will increase its chances of winning departmental recognition in that subject. Such is the case of boys specializing in advanced math courses, thereby increasing their chances of earning Math prizes.

At the end of each school-wide academic year, prizes are awarded at a Prize Assembly and others are given at the Commencement exercises. It might be expected, since girls make up two-fifths of the student body and boys three-fifths and the two groups have the same overall ability and performance characteristics, that prizes might be awarded in ap-proximate proportion to the two-fifths to three-fifths ratio.

However, such is not the case with graduation prizes, for in a com-bined tally of prizes awarded in '82, '83, and '84 girls and boys each earned 50% of the prizes, including those specifically designated to rec-ognize excellence in athletic achievement. Thus, girls are proportionate-ly overrepresented in graduation awards. The reason for girls' overre-presentation may be found in the prize donors' definition of the characteristics they wish to recognize. For example, the Isabel Hancock Award each year recognizes a student who "has shown depth of under-standing, sensitivity, and response to the needs of others, and concern for the welfare of all" and the Schweppe prize is defined to award stu-dents for "cooperation and friendliness." In the opinion of the Prize Committee an equal number of girls and boys have been deserving of recognition in these areas.

Students' Self-Evaluation of Confidence

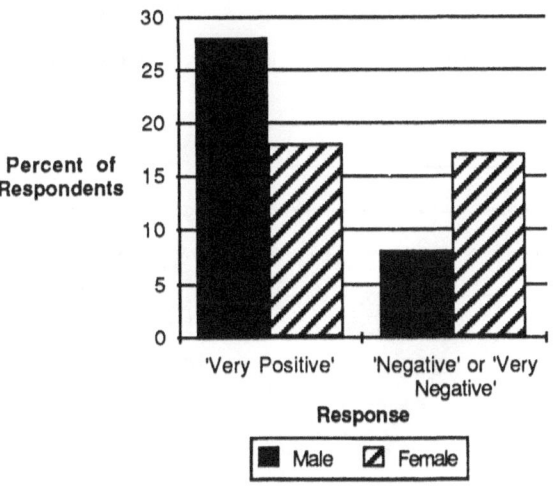

SQ#40. What kind of rating would you give yourself on [CONFIDENCE]? (possible answers: very positive, positive, average, negative, very negative)

ACADEMIC SELF-CONFIDENCE

Though we have seen that Andover girls have outstanding abilities and perform well academically, we find that they continue to underrate themselves. The disparity between girls' proven abilities and their self-evaluations is stark. When students were asked to rate themselves on the basis of their own confidence, girls in every class showed themselves to be less self-confident than boys. They were consistently more likely than boys to rate their confidence in the "negative" and "very negative" range, and they were quite a bit less likely than boys to refer to their confidence as "very positive."

The same relative lack of confidence felt by girls cropped up when students were asked to rate their own intelligence: 33% of the boys rated their intelligence as "very positive" compared to 20% of the girls. Though very few Andover students saw their intelligence in "negative" terms, girls did so twice as often as boys. Every objective indicator, such as SSATs, SATs, and grades put Andover boys and girls in the same high range of ability and performance. Their overall grade point averages were virtually identical in '77-'78, '79-'80, and '82-'83. Yet, girls are almost twice as likely as boys to see their intelligence as merely "average." Furthermore, gender matters more than race or ethnicity in affecting a student's rating of his/her own intelligence as "very positive." Girls in every ethnic and racial group studied were less likely than their male peers to see their intelligence as "very positive." Girls in every group studied rated their success at grades lower than their male counterparts. Lesser female self-confidence was evident throughout the survey results, and sociologists Janet Giele and her assistants Mary Gilfus and Peter Dunn discovered that female students also had lower overall self-concept than male students at Andover.[128]

Educational Aspirations: All Levels

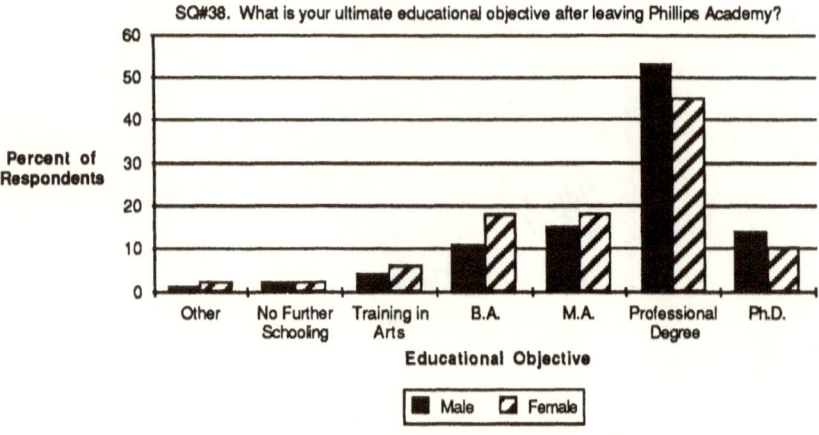

SQ#38. What is your ultimate educational objective after leaving Phillips Academy?

Percent of Respondents — Educational Objective

Male Female

Why should it make any differences how much self-confidence a student possesses as s/he walks into class each day? Self-confidence, it turns out, is closely related to a student's willingness to pursue further educational goals.[129] Probably as a result of their lower self-confidence, P.A. girls have less ambitious educational aspirations than the boys do. Though a great many Andover students of both sexes aim to get Ph.Ds or professional degrees, girls with the same ability and record of achievement set less demanding goals for themselves. Furthermore, Andover girls with the lowest self-concepts, i.e. least self-confidence, have the lowest level of educational aspiration.

Self-confidence also affects the college application process. A greater number of boys apply to "Line One" selective colleges: in fact, boys may at times set their sights unrealistically high. For most years studied, over 70% of the males in the senior class applied to one or more "Line One" colleges, while around 60% of the females did. Despite the differences in application rates about the same percentage of each gender is admitted each year. While girls may simply be more realistic or subject to less parental pressure, they also may be more open to counseling and less eager to risk rejection. Records of college admissions patterns at Andover show that girls need higher grades than boys to get into the same colleges, perhaps because females' test scores are slightly lower.[130] Of course, aside from issues of sex discrimination, grades are not the only factor in college admissions, and, as the chapter on student social life will show, P.A. girls are less likely than boys to be able to strengthen

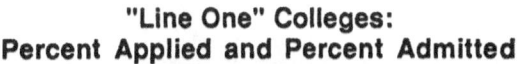

"Line One" Colleges:
Percent Applied and Percent Admitted

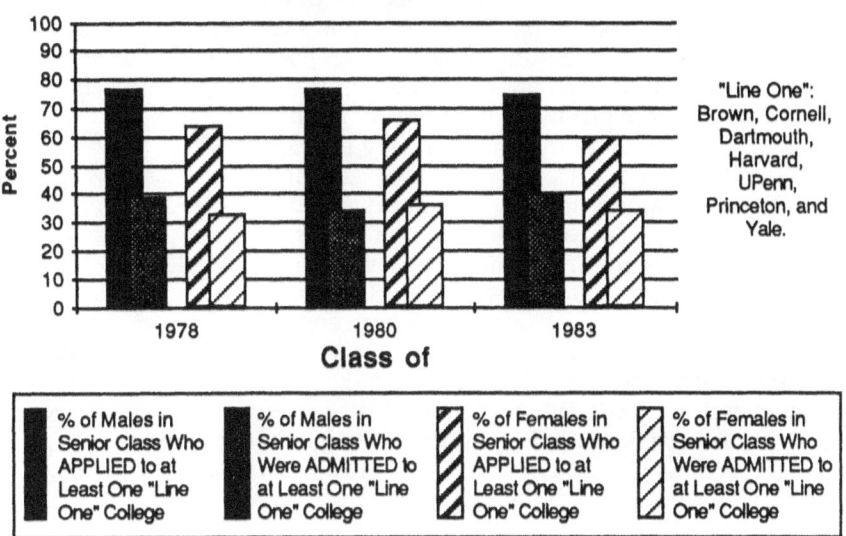

"Line One":
Brown, Cornell,
Dartmouth,
Harvard,
UPenn,
Princeton, and
Yale.

% of Males in Senior Class Who APPLIED to at Least One "Line One" College	% of Males in Senior Class Who Were ADMITTED to at Least One "Line One" College	% of Females in Senior Class Who APPLIED to at Least One "Line One" College	% of Females in Senior Class Who Were ADMITTED to at Least One "Line One" College

their college admissions candidacies with experience in student government or extracurricular leadership. When asked to rate their personal success at getting into college, senior girls were less likely than senior boys to indicate that they were successful or very successful, although a majority of both sexes saw themselves as successful in this endeavor.

Of course, these trends are not unique to Andover. When the Brown Project matched male and female students in terms of grade average and graduate plans they found that men and women with equivalent g.p.a.'s and similar aspirations differed in academic self-confidence. At the six colleges they studied men were more confident than women about their academic abilities.[131] In many challenging academic environments the "frog pond" effect occurs, according to the Brown Project, for new students find themselves feeling like smaller and less accomplished frogs in a large and more intimidating pond. The "frog pond" effect apparently alters the self-confidence of females more than males.[132] And lesser self-confidence may have serious long term effects on females' willingness to try new subjects or to venture into new careers. Underrating themselves may also influence their college and educational aspirations, and perhaps even what they ultimately accomplish in life.

Andover is not very different from other coeducational environments when it comes to the ways that gender can affect teachers' evaluations of students, students' classroom behavior, teaching styles, students' and teachers' vulnerability to certain forms of gender bias, and course selection patterns. Our school has been as unaware of some of these gender differences as most other schools are. But Andover, unlike many schools before the equity earthquake and a few schools today, does not make courses unavailable to any students because of their gender.[133] In fact, teachers, academic advisors, deans, and house counselors often urge students to leave behind them subject preferences based on gender stereotypes. Moral support is often available for the boy who enrolls in gender studies and the girl who elects to take Math 65.

While a number of academic sex equity problems remain unresolved at Andover, many faculty members are beginning to discuss how to address these issues. For they have realized the educational significance of gender-stereotyped course selection patterns and the lack of a gender-balanced curriculum. Throughout Andover's academic life new initiatives are being formulated in the attempt to offer encouragement to students of both sexes: off-sequence and term contained courses are being increased to encourage students to try subjects that in the past intimidated them; a few academic advisors have talked informally about ways to support, without pushing, students' efforts to venture beyond stereotypical course selection. Andover is on the verge of many possible changes, but, as yet, no clear-cut solutions have emerged for the problem of lesser female academic self-confidence.

Chapter Four:
THE COMPETITIVE ATHLETIC TRADITION UPDATED

Does the athletic program serve the needs of boys and
girls equally well?

THE CHARACTER-BUILDING ATHLETIC TRADITION AND ITS
ADJUSTMENT TO COEDUCATION

Before the merger athletics had been much more central to boys' educational experience at P.A. than it had been at Abbot. In the Office of Research and Evaluation Study done the year before the merger, Abbot
girls and P.A. boys were asked what their "clearest impressions" were
about their respective schools when they began their education. Eighty-
three percent of the boys viewed P.A. as a school where "the physical
education and sports programs are good," and many boys chose Andover over similar boarding schools simply because of the strength of
Andover's competitive athletic program. In contrast, 55% of the girls
surveyed viewed Abbot's athletic program as one of the striking attributes they noticed at the outset of their enrollment.[134] At Abbot, dance,
riding, and recreational activities were emphasized, rather than competitive team sports.

Historically, athletics also had a different meaning at Abbot and P.A.
At Abbot, as in many girls' boarding schools, competition and rigorous
athletic training were not integral parts of female education. In contrast,
within the boys' boarding school tradition, at Andover and elsewhere,
athletics were assumed to be "of fundamental importance to a student's
educational experience."[135] English and American boys' boarding
schools ever since the mid-Victorian era have had a tradition that athletic
competition was an essential character-building tool; popular articles de-
fended "Football as a Moral Agent."[136] Groton's famous Reverend Endi-
cott Peabody outlined the essentially Victorian goals of the character-
building tradition in athletics:

> It seems to me of the utmost importance that there should be noth-
> ing of the nature of loafing in a school...You can avoid that easily in
> a school, because you have the great advantage of athletics. One

has not the slightest hesitation in saying that to run a school on a high standard of morality without athletics would be a practical impossibility. Athletics are of the most importance in establishing righteousness in the school.... For moral evil you have got to consider the care of the body, and the best thing for a boy is to work hard and then, after a short interval, to play hard, and then to work hard again and then to play hard again and then, when the end of the day has come, to be so tired that he wants to go to bed and go to sleep. That is the healthy and good way for a boy to live.[137]

Vigorous athletic endeavor taught self-discipline and perseverance, but it served other Victorian purposes as well, including tiring out boys enough to dull their sexual impulses, to assure that they indulged only in "pure and clean and righteous living in the school."[138]

Long after certain Victorian goals had faded, the character-building athletic tradition lived on at Andover. For many years athletics held center stage in school life. Consequently, news of athletic victories and defeats took precedence over all other subjects covered by the *Phillipian* until 1929, when sports were moved off the front page.[139] Beginning in 1878 Andover's athletic rivalry with Exeter aroused the fierce loyalties of enthusiastic spectators, and the festivities of the Andover-Exeter football week provided generations of Andover graduates with some of their fondest memories.[140]

Modern P.A. still believed that a boy's character could be strengthened, if not built, by the self-discipline learned by meeting athletic challenges, by the testing of his courage against opposing teams, and by the good fellowship of cooperative team play. Athletics were also valued as a great equalizer where boys from every background competed as peers. Defending the character-building potential of competitive sports, athletic historian, former P.A. history teacher, and former Athletic Director Ted Harrison wrote that "athletics offer the student a chance to meet his own inadequacy head-on and do something about it, as no other activity does."[141] With athletics required each term, every boy was encouraged to try out for varsity or JV competition or at least intramural sports at some time during his career.

How would Abbot girls fit into Andover's strong tradition of required athletics? Would females readily accept the school's belief in the positive value of competition? Would they be welcomed as automatic equals or would they have to earn a place in the athletic program? Many of the students and teachers in the new coeducational school had grown up in the fifties and sixties when women were often discouraged at an early age from being competitive about athletics or career achievement. Besides being unfeminine, female competitiveness was judged by some medical and psychiatric experts to be a sign of precarious mental health or even penis envy, and some believed that participating in competitive athletics could "interfere with childbearing."[142] Andover's coeducational athletics began at the same time that the women's liberation movement was struggling to revise these old beliefs about the alleged dichotomy between femininity and competitiveness. As Abbot and P.A. merged, the nation at large was debating whether the locker room should open up to women. Women athletes were fighting for the right to compete in professional contests, and television audiences placed bets on Billie Jean King's tennis match against Bobby Riggs, a symbolic contest over women's right to be taken seriously as athletic competitors.

Initial logistical problems loomed large as Andover struggled to build a coeducational athletic program without a girls' locker room and without adequate facilities. The athletic department had to work fast to find room, let alone coaches for the newcomers. Flexibility was required of everyone, and new sports and activities were offered as new needs were discovered. While some girls thought the athletic department too slow in responding to their requests for a girls' ice hockey team, others thought they were being given opportunities they had never dreamed of at Abbot. But it remained to be seen if Andover's competitive athletic tradition was a suitable home for all female students. According to Harrison's history of Andover athletics, some of the "pioneer generation" of former Abbot students at P.A. were put off at first by the "overemphasis on competition everywhere in their new environment."[143]

The Merger Study found that many people were concerned about the lack of locker rooms for girls. Some members of the community also stated that the "athletic program does not provide equal opportunities for boys and girls, that the boys' program, to the detriment of the girls', appears to have first priority in scheduling, assignment of athletic areas, and in coaching."[144] A majority of the groups studied—old P.A., former Abbot, new, male, female, faculty and students—agreed that the following statements were true:

1. Boys have better athletic facilities than girls.
2. The athletic program is adequate for boys.
3. Boys generally receive more recognition than girls for athletic achievements.
4. Boys generally receive adequate instruction and coaching.
5. More coeducational athletics are desirable.[145]

With time old ideas were modified and new facilities were built for girls. Gradually a compromise was worked out between the competitive athletic tradition and the less competitive female tradition: they met each other halfway, especially after Joe Wennik made creating a more coeducational program a central goal in his term as Athletic Director from 1977-1984. First, the athletic program was diversified and expanded to accommodate the new students. Many new noncompetitive coeducational sports were made available to boys and girls alike. Students were also permitted to substitute music activity, ceramics, or community service for one term of athletics. Girls' interscholastic teams and coaches were added, too, to expand further the options available to students.[146]

Interscholastic Sports Added Since 1975:
  Girls' Hockey
  Boys' Gymnastics
  Girls' Volleyball
  Team Cycling
Non-Interscholastic Co-Ed Options Added Since 1973:
  Ballet
  Modern Dance
  Instructional Squash
  Swim Fitness *
  Frisbee *
  River Running
  Paddle Tennis
  Instructional Cross Country Skiing
  Fencing
  New Games *
  Yoga
  Fitness
  Tai Chi *
  Medical Swim
  Speedball
  Stxball (sic)
  Water Polo
  Aikido
(*Since discontinued)

In addition, with each passing year more girls welcomed the opportunity to compete athletically. Female athletes began to apply to Andover because of the strength of its athletic program, just as male athletes had done for generations. Some girls thrived as competitors within Andover's athletic tradition, while others found ways to enjoy sports without competing. Fewer and fewer girls experienced culture shock when they entered the diversified P.A. athletic program, for there were many alternatives to competitive athletics, and, as the years went by, it became more and more comfortable for girls, and even a few boys, to take dance one term and hockey the next. Boys, too, benefited from the increased variety in the program.

RECONCILING THE COMPETITIVE TRADITION WITH THE COEDUCATIONAL REALITY

The Athletic program has moved beyond the initial adjustment problems of the seventies. Today it is simultaneously an heir to Andover's character-building competitive athletic tradition and a fully coeducational program designed to welcome both sexes. The P.A. *Blue Book* of basic rules for students still reaffirms the school's competitive tradition by stating to boys and girls alike that they are "strongly encouraged to play at least one competitive team sport while at Andover."[148] In its statement of objectives the Athletic Department defends the educational value "inherent in well-coached competitive athletics" and the "beneficial effects of that competition." But at the same time, the department has committed itself to another goal: to have students learn "through coeducational facilities and options, the mutual acceptance and respect of the athletic capabilities of the opposite sex."[149]

The athletic program at Andover has blended its two goals of maintaining the competitive tradition and providing a coeducational program in which the abilities of both sexes are respected. In the 1983-84 school year an average of 47% of the female students responding to the student questionnaire indicated that they had competed in interscholastic (varsity and JV) or intramural (cluster A or B) sports each term. While this is less than the 63% of the male students who played competitive sports, it is strong evidence that about half of the girls at P.A. today elect to compete each term and that *at least half* feel comfortable with the competitive tradition. Girls registered a high rate of satisfaction with their participation in varsity, JV, and cluster A programs —in the case of varsity sports a higher rate of satisfaction than the boys.

Gender is less important than other factors when levels of satisfaction with competitive sports are examined. Both male and female junior varsity athletes are slightly less satisfied than are varsity athletes, which is probably due to the fact that most JV players of both sexes would have been happier if they had been chosen for varsity teams. The older the students of both sexes are, the more likely they are to be chosen for interscholastic competition, and the older they are, the more likely they are to express satisfaction with their interscholastic participation.

Success has also come to the athletic program because it has tried to recognize when to deemphasize the competitive tradition in the interest of creating an environment conducive to coeducational activity. The competitive tradition is much less evident in the wide range of instructional and recreational activities offered, and so this group of "sports" is lumped together with the title noncompetitive sports. This group includes a long list of noncompetitive options ranging from instructional tennis to yoga, karate, dance, and jogging and fitness. One noncompetitive sport, Search and Rescue, is a descendant of the Outward Bound Program which former P.A. Admissions Director Josh Miner introduced in America. Like Outward Bound, Search and Rescue retains the cooperative team spirit of competitive athletics, but, instead of competition against opposing teams it encourages students to offer encouragement to their peers as they struggle with new challenges. In addition, more than most sports, it carries out the character-building goals of the P.A. athletic tradition, for Search and Rescue self-consciously teaches students to help each other and to support each other's efforts to overcome fears.[150]

Noncompetitive sports are also an important alternative to the competitive tradition for both sexes. However, girls are more likely to elect noncompetitive activities. An average of 53% of the females surveyed in 1984 had taken noncompetitive sports each term compared to 37% of the males. Both males and females report a high level of satisfaction with the noncompetitive sports they elect, and a greater percentage of girls than boys are satisfied with them. Gender differences exist in student selection of noncompetitive sports. For example, more boys than girls elect to take karate and very few boys have ventured into the dance classes.

Athletic Participation 1983-84

SQ#21. Please describe your partcipation in athletics at Phillips Academy.

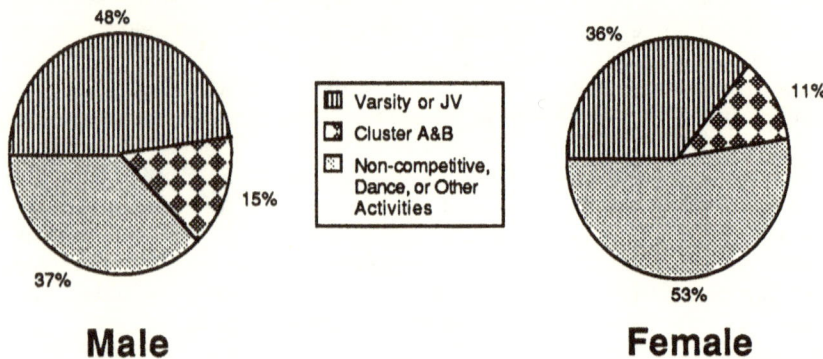

Male   **Female**

Problems remain in Andover's athletics in areas where coeducation and the competitive tradition have not been reconciled easily. The most vivid example of the contradictions inherent in blending the competitive tradition with coeducation is Cluster sports. The purpose of creating Cluster sports was to encourage Cluster spirit and to mix boys and girls on the same teams in order to encourage, as the Athletic Department's objectives state, "the mutual acceptance and respect of the athletic capabilities of the opposite sex." However, to maintain the competitive tradition and to encourage excellence, Cluster sports have been stratified by putting the best players in Cluster A and the other players in Cluster B. Though Cluster teams were planned to be fully coeducational, a pattern of sex segregation has emerged, with many Cluster A teams being predominantly male and Cluster B teams having more females. For example, in the 1981-82 school year, Cluster A softball was 100% male, and, in other recent years Cluster A soccer and basketball have been 90% male. The ratios in Cluster B vary : one Cluster B soccer team was 52% female, while the Cluster B basketball roster was only 28% female.[151]

We might expect a fairly high level of dissatisfaction among females in Cluster sports as a result of the segregation, but, perhaps because they did have the option to choose not to take Cluster sports, there is no such outcome. Girls were less likely to be satisfied with their Cluster A experience than boys were, but 61% still registered satisfaction. Students of both sexes were less satisfied with Cluster B sports than with Cluster A, but we can assume that, as may be the case in JV sports, being cut from the best team may be a factor in lower levels of satisfaction among these students. Boys seem to be slightly less satisfied with their participation in Cluster B. Athletic Director Paul Kalkstein has been working on the problem of sex segregation in Cluster sports, and he has cancelled some sports and opened others, such as speedball, in hopes of enabling female athletes to compete at the A level more often.[152]

A certain amount of male discontent has also resulted from the athletic program's attempts to blend coeducation with the competitive tradition. Years ago at Andover and at many high schools today, male athletes could expect to be honored in a special way by cheering crowds. In many high schools the captain of the football team is a hero, and school spirit often depends on the victories or defeats of the boys' teams, especially the football team. Through the years—starting long before the merger—Andover has become less football-centered, and since there have been so many boys' and girls' athletic contests to attend, spectator support has thinned out. In fact, the academic and extracurricular demands on most students' time preclude faithful attendance at athletic contests.

Student Satisfaction With the Athletic Program

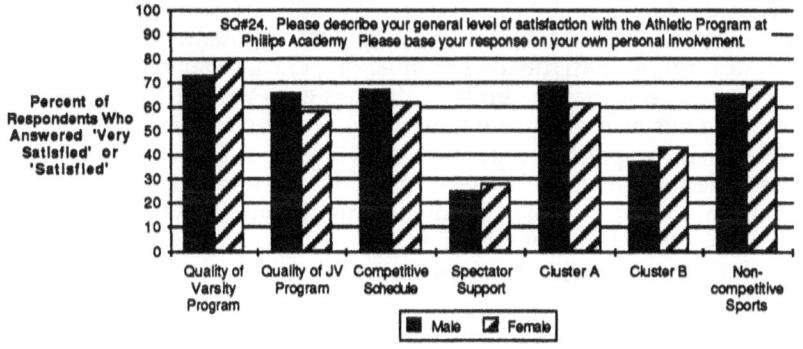

The result is a significant amount of dissatisfaction among boys with the degree of spectator support : 40% registered dissatisfaction with the degree of spectator support their teams received. Boys' disappointment with spectator support became a campus-wide issue in the past few years because school spirit seemed to be lacking during Andover-Exeter week, and the spotlight was to be shared with girls.

Members of Blue Key and other student leaders, working with the Athletic Director and the Headmaster, decided to continue to include girls' sports teams in Andover-Exeter week rallies, which traditionally had been football rallies that recognized only male athletes. In previous years sexist and obscene cheers as well as one belly dancer had graced Andover-Exeter week festivities, but now they were banned. When new rules banned obscenity and sexism at the rallies, some team members felt the spontaneity of the rallies was lost. In 1984 when the top scorer of the often victorious girls' soccer team stood up to speak to the crowd at an Andover-Exeter week rally, she was injured by a hurled toilet paper roll. Nevertheless, female athletes drew cheers from the crowd, and for a few it was an exhilarating new experience. Some football players had expected, possibly from their experiences at other schools, to receive more support from larger crowds, and some students and faculty thought the rallies were too controlled.

Within the Andover-Exeter week debate dwelled part of the dilemma of coeducational athletics at P.A.: how can a tradition that was once exclusively male welcome female participation on equal terms without dilution (or at least redirection) of the tradition? Some faculty members regretted that the long-standing "male tradition" of football-centered school spirit and unregulated Andover-Exeter rallies had been modified.[153] Others hoped that a new tradition could emerge, without sexism or obscenity, and with renewed school spirit on behalf of athletes of both sexes.

A much more minor degree of disappointment showed up when students were asked to rate their competitive schedules: 10% of the boys and 8% of the girls noted dissatisfaction with their teams' schedules. In doing so they may have been taking issue with the quality or choice of the schedule rather than the total number of games. Despite the fact that girls overall have a smaller number of games each year (though some girls' teams have *more* extensive schedules), they noted less dissatisfaction with their competitive schedules than boys did. The number of girls' athletic contests has increased markedly since the early years of coeducation. In 1973-74 only 15% of all athletic contests were girls' contests, but by 1983-84 41% of all athletic contests were girls' contests, a proportion that was roughly equivalent to the ratio of girls in the school.

THE NEED FOR MORE WOMEN COACHES

While the Athletic program has been increasing the number of girls' teams and the number of girls' athletic contests, it has not been able to solve the problem of a predominance of male interscholastic coaches. In recent years, roughly half of all coaching of girls' teams has been done by men. In the years studied, for every woman coaching more than one varsity or JV sport each year there were 5.8 men coaching, and for every woman coaching one varsity sport there were 3.8 men doing so. Trends

Interscholastic Competitions: Total Contests Over Time

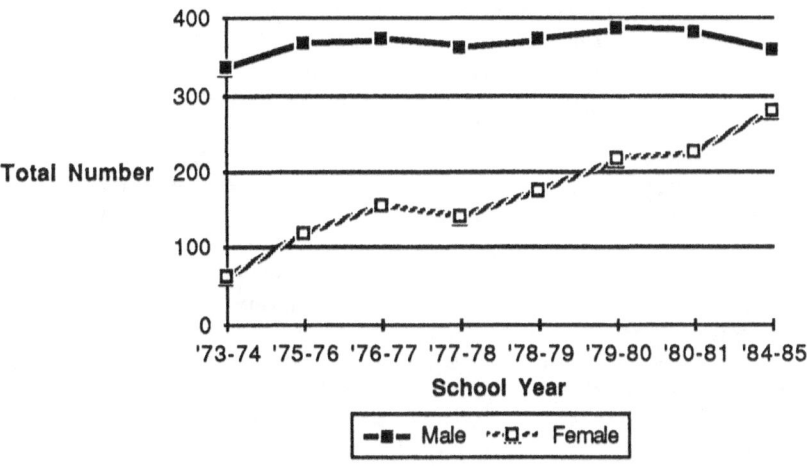

Data From Athletic Office (certain years deleted due to incomplete records)

changed little until the 1984-85 academic year when more female P.E. instructors and other female faculty interested in coaching were hired. As a result, in 1984-85, for every woman coaching more than one varsity or JV sport there were 3.2 men doing so, and for every woman coaching one varsity sport there were 3.2 men doing so. The biggest increase was in females coaching more than one interscholastic sport.

Out of the nine females coaching more than one varsity or JV sport, seven were new to the school in 1984. The increase in females coaching interscholastic sports in 1984-85 is encouraging, but five of the seven new female coaches were not returning to P.A. for the '85-86 school year. As we will see in the section on faculty attrition, the school has recruited and hired women at significant rates recently, but high hiring rates have not guaranteed that women faculty will always stay at P.A. In addition, the high turnover rate among female coaches has created a serious lack of continuity in the female portion of the athletic program. For example, girls' lacrosse went through seven coaches in seven years, and this pattern of disruption makes it harder to build apprenticeship into the program, whereby a junior coach would learn from working with a senior coach for a year or two before assuming full responsibility herself. While the athletic program offers some training programs as well as support for coaching education outside the school, the discontinuity problem in the coaching of girls' sports makes it hard to create apprenticeships. Kalkstein anticipated the arrival of four new female interscholastic coaches in September 1985, and a central goal of his directorship is increasing the number of female coaches.[154]

Like female students choosing their sports, female faculty most often elect to coach noncompetitive rather than competitive sports. While some do coach Cluster competitive sports, most Cluster coaching is done by men. There has been some disagreement about why female faculty often prefer not to coach interscholastic sports. One observer viewed it as a lack of qualifications for, he wrote, "there are not enough competent women coaches for the established varsity and JV girls' teams."[155] This is a misleading argument, however. Many male faculty do not begin their careers at P.A. fully qualified as coaches, but they learn on the job. Few women faculty follow this path, not because of incompetence, but because of lack of experience and because they may be intimidated by the prospect of acquiring a new skill in an unfamiliar realm. The idea of varsity and JV coaching seemed unappealing to many female faculty over 30, most likely because competitive athletics were not a part of their educations. The extensive time commitment required of varsity and JV coaches also serves as a disincentive to prospective female coaches. Some varsity coaches spend as much as 25 hours a week in practices and traveling to away games, and such a time commitment would be different for women faculty with full teaching loads, children, domestic responsibilities, or dorm or counseling demands elsewhere in the school. Of course, the same is true for many male faculty as well. Currently there are 2.1 men for every one woman coaching. Because that ratio is consistent with the overall male-female ratio in the full-time faculty, it can be certified that women fill their share of coaching slots at P.A.. However, women are still less at home coaching within the competitive athletic tradition than men are.

Coaching Assignments 1984-85*

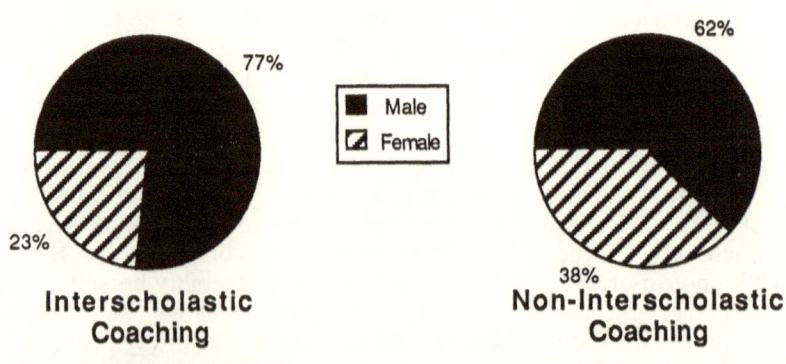

Interscholastic Coaching

(e.g. Varsity and JV Football, Field Hockey, Tennis Team)

Non-Interscholastic Coaching

(e.g. Cluster, Search and Rescue, Karate, Cycling, Yoga, Dance)

*Based on total coaching slots for the entire year.

Despite the time it may take, coaching on any level of the athletic program has special rewards as both coach and student escape the graded expectations of the classroom and find more informal ways to work together. When students were asked what roles their coaches played for them, they described their coaches most often as friends and as morale builders. Great coaches can and do influence students in profound ways. When students were asked to rate the quality of their coaching they generally responded that they were satisfied. When the faculty was asked to rate how rewarding coaching was to them, most viewed it as very rewarding or rewarding. And yet, despite the special rewards of being a coach, 37% of the males and 27% of the females on the faculty rated their coaching experience as stressful, somewhat stressful or very stressful.

OFFICIAL POLICIES VERSUS COMMUNITY ATTITUDES

The reconciliation between the competitive athletic tradition and the new coeducational reality has been most difficult to effect in the area of attitudes and stereotypes. Even if the athletic program gave each student a lecture on sexism each term it would not change everyone's attitudes. When Paul Kalkstein and his Athletic Advisory Committee did a brief study of charges of sexism in the athletic program, they found the problem was hard to pin down and they could not find any official policy that would cause or put an end to sexism. Obviously, the problem was too elusive to be cured only by official policies, for the attitudes were embedded, often unconsciously, in student and faculty culture.

Two good examples of the inadequacy of official policies to change quickly student and faculty culture are a) the higher status which male interscholastic athletes enjoy within the student community and b) the male aura of the weight room. The Athletic Department has become increasingly sensitive to the importance of recognizing the athletic achievements of both sexes. Years ago most athletic awards went to boys; now it is official policy to recognize excellence as fairly as possible.[156] But, despite official policies, equivalent peer recognition of athletes of both sexes has not been forthcoming. Being a noted female athlete wins respect at P.A., but it carries with it much less social status than being a male "jock." Although the *Phillipian* has been careful to recognize a male and female athlete each term, boys' sports have usually gained greater recognition in line-by-line news coverage, even in seasons when there were especially strong girls' teams.

A similar example of the distance between official policies and student and faculty culture is provided by the weight room. Because of federal laws and media interest in equal access to athletic facilities, the Coeducation Committee looked into the use of all athletic facilities at P.A. Jon Stableford found that the playing fields, pool, gym, cage and rink time are "split equitably." He also discovered that the training room was used equally by both sexes, but not the weight room. According to Stableford's 1984 preliminary report on coeducation in athletics, "Weight training has become an essential part of all athletic training, but most female athletes are not comfortable using our weight room because of the behavior of some male athletes and the lack of supervision."[157]

So, in the 1984-85 school year Paul Kalkstein and Assistant Athletic Director Kathy Henderson tried to create a less threatening atmosphere in the weight room by planning a renovation of the room and providing more supervision. According to Kalkstein, "In the summer of 1985 the Athletic Department commenced a major project in the weight room. Expansion will allow the 'free weights,' used almost solely by males, to be placed in a separate room from the machines. Several new Eagle machines will be added; these are adjustable and particularly adaptable to women. These two changes will greatly diminish the 'men only' mystique of the weight room."[158] Additional "change of atmosphere" was provided by a number of recently hired young female faculty who went to the weight room to work out together regularly. But even if full-time supervision were provided, many female students and faculty would remain uncomfortable using the weight room because of memories of past experiences being heckled or because of their own stereotypes about what females can expect from groups of muscular males.[159]

Despite the conscientious efforts of the athletic program, certain attitudes still cloud the progress P.A. has made in blending the tradition of competitive athletics with coeducation. Some boys persist in referring to noncompetitive sports as "hacks," and thus, the 53% of the girls who elect these sports may feel that their noncompetitive accomplishments are diminished in the eyes of the community.

As far as spending goes, more money is spent on interscholastic sports than noncompetitive sports. All-male sports like football are the most expensive, but when new girls' teams are created, extra expense is also incurred because brand new equipment has to be purchased. In one recent athletic director's report it was stated that "over 90% of the 'sports account' budget and about 40% of the 'sports-related' budget is spent for the 40% of the student body playing interscholastic sports."[160] But we cannot assume that a smaller expenditure for noncompetitive sports implies that less value is placed on them by the athletic program. Today a smaller portion of the total athletic budget is devoted to interscholastic expenses than in the earlier days of coeducation.

The Coeducation Study's survey results show clearly that the majority of male and female students are satisfied with the athletic program, and the majority of the faculty approves of the "priority placed on athletics and fitness activities as reflected by time, effort, and money spent." Yet other data raise questions about athletics at P.A. that we cannot answer fully. Perhaps most unsettling was the faculty's response to the question "In general, how do you feel the athletic program treats females and males?" Sixty-two percent of the women and 29% of the men surveyed on the faculty answered that they believed the program "favors males" or "greatly favors males." No one believed that the program favored females, but the vast majority of men believed that the program was equal. Beyond the frequency of the belief that the program favors males, the fascinating part of this data is the striking difference in male and female perceptions of the program.

Faculty View of the Athletic Program's Treatment of Male and Female Students

FQ#21 In general, how do you feel the athletic program treats females and males?

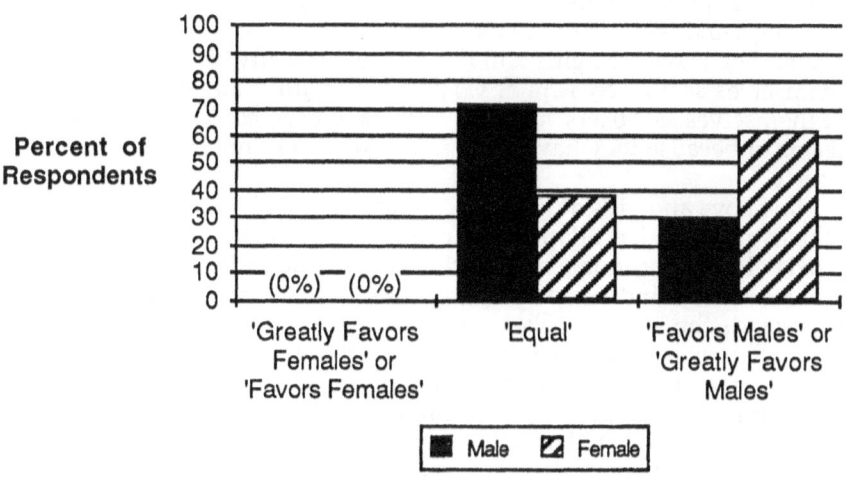

The only survey data that sheds any light on the meaning of this alleged "favoritism" perceived by the majority of the female faculty appeared in the open-ended responses at the back of the student questionnaire. One student wrote that "girls' sports are also treated less seriously than boys. Some teachers will excuse a boy from class because of a game or an 'important' practice, but not do the same for a girl." Another student asserted that "discrimination is still prevalent in sports." She also pointed out that inequality existed because of the lack of women coaches and because sweat clothes indicate that "boys play *Basketball*" but "girls play *Girls Basketball*."

When students refer to teachers who allegedly will excuse male but not female athletes from class, they raise the important question: does the faculty take girls' athletic efforts less seriously than boys'? We have no data that answers such a question. All we have is data on the way the faculty rated the importance of sports in students' lives. When the faculty was asked to rate the importance of sports in students' lives, 22%

rated sports as highly important to boys and 7% rated them as "highly important" for girls. In contrast, the majority of students rated athletics and physical fitness as very important to them. Thus, the faculty may underrate how important sports are to many Andover girls. Of course, being unaware of the real importance of athletics to girls is different from taking girls' athletic efforts less seriously than boys.

Another concern is the fact that female students surveyed feel less personally successful at athletics than their male peers. When asked on the student questionnaire to rate their personal success at athletics, 49% of the males and 37% of the females answered that they were "very successful" or "successful." It may well be that, because of the continuing emphasis put on interscholastic competition, the only students at Andover who judge themselves to be "winners" at athletics are the same 48% boys and 36% girls who have made their way onto varsity or JV teams. The 19% of the girls and 17% of the boys surveyed who define themselves as unsuccessful or very unsuccessful at athletics may think of themselves as "losers" because they have been cut from JV or varsity teams or because they have chosen to take "hack" noncompetitive sports.

Most boys and girls at P.A. have benefited greatly from the way the athletic program has adapted the competitive athletic tradition to the needs of a coeducational school. Bringing the opportunity to compete athletically to hundreds of girls each year is an accomplishment that transcends the school's belief in the character-building power of competition. Research shows that women who grow up with such athletic experience may feel stronger and more positive about their own bodies.[161] In a comparative study of coeducational and single-sex private high schools, psychologist Martha Hennessey found that females at coeducational institutions played on more athletic teams, rated the importance of athletics higher, enjoyed playing sports more, and viewed themselves as competent at athletics more frequently than females at single-sex schools. This trend has also been documented in studies of coeducational and single-sex colleges.[162]

When we return to the central question "Does the athletic program serve the needs of boys and girls equally well?" we are again facing complicated answers. There is no question that the athletic program has tried very hard to serve both boys and girls, but they have sometimes felt helpless when faced with the common perception that the program favors boys or is male-oriented. The perception that the program is male-oriented probably comes from the fact that most of the visible administrators, coaches, and even athletes are male. Males outnumber females in athletics as in almost every other area of school life. Because many people still perceive competition as male, the persistence of the competitive athletic tradition may seem like trying to pour current male and female students into an old male mold. Beyond such perceptions, there is the reality that after a decade of coeducation females still feel less successful at athletics.

How Students Rate Their Own Athletic Success at PA

SQ#39. How do you rate your personal success at Phillips Academy at athletics?

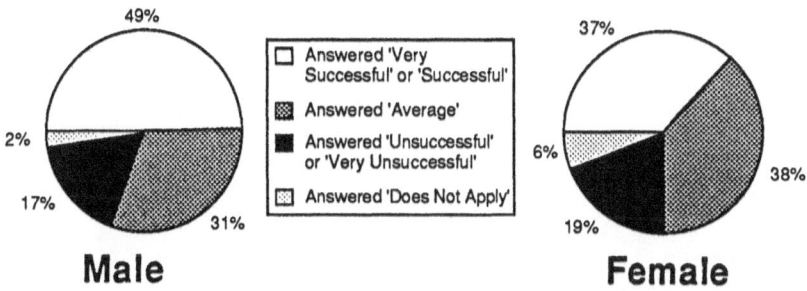

Male   **Female**

The Andover athletic program deserves praise for working hard to create an environment of equity in many areas: in recognizing excellence in athletes of both sexes, in urging the administration and department chairs to hire women faculty who want to coach interscholastic sports, in giving moral support to many female athletes and women coaches, in realizing the importance of female role models on the athletic field, in creating noncompetitive options for both sexes who do not care to fit into the competitive athletic tradition, and in attempting to encourage equal access to all facilities. Leaders within the athletic program have pursued these goals with varying degrees of success even when students and their peers were resistant to change.

Andover may offer one of the most varied and wide-ranging athletic programs in America; certainly it remains an excellent place for the development of competitive athletes of both sexes. Unlike many high schools, Andover lacks one of the most blatant forms of anti-male sexism. Male athletes are very rarely stereotyped as "dumb jocks" at P.A. Because it is now taken for granted that everybody is smart at Andover, no one looks askance when abundant brains and muscles coexist in the same body. Furthermore, no scantily clad cheerleaders imitate the Dallas cowgirls at P.A.; only an ad hoc group of male and female cheerers leads the crowd during Andover-Exeter week. Certainly the school is free of many sex role stereotypes that characterize athletic programs elsewhere, but as long as female students are less likely to feel personally successful at athletics we cannot say for sure that the program serves the needs of both sexes equally well.

Chapter Five:
EQUALITY, AUTONOMY, AND AFFILIATION IN
STUDENT SOCIAL LIFE

Does the school encourage male and female students'
urges to lead, to enjoy recreation and social life, to build
friendships, and to pursue special extracurricular
interests?

GENDER DIFFERENCES IN SELF-DESCRIPTIONS

The differences between boys and girls at Andover are not evident in
external sociological characteristics: male students do not differ significantly from female students in age, religion, ethnicity, or parents' occupation.[163] Instead, differences of identity, values, and concerns begin to
appear when students describe themselves. For example, though girls
see themselves more often as being personally successful at friendships
and service to others, boys are more likely to see themselves as personally successful at leadership, grades, athletics, and getting into the right
college. Thus, sex differences in self-ratings of success follow traditional
sex-role patterns that might have existed twenty years ago.

In describing their own characteristic traits, boys and girls also
showed that they often see themselves as possessing culturally defined
"sex-appropriate" traits. A higher percentage of girls than boys saw
themselves as sympathetic, understanding, sensitive to the needs of
others, and gentle. Conversely, a higher proportion of the boys saw
themselves as competitive and willing to take risks. However, boys and
girls rated themselves as assertive and independent at almost the same
rates, and over half the boys saw themselves as sympathetic, understanding, and sensitive to the needs of others.

The trend we have seen toward lower female self-confidence in athletics and academics and lower overall female self-concept is paralleled by
lesser female personal and social self-confidence. Boys rate themselves
more positively than girls do in terms of appearance, intelligence, popularity, confidence, and health. Over half the girls surveyed rated their

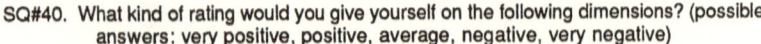

Students Who View Themselves as "Very Positive"

SQ#40. What kind of rating would you give yourself on the following dimensions? (possible answers: very positive, positive, average, negative, very negative)

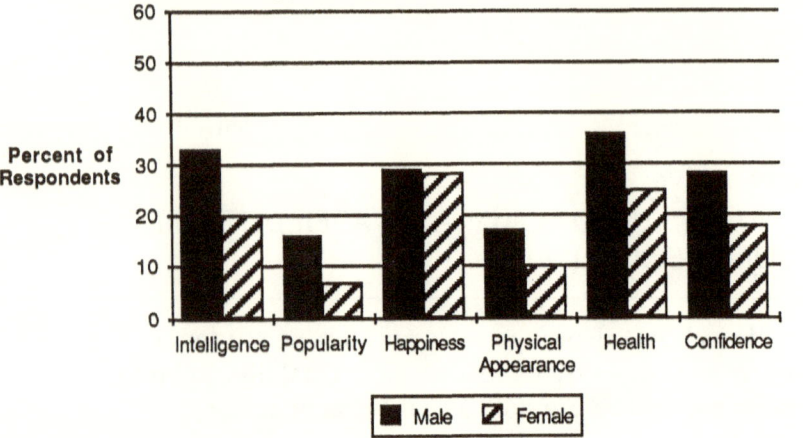

popularity as negative or very negative, and over a third rated their physical appearance in the same negative manner.

Lower female self-confidence is not new at Andover. Although no complex self-concept scale was used in P.A.'s 1972 O.R.E. study, research showed that girls at Abbot rated themselves lower than boys did in several areas including science, math, perseverance in spite of hurt feelings, knowledge of own abilities, physical development, common sense, and, to a less marked degree, athletics, leadership, making friends, self-discipline, handling worries, and relating to the opposite sex. Girls rated themselves higher in art, general imagination, writing, foreign languages, independent work, dramatics, and religious development.[164] Boys clearly saw themselves in positive terms in more areas than girls in 1972, as they do today.

GENDER DIFFERENCES IN ATTITUDES TOWARD LIFE GOALS, WORK AND MARRIAGE

The tendency for girls to rate their abilities lower than boys may not have changed much since the beginning of coeducation, but female values and goals have changed. In the eighties Andover females are more willing to see themselves as interested in career achievement and educational advancement than females were when coeducation began. For example, in the 1972 O.R.E. study only 41% of the girls planned to earn graduate degrees, but in the 1984 Coeducation Study 73% of the girls, compared to 82% of the boys, indicated that they planned to get Masters, Professional or Ph.D. degrees.

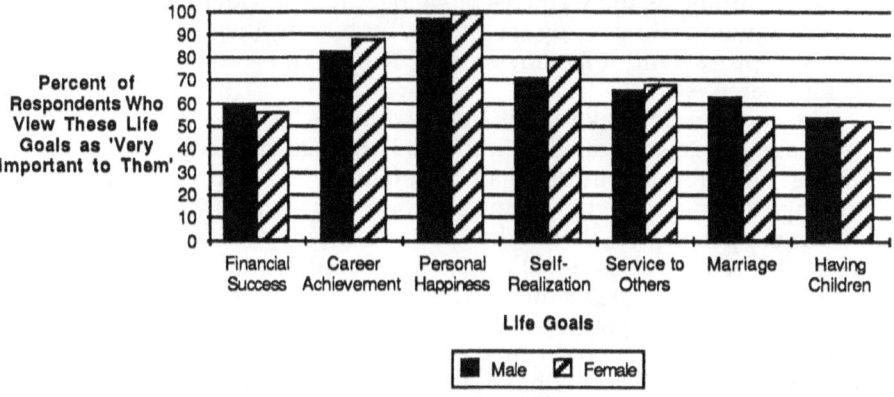

Students' Very Important Life Goals

SQ#37. Please rate the importance of the following goals in your life: (possible answers: very important to me, no opinion, very unimportant to me)

Percent of Respondents Who View These Life Goals as 'Very Important to Them'

Life Goals

■ Male ☑ Female

Financial success or making money has become less important to boys and slightly more important to girls since coeducation began. Fifty percent of the girls in 1972 viewed making a lot of money as an important lifetime goal, while in 1984 56% said financial success was very important. In 1972 74% of the boys valued making a lot of money, compared with only 60% in 1984.

Increased concern with career achievement and success indicate important changes in goals and values for both boys and girls in the last decade. In 1972 46% of the girls and 75% of the boys valued highly becoming "important and successful," and we can safely assume from the data that they meant career success and public recognition rather than private achievement or personal importance. In 1984 88% of the girls and 82% of the boys ranked career achievement as "very important to me," and 90% of the senior girls, compared to 74% of the senior boys, rated career achievement this way. Clearly, career achievement has become much more important to girls in the last decade and to a lesser degree, to boys.

Career achievement has also become more important than marriage for both sexes at Andover. Girls in 1972 valued marriage more than they valued being important and successful. In 1984 girls valued career achievement much more highly as a life goal than they valued marriage. In fact, in the Coeducation Study questionnaire 88% of the girls indicated that they valued career achievement, compared with 54% who valued marriage. Eighty-two percent of the boys valued career achievement compared to 63% valuing marriage. The trend toward valuing career achievement more than marriage has been more marked among females, but males in 1984 definitely value career achievement over marriage more than they did in 1972.

Why should girls, in particular, have changed the way they value career achievement and marriage between 1972 and 1984? As more women have entered the work place and gained acceptance in traditionally male professions and as the women's movement has provided encouragement for women to develop their career ambitions, there has been more social approval (and sometimes social pressure) for women to build successful careers.

The equity earthquake shook many women's life goals away from marriage and toward careers. In the mid-eighties the countercultural attitudes still prevalent in 1972 had been replaced by an urgent concern among students that a tightening economy might offer a narrower range of career openings for them. The "pressured generation" often sees career achievement as essential to gain a foothold in an unwelcoming professional world. Thus, valuing career achievement more than marriage may reflect societal pressure on this generation to establish careers before marrying. The high divorce rate may also affect the value they put on marriage. On the other hand, both sexes may also have rated marriage lower than career achievement because they perceive marriage less as a planned "life goal" than as something that will happen naturally when and if the right mate comes along.[165]

The same historical trends may also affect the degree to which girls of the "pressured generation" value having children. By 1984 dual career marriages have become economic necessities for some, and the new cultural ideal of the "superwoman" often creates the expectation that women should combine marriage and children with a high level of career achievement. But marriage and having children may look like the problematic side of the "superwoman" formula to the girls, influencing them to be less likely to view them as life goals than career achievement. Andover boys may be less likely than girls to feel such a conflict between their career ambitions and their personal lives. The Brown Project found that combining marriage and career appeared more complicated to female students. In their study two-thirds of the women wanted to have full-time careers, but only two-fifths of the men wanted to marry women who worked full-time.[166]

Coeducation at Phillips Academy has grown up in an era when women have become less willing to define marriage and having children as their primary life goals. In fact, the traditional expectation that men should pursue career achievement and women should concern themselves with marriage and children seems to have declined sharply since coeducation began. The Academy has responded to the changing roles of women by welcoming female achievement, but the school has not yet taken Jon Stableford's advice about sponsoring "discussions of the issues related to combining parenthood and careers." Realization of career aspirations may be more difficult for girls who expect themselves to become "superwoman" or who define their career aspirations as barriers to the creation of a happy family life. Career aspirations remain more complicated for young women than for young men.

ADDITIONAL GENDER DIFFERENCES IN USE OF LEISURE TIME
AND OTHER ATTITUDES

Our Coeducation Study data shows other, perhaps less profound gender differences that are worth noting. Since coeducation began in 1973, non-conformity appears to have declined as a value for both sexes, but placing importance on creativity and involvement in arts appears to have remained the same for girls and increased for boys.

Boys and girls also use their free time in different ways. Females reported most often using free time to spend with friends, and males reported using it to play sports. Boys are more likely to read daily newspapers and science fiction than girls are, while girls are more likely to read newsmagazines, nonfiction, and fiction than boys are. Girls tend to be less satisfied than boys with the amount of free time that they have outside of class and sports. A larger proportion of boys eat all their meals at Commons, yet they were more likely to rate the quality and quantity of the food at P.A. as one of the things they liked least about P.A.

Student Satisfaction With PA

SQ#47. Please rate your overall satisfaction with PA.

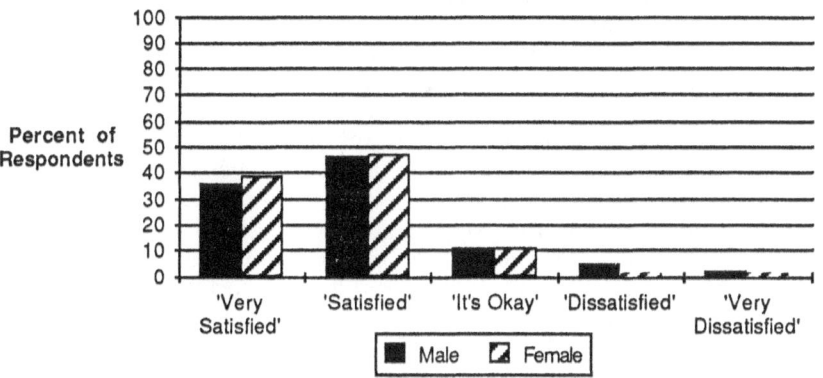

Only dissatisfaction above 2% is: 5% senior females, 6% senior males, 7% upper males, 9% lower males, 6% junior males.

Ironically, though Andover girls have less enthusiasm about themselves than boys do, they tended to view most aspects of their educational experience in a more positive light than boys do. Girls were more likely than boys to report being satisfied with social functions, friendships, rules, the work program and with life at P.A. overall. The two areas in which girls were less likely to express positive feelings were academic workload and relations between the sexes. Seventy-six percent of the girls viewed the workload as too heavy, compared with 63% of the boys. Twenty-eight percent of the girls, compared with 15% of the boys, perceived the relations between the sexes at Andover as sexist or tending toward sexism. In general, however, girls' survey responses indicated they were slightly more satisfied with their P.A. experience than boys were.

ADULT GUIDANCE OF STUDENT SOCIAL LIFE AND THE ATTAINMENT OF EQUITY

One of the central questions that adults at P.A. ask themselves when examining student life outside of academics and athletics is: "To what degree can we guide, influence, or regulate what students do?" Regulation of student social life can—on the surface at least—be managed by setting up clear expectations and enforcing specific rules about sign-in, parietals, drinking and drugs, honesty, and consideration of others. If students knowingly disobey the rules, then reasonable punishments from room restriction to dismissal can be chosen by discipline committees made up of students and teachers.

But student life involves much more than rule obedience or rule breaking. Student social life at P.A. is filled with educational opportunities. For example, students gain an education via extracurricular activities, by discovering their leadership potential through student government, by learning about the dangers of drug and alcohol abuse through counseling groups, and by making choices about their own recreation. Students also can learn a great deal outside the classroom by overcoming fairly common emotional setbacks like depression, homesickness, or eating problems through personal counseling at Graham House and Isham Infirmary or through the student peer counseling system.

Education can also be furthered by other out-of-the-classroom learning experiences: doing community service and volunteer work, pursuing their religious beliefs and learning about the faith that others follow, living with students of different racial, ethnic, economic, and cultural backgrounds and imagining what life in different worlds would be like. Just as students try to find themselves and their values through informal talks with peers and adults, an important part of their education occurs when they learn to be friends with the opposite sex and begin to understand the closeness and mutual respect that can exist between the sexes.

Although the school is proud to offer such a richly varied social life to its students, much of students' social experience at Andover occurs outside of direct adult supervision: peer cultures set the tone in some areas. And that tone is not always what the adults in the community want. Most adults at Andover recognize that rule enforcement is not the best way to have an influence on student social life. But outside of enforcing rules, how are adults at Andover to define the comprehensive commitment they have made to educate and guide the development of young people?

Influencing and guiding youthful peer cultures, let alone uniformly regulating them, is a challenge for any adult in modern American society. Simply drawing the line and punishing offenses is never enough.

The instilling of values and the nurturance of self-respect and of respect for others cannot be initiated until a working relationship between the adult and the adolescent has been built. How much influence over student social and extracurricular life can the adults at P.A. have and how much should they try to have? How does adult guidance or the absence of it affect boys and girls and the quality of the coeducational social experiences they have together?

Coeducation Study data clearly indicates that the greatest gender equity—full and equal participation of both sexes—exists in the areas of student life where guiding adults play the most active role. In other words, when the adults get involved in student life, as they do in counseling, supervising certain extracurriculars, and enforcing discipline, students of both genders are usually treated fairly and equally. When students have near complete autonomy in making decisions and governing their own activities, as they do in many extracurricular organizations and student elections, boys often dominate in leadership positions and girls sometimes complain about being left out.

Perhaps the most striking example is the underrepresentation of females among the student leadership. Andover's *Catalogue* explicitly promises to cultivate the leadership potential in all its students: "We presume to forward the learning of leaders here, and leaders in our day must understand racial, social, national and religious differences, and see for themselves how significant is the unity in humanity."[167] Building the "courage to lead" in students is also stated as an explicit part of the school's educational purpose, and in 1979 the faculty voted to encourage "demonstrably responsible students to assume leadership and initiative in academic, residential, and athletic life at the school."[168]

However, a long-standing tradition at Andover has held that students learn leadership best when they are given the freedom and responsibility to run their own organizations. Thus, despite the fact that most organizations have faculty advisers, most extracurricular clubs and organizations are primarily student run. For example, no adult censorship or prepublication editing of the *Phillipian* occurs; in fact, students make all the editorial judgments about what to cover and who to put on the staff. Most clubs are self-perpetuating, i.e. the members at the end of one school year elect or appoint the officers for the following year.

As a result of the tradition of students running—without faculty interference—their own extracurricular activities, male student leadership has been encouraged more successfully than female student leadership. According to former Dean of Residence David Cobb, out of ninety clubs, activities, and organizations 84% of the leaders were male. He found that in most cases females were consigned to "middle management jobs."[169] Females are less likely than males to hold leadership positions in a number of student organizations. For example, since coeducation began *The Phillipian* has had, with only two exceptions, all male presidents. Males have usually outnumbered females on the board and the staff of the newspaper, too. The same trends are evident in the leadership of the *Pot Pourri*. When students were asked how many offices they held in extracurriculars, 9% more boys than girls reported holding one or more offices in student publications. One hundred forty-four boys indicated they held one or more offices in clubs, compared to 73 girls.

THE PHILLIPIAN CONTROVERSY: GENDER INEQUITIES IN EXTRACURRICULARS

The problem of male predominance in extracurricular organizations was brought to school-wide attention in early 1985 by a public letter to the Coeducation Committee from Rabbi Everett Gendler which outlined examples of bias in the *Phillipian* and in the debate society. He wrote the letter because he was "troubled by indicators that we're not succeeding on the Coed issue as well as we might have hoped."[170] The underrepresentation of females on the *Phillipian* board concerned him, for no females were included in the top seven editorial posts at that time.

In the community discussion that followed, the faculty advisor to the newspaper Tom Lyons added that he was also concerned about the total absence of blacks on the *Phillipian* staff. David Cobb called the *Phillipian* "woefully sexist," and he suggested that the paper should try to include more women. However, because of the tradition of allowing students to manage their own organizations without much adult influence, other faculty viewed the problem of male predominance at the *Phillipian* as solely an issue for student concern and for redress by students.[171]

Alerting the community to the fact that the numbers of extracurricular participants were clearly skewed toward males, Rabbi Gendler also hoped to raise the more subtle gender issue of values and language. He pointed out that the rhetoric used in the *Phillipian* to describe the debate society's performance at the Exeter Invitational Debate included unusually aggressive language: "trounced opponents . . . battered demand-side opponents . . . incensed over his one point loss . . . gloat after their studly performance." This bellicose description made Rabbi Gendler ask: "Is this independent school debating, or the Pittsburgh Steelers on a Sunday afternoon bone-crushing expedition?" Andover had lost the debate in question in part because of the performance of a female debater from Milton, but the contribution of females to the debate was virtually overlooked in the *Phillipian* article. Rabbi Gendler asked if the debate society was becoming "a predominantly male preserve?"[172]

Others agreed that values and style were at the heart of the problem of the predominance of males in extracurriculars. Susan Lloyd pointed out that the model of the hard-boiled newspaperman admired most by the top *Phillipian* staffers made them emulate a journalistic style that was "action-oriented, and competitive," "not oversensitive to criticism." She added that although girls were more likely than boys to be put off by this model, "boys who don't fit this stereotype are just as vulnerable to intimidation as girls are." *Phillipian* features editor Melanie Sarino did not attribute the problem to values or style directly, but she did note that "four female board members have felt oppressed by the male-dominated atmosphere of the organization."[173]

Although Rabbi Gendler called for all student organizations to talk with the faculty about these issues, few did so.[174] At the next *Phillipian* staff meeting, advisor Lyons spoke out strongly against any form of discrimination on the newspaper staff. In response the staff wrote a long story called "Sexism: An Andover Dilemma?" The student journalists also published a thoughtful editorial about the difference between real sexism and incomplete coeducation which explained that:

> . . . the problem we face now is that extracurriculars are older than coeducation. When a group is predominantly male, it tends to take on, even unintentionally, male attitudes and feelings. This situation creates a male-oriented atmosphere which can be justifiably uncomfortable to females. Thus fewer females feel inclined to join or those that do are less apt to stick with the activity. And since the board of each organization operates without quotas, it inevitably chooses a larger percentage of males than females for the subsequent board.[175]

But later the few female reporters who had gone public with complaints about sex bias had to face negative peer pressure: hostile graffiti were scribbled across the newsroom wall stating that the newspaper did not need any "f-g feminists."[176]

EXCEPTIONS TO MALE PREDOMINANCE IN EXTRACURRICULARS

While many student-run extracurriculars are dominated by boys, there are exceptions to this rule. For instance, because the faculty requires that there be male and female co-heads of the student service organization Blue Key, girls have played important leadership roles there each year. The student-run literary magazine *The Mirror* has also offered leadership roles to both sexes.

Where adult guidance of extracurriculars has been strong, female participation has been quite active, especially in Drama Lab, theatre productions, music activities, arts organizations, and Social Functions Committees. In fact, adults appoint leaders of Social Functions, and so girls are often given leadership opportunities there. Music activities run by the department can be taken for credit, so activities such as Chorus, Cantata, Orchestra, Band, Fidelio, and Chamber music are supervised like classes. Therefore, they are directly led by the Music Department's faculty, and attempts are made to include both sexes in public performances and leadership roles. In addition, almost equal percentages of boys and girls (11% male, 12% female) report holding one or more offices in arts organizations.

STUDENT GOVERNMENT

In student government, which is elected and run by students without adult involvement, males have predominated since 1973. In the first ten years of coeducation only 9 girls were elected cluster president compared to 57 boys. In the same time period only one girl has been elected student body president. One student wrote in the back of the questionnaire that the "only marked area of sexism at P.A." was that "it is generally expected that a male student will become school president, etc." For many years when most student participation in community discussions and governance occurred largely through the Cluster Presidents and the Committee on Residential Life, boys were represented far beyond the male ratio in the student body. Many faculty believe, as Jon Stableford wrote in his response to the Visiting Committee, that males tend to vote for candidates of their own sex even when female candidates are more qualified. If this is so, then boys, who have constituted about 60% of the student body in recent years, can easily win student elections with same-sex loyalty and the strength of numbers working in their favor.

Besides the unequal ratio in the student body, males may get elected more often because students believe that they exhibit "leadership qualities" better than females do. For example, students of both sexes reported that the most important attributes they look for in student leaders are assertiveness, willingness to take risks, and sensitivity to the needs of others. The first two of these attributes are ones boys are more likely to report possessing. Sixty-nine percent of the boys and 53% of the girls believed competitiveness is important in student leaders, and males were more likely than females to describe themselves as being competitive. Therefore, if the job description for a student leader reads assertive, risk-taking, and competitive, boys are more likely than girls to see themselves as fitting the description.

However, students of both sexes also value sensitivity to the needs of others, sympathy, and, to a much lesser degree, gentleness in their leaders, so the attributes they associate with leadership are not solely ones that fit best with boys' self-descriptions. Nevertheless, like many adults in our society, P.A. students, if asked to choose between gentle, sensitive, and sympathetic leaders and leaders who are assertive, competitive, and risk-taking, would pick the latter.

The theory that both sexes are biased in favor of male leadership is upheld by students' rating of the effectiveness of male and female leaders. Both sexes rate male leaders as "very effective" more often than they do female leaders. Furthermore, boys rate female leaders as "ineffective" four times as often as girls. Faculty ratings of student leaders of both sexes tend to be more positive than student ratings. While male faculty rate leaders' effectiveness among both sexes at about the same level, female faculty are more likely to rate female rather than male student leaders as effective. But in student elections, students, not faculty, do the voting, and since coeducation began students have voted many more males into office.

Students and faculty were asked what they thought about the proportion of male to female student leaders, and female students and female faculty were much more likely than their male counterparts to think that there were too many male leaders. Sixty-six percent of the boys viewed the current proportion of male/female student leaders as "about right," and 37% of the male faculty agreed with them. Eighty-four percent of the female faculty thought that there were too many male leaders, and 59% of the female students and 63% of the male faculty agreed with them. Seven percent of the boys answered, however, that there were too many female leaders.

A trend toward increased female leadership in student government may be building, however. In the past few years the Student Council has been more gender balanced, and four cluster presidents out of six elected in 1985 were females. More girls appeared to be willing to run for office in 1985, and, at least for Cluster President, more girls than boys were elected. Though more boys reported holding student government jobs, and many more boys held the top jobs, by 1984 almost the same percentage of girls and boys reported gaining some leadership experience in student government. Adults were unwilling to intrude on the students' right to choose their own leadership, but the Student Leadership Conference sponsored each year by the school has trained already elected leaders and brought gender issues to their attention. Less has been done about the problem of male predominance in other extracurriculars.

The problem of male predominance in extracurriculars and student government is more than an equity issue and more than a discrepancy in the school's stated promise to open up leadership opportunities to everyone. Perhaps because they have had less access to leadership experience at Andover, girls rated themselves as less personally successful at leadership than boys did. Forty-two percent of the boys surveyed and 32% of the girls see themselves as personally successful at leadership. Because educational researchers have found that "opportunities to demonstrate leadership" tend to increase self-confidence among students, inequality in some extracurriculars and in student leadership at Andover has great educational and developmental significance, especially for female students.[177]

AREAS OF EQUALITY IN STUDENT LIFE

Much more equity exists in other areas of student social life. For example, gender bias is absent in areas of student life governed by the Office of the Dean of Residence, where official policies governing students are made. Although on occasion students have asserted that males were given better dorms than females, there is no evidence that this charge is true. Both sexes are assigned to roughly similar dorms in each cluster. If there has been any tendency toward gender-biased assignment, it has been to assign a few more small dorms to girls than boys. In the '77-78 school year the average number of boys per boys dorm was 16.4, compared to 13 girls per girls dorm. However, the trend toward girls being assigned more often to small dorms has been halted. In 1983-84, there was an average of 15.8 boys per boys dorm and 15.6 girls per girls dorm. Not all clusters have equal numbers of girls and boys, but that is due to the unequal ratio in the student body and to the fact that dorm conversion has occurred more quickly in certain clusters.

Male and female student participation in cluster discipline committee decision-making has been assured because the Cluster Deans have "traditionally agreed" to have two student members, one male and one female. As a result, students are hardly ever required to appear before cluster discipline committees in which they are faced only by members of the opposite sex. A study of the punishments given by discipline committees over the course of several years starting in 1977 showed that no sex discrimination existed. For example, boys committed 74% of the rule violations in 1979-80—and received 71% of the probations, 75% of the restrictions and 71% of the work duty hours.

As these percentages show, significant gender differences do exist in rule violation. Boys were caught violating minor and major school rules at nearly twice the rate than girls were. A study of student offenses in the years 1977-78, 1979-80, and 1983-84 showed boys committed about three quarters of all major offenses that were dealt with through the official discipline process.[178] Major rule violations include dishonesty, cheating, use or possession of drugs or alcohol, unauthorized parietals, repeated or serious sign-in violations, "malicious harassment," "racial or religious intolerance," "willful infliction of personal injury," or "destruction of property."[179] Females are less likely than males to be caught committing offenses such as selling drugs, or causing personal injury, property destruction, or harassment. Boys committed 100% of all late sign-in and irresponsible work duty performances recorded, as well as 91% of all disruptive or inconsiderate behavior violations. In addition, boys exceed the limit on class-cutting more than girls. Girls were more likely to be caught breaking the parietal rules than any other major rule. While drug-related rule violations by both sexes have declined in recent years, girls remain less likely than boys to be caught using drugs.

As house counselors and cluster deans respond to different kinds of rule violations among boys and girls, the structure of the discipline system encourages them to treat both sexes fairly. The system requires that a student have an opportunity to defend him/herself and that responsible adults counsel the student and attempt to turn the incident into a learning experience, if possible. Finally, except in extreme cases, students are usually given a second chance—to learn from their first mistake—before they are dismissed. Boys are dismissed more often than girls, which may suggest that the disciplinary counseling system does not work as well to discourage rule breaking in boys.

Why should rule breaking and dismissals be so much more common among boys? Acting out against rules (possibly rebelling against the expected male role of responsible achiever) may serve a developmental function for boys: by breaking rules they experiment with asserting their adult autonomy. According to researchers, many schools reward compliance, docility, and conformity in students, and because of their previous sex role socialization, boys are less able than girls to live within the confines of the "good student" role. Thus, rule breaking may appeal to boys who feel too much pressure to be "good boys" who do all the right things. In the case of alcohol and drug use it may also be a way of gaining respect within certain male peer subcultures.[180] Whatever the sources of the more frequent male rule breaking, our evidence shows that the adults involved work hard to provide equitable counseling and discipline for both sexes.

FOSTERING AUTONOMY OR AFFILIATION IN STUDENT SOCIAL LIFE

When specialists in adolescent psychology write about the common developmental issues American teenagers face today, they are less likely than earlier scholars to emphasize inevitable stressful identity crises or "sturm and drang" tumult.[181] But psychologists and psychiatrists continue to see adolescence as a time when the search for individual identity is connected to a) defining a new and more independent bond with parents, b) coming to terms with the larger social structure by finding a place with the peer group, and c) moving toward an adult sexual identity. Previous developmental psychologists believed the central emotional task for all adolescents was separation-individuation (building a separate individual identity by letting go of child-like ties to parents). But recently scholars Nancy Chodorow, Jean Baker Miller, and Carol Gilligan have challenged this earlier emphasis on separation-individuation as being too biased toward male experience pointing out that males more than females are socialized to define their maturity in terms of separation from parents, autonomous action, and the ability to live independently; Gilligan, in particular, insists that separation-individuation has not been at the core of female adolescent development. Instead, she sees girls developing through the search for a new level of meaningful attachments during adolescence. From Gilligan's perspective boys view attachment to others as a threat to their individual identity while girls view the growth of their individual identity as being threatened instead by isolation from others or from loss of attachment.[182]

Perhaps, in reality, adolescent boys and girls are not always as different as these theories suggest, for within both sexes we see needs for autonomy or separation-individuation coexisting with urgent needs to affiliate, to be close to others, to be loved, to belong, and to be accepted within a larger social group.[183] Of course, boys in our culture are often socialized not to be too dependent or attached to others, while girls are often socialized to view too much autonomy as self-centered. But despite these pressures both sexes need to work on the developmental tasks of separation-individuation and affiliation (building bonds with others) in their teenage years in order to reach psychological adulthood.[184]

The outside pressure or support young people receive as they try to build both their autonomous and affiliative selves is crucial to their emotional development. When educators look at the needs of adolescent development in a boarding school context, it appears easier to set up residential boarding school social structures that facilitate separation-individuation than it is to establish those that support affiliation.[185] Students' striving for autonomy can be encouraged easily in an educational setting that gives them important choices to make about their lives and that teaches them to live with the consequences of their choices. Some separation from parents happens naturally during these years, but having a separate life away from home enables many boarding students to define how they want to be the same or how they want to be different from their parents. In that way a school like Andover can aid the growth of students' autonomy simply by offering them a residental setting away from home.

Asserting autonomy and refusing to be bound by limits set by adults are familiar ways that adolescents try out their independent potentials. A boarding school often creates an environment in which adolescents of both sexes can be aided by house counselors and other adults as they learn to make responsible autonomous choices and to become more independent. Evidence shows that Andover does an excellent job of encouraging boys and girls to work on the developmental task of building their autonomous selves. Adult guidance in many forms is available for students who are independent enough to take the initiative to ask for it. Students make important choices about courses, sports, activities, and social life without a great deal of interference from adults. They decide with only a few limitations how to decorate their rooms and how to choose their sleep hours and their study habits. In fact, the freedom to choose for themselves among all the opportunities that Andover offers is one of the things that students like best about the school.

Despite the support Andover gives them in defining their autonomy, students are often lukewarm or dissatisfied with the amount of privacy and personal freedom they are given at Andover. Only 40% of the boys and 46% of the girls said they were satisfied with the privacy and personal freedom they have. These figures suggest that, like other adolescents, Andover students are eager for more freedom and autonomy than the adults who care for them are willing to provide. The older a student is, the more likely s/he is to be dissatisfied with his/her privacy and personal freedom at P.A. A majority of 9th graders reported being satisfied with their privacy and personal freedom, but about a third of the seniors of both sexes reported being dissatisfied and another near third of the seniors viewed their privacy and personal freedom at P.A. as merely

O.K. Unlike some schools that take a more protective stance toward girls than boys, Andover provides an educational setting that encourages autonomous growth in both sexes, even if that freedom does not fully satisfy all students.

ENCOURAGEMENT OF AFFILIATION AND ITS GENDER IMPLICATIONS

At the same time as it does well in supporting students' separation-individuation, does the school also foster connectedness, affiliation, friendships, and close attachment in order to facilitate the other side of adolescent development? Andover prides itself on having a strong sense of community, and students report that the friendships and the wonderful people they have known at P.A. have been the best part of their experience at the school. Certainly a lot of attachment and connectedness comes spontaneously out of the shared experiences and the growing up that students do together at Andover.

However, the school seems to provide an environment which encourages affiliation among girls more successfully than affiliation among boys. A majority of students of both sexes reported that they were satisfied or very satisfied with friendships and the sense of community at Andover, but girls were more likely to be satisfied than boys. Almost a third of the boys responded with a lukewarm "it's okay." Evidently affiliation in the form of friendships and having a sense of community is made more difficult for boys because they may be socialized to be independent and/or because there may be unidentified factors in the Andover environment that slow male affiliative development. [186]

What could these unidentified anti-affiliative factors be? All we have are clues. In the questionnaire one boy described how his desire to build close attachments seemed to be at odds with the high value placed on autonomy and individualism at Andover:

> The things that make people unique are often considered blemishes that ought to be smoothed out. This attitude manifests itself most of all in the pressure to be independent. People are often unwilling to become close to one another. So I have seen many short-lived friendships that turn sour, and relationships in which people remain aloof and careless. In short, I see a lack of devotion and faithfulness. I believe this is a result of a general attitude that pushes [us] to be the best, to be normal, that makes people hide the weaknesses and emotions that make them human.

While his viewpoint may not be representative, it does suggest that some boys feel that "pressure to be independent" in the environment takes a toll on their interpersonal relationships.

At Andover, boys more than girls may feel the pressure to "hide the weaknesses and emotions that make them human," for they are less likely than girls to ask for help in times of trouble. In 1982-83 only 27% of the students seeking help at Graham House were boys, although by the first half of 1983-84 the male percentage had increased to 42%. Some boys reported feeling uncomfortable admitting they need counseling help to solve a personal problem, and boys more than girls may feel that a negative stigma is attached to talking with Graham House psychologists. Boys typically have longer courses of counseling than girls do once they finally come to Graham House. Psychologist Jonathan Marlowe believes that boys' longer terms of counseling may occur because they wait to seek help until a problem has reached a more severe stage.[187]

Despite societal pressure on them to be self-sufficient, most boys do seek some help from adults. When they were asked "how often in a typical month do you use the following to help you with personal, physical, or academic problems?" boys and girls alike reported that they turned most often to friends, parents, teachers, and house counselors. Yet girls were more likely to report seeking help "frequently" while boys reported turning for help "occasionally." Boys, in keeping with the sex role expectation that they be independent even when in need, were more likely than girls to report that they would be "not at all" likely to seek help from others. Six percent of the boys compared with 1% of the girls indicated they would not turn to friends for help in a typical month. Eighteen percent of the boys compared with 10% of the girls said they would not turn to their parents for help in a typical month. Some boys report turning to athletic trainers for help with physical, personal, or academic problems; they may feel more comfortable talking about problems in an athletic setting.[188]

AFFILIATION AND SUPPORT IN DORMITORY LIVING

Is there a conscious part of the school's educational philosophy that is devoted to supporting boarding students' developmental need to build close ties to other people? Every boarding student has at least one house counselor to turn to for help, and the expectation exists that the house counselor or another adult nearby can be sought out in times of trouble, ill health, or sadness 24 hours a day. The *Catalogue* states that all dorms are "small enough to encourage close relationships among students and between students and house counselor." [189] But several dorms have just two house counselors for forty students, and it is sometimes difficult for busy house counselors to establish a close relationship with each of the twenty students in the dorm. Not all students allow their counselors to become their friends even when house counselors have time to spend with them.

At many residential schools like Andover, house counselors commonly believe that boys' dorms are relatively easy to supervise compared to girls' dorms. When P.A. faculty members were asked whether they *thought* girls' or boys' dorms took more time, the majority of the faculty (62%) expressed the belief that girls' dorms took more time. Faculty members often view boys' apparent unwillingness to ask for help as an advantage that makes boys' dorms less work for adults. By viewing boys as less likely to have problems that require intervention by house counselors, many adults at Andover accept the belief that boys are by nature self-sufficient and unaffiliative. Girls' dorms, on the contrary, are often viewed as carrying with them the expectation of constant student interaction with house counselors which makes some faculty view girls' dorms as demanding.

According to evidence from the student questionnaire, this common belief in demanding girls' dorms and self-sufficient boys' dorms may be a partial myth, possibly a self-fulfilling prophecy through which the house counselor may invite exactly the student behavior that s/he expects to get. Indeed, our survey results suggests that boys and girls have similar needs for affiliation and support from adults. For example, male and female students reported at the same rate that they turn to house counselors for help frequently. Nine percent of the boys and girls said they turn to their house counselor frequently. Fifty-two percent of the boys and 54% of the girls reported asking for occasional help. Younger students are more likely to ask for frequent help, but the group that is least likely to report asking for frequent help from house counselors is senior girls. Though boys and girls may ask for different kinds of help from adults, there may be more basic similarities between girls' and boys' need for adult contact in dorms than the faculty recognizes.

Boys and girls evaluated their house counselors in the same way, too. Most were satisfied with the degree to which their house counselors fulfilled important caring roles for them. Nevertheless, 28% of the boys and 27% of the girls surveyed felt that their house counselors did not play the role of parent substitute often enough. The student group reporting the highest degree of concern about house counselors not playing parent substitute often enough were 9th grade boys. Boys also reported at a slightly higher rate than girls that their housecounselors did not fulfill the role of personal counselor for them (20% girls, 25% boys). Because many boys and girls gave similar answers to questions about their attitudes toward their house counselors, we are forced to conclude that boys and girls are more alike in their expectations of housecounselors than the myth suggests.

HOURS SPENT HOUSECOUNSELING

FQ #25: About how many hours per week do you spend housecounseling or on dorm-related tasks (e.g., shopping, phone calls, consulting with teachers, etc.)?

Hours: per week	0-5	5-10	10-15	15-20	More than 20
Males	9%	31%	36%	22%	3%
Females	9%	29%	32%	27%	3%

How about the actual hours house counselors spend working with their dorms—do women spend more time with their dorms than men do? According to survey evidence, boys' and girls' dorms take roughly the same amount of supervision time. The majority of house counselors—58% of the males and 59% of the females—spend between 10 and 20 hours per week on dorm work. Five percent more women than men do spend 15-20 hours per week in dorm work, but, overall, the pattern of time spent by both sexes is quite similar. Thus the statistics undermine the myth of boys dorms being easier to run.

Despite the similarity in time spent house counseling in dorms, males and females perceive their performance in dorm interactions in different ways. Males were more likely than females to report feeling they are too often disciplinarians in the dorm (15% to 6%) and that they do not act often enough as personal counselors (29% to 18%). Female house counselors, however, were twice as likely as male house counselors to report that they do not serve often enough as liasons with parents (46% to 23%) and as social arrangers (27% to 13%). Of course, susceptibility to guilt and variations in self-expectations could cause these results, rather than actual behavior.

Males are somewhat more likely than females to feel they spend too much time on dorm work. No females reported spending "far too much" time on housecounseling, compared to 8% of the males. But these responses may have a lot to do with the expectations created by the myth. If almost two-thirds of the male faculty believe in the myth, some of them may feel, as a result, that 10-20 hours a week is "too much" to spend working with an allegedly self-sufficient dorm. Similarly, it may be that no females reported spending "far too much" time on house counseling because the myth tells them to expect to spend a lot of time. Admittedly, there may be some significant gender differences in actual dorm interaction with house counselors, which our survey data did not reveal. But our findings suggest that the myth of the demanding girls' dorm and the self-sufficient boys' dorm may set up gender-typed norms which interfere with student-house counselor relationships. For example, if girls' dorms are defined within the community as inevitably demanding, will a female house counselor with a self-sufficient group of girls feel that she is somehow failing to meet all the needs of the dorm? If boys' dorms are defined as inherently self-sufficient will a male house counselor facing a group of homesick, lonely, or emotionally needy boys feel that the boys are deviating from "normal" male behavior?[190]

Perhaps the myth of the self-sufficient boys' dorm and the demanding girls' dorm reveals the positive value the school sometimes places on self-sufficiency and autonomy among students and the negative connotation that needs for support and affiliation sometimes have. Viewing self-sufficiency positively and needs for support negatively fit larger American cultural patterns, for, according to Gilligan, we live in a society where "maturity is equated with personal autonomy (and) concern with relationships appears as a weakness of women rather than as a human strength."[191] Even though the myth of the self-sufficient boys' dorm may suggest that some adults underestimate boys' need for nurturance and care, evidence shows that the myth does not stop house-counselors from spending time caring for the boys. Similarly, even if the myth of the demanding girls' dorm suggests that some adults may view girls' eagerness for adult guidance as a nuisance, evidence shows that house counselors also take time for them.

AFFILIATION AND SUPPORT FOR DAY STUDENTS

Affiliation and connectedness is a special issue for day students who, by and large, do not share in the experience of dormitory life at P.A. In particular, day students, especially males, may have less access to the common channels for student affiliation. When day students were asked whether they were satisfied with their integration into the school, 42% of the girls and 39% of the boys replied that they were not satisfied. More than a third of the day students reported that one of the effects of living at home is the fact that they will have very unsatisfactory integration into the P.A. community. On the other hand, they did not see living at home as a problem for friendships and social life, which sometimes take place outside of the P.A. community.

Whereas the lack of day student affiliation and sense of belonging to student social life has long been recognized as a problem, nothing has completely solved it. Assigning day students to dorms as associate members has worked very well in some cases, but it has helped girls more than boys. Sixty-three percent of the female day students surveyed were affiliated with a girls dorm, but only 28% of their male peers were. Boys may be less willing to affiliate with dorms or the school may not have urged dorms sufficiently to welcome them as members.

Day students' feelings of being insufficiently integrated into the school community, of course, reflect a larger contradiction between affiliation and achievement at Andover. Nurturance, community, and affiliation are valued very highly by faculty at Andover—perhaps more now than any other time since 1973. Yet the intensity of the academic and extracurricular lives community members lead often takes precedence over the formation of close relationships, especially in boys' lives. Achievement, the central goal of most students, takes so much time that affiliation occasionally has to be postponed for vacations. The most vivid example of the "affiliation gap" at Andover is the request by students' for more attention from faculty. At the 1985 Pace of Life conference and in open-ended responses to the student questionnaire, some students expressed the view that "more adult-student interaction must take place." According to one student, while students are "going through a tough adolescence" and getting used to a school that is "highly stressful and competitive," "it doubles their difficulties by having no parent figures to keep things in proportion. Phillips is too large a school to be socially supportive." While the school offers a great deal of support to its students, and house counselors sometimes serve as parental figures, some students feel a need for even more adult contact.

One boy wrote on his student questionnaire that "there should be more close, personal relationships between students and faculty." While girls are often socialized to find time for affiliation even under academic pressure, boys are often socialized to make achievement a higher priority than building close relationships. Because some members of the P.A. community have type-cast boys as inevitably self-sufficient, they may not be able to assist boys in overcoming the social pressure which constrains them from seeking help or closer bonds. Thus, some boys may suffer when Andover emphasizes autonomy and separation-individuation over affiliation in student social life. Ironically, many of the same adolescents who complain that adult guidance and rule enforcement are restricting their personal freedom at Andover also want closer and more supportive relationships with the same adults.

STUDENT RELATIONSHIPS: ADULT SUPERVISION OF MALE-FEMALE FRIENDSHIPS AND SEXUALITY

Before coeducation began, meetings were held by the P.A./Abbot Boy-Girl Relations Committee to discuss what school policy should be if boys and girls became "dangerously involved with one another." The committee worked toward a room visiting policy which "discourages sexual license."[192] The eventual result of that policy is the current parietals or room visiting system which allows students to enter the opposite sex's rooms only if they have received the house counselor's approval and if they have signed in.

Since coeducation began the school has never been supportive of male-female romantic and/or sexual relationships. Ted Sizer once told the student body "If you're old enough for sex, you're too old for Andover." Sexual relations have been removed from the list of punishable offenses only recently, though the school still does not condone them. As David Cobb wrote to the Faculty Advisory Committee:

> though sex is not explicitly prohibited, it is hardly a pervasive problem in our community, and it seems more positive, constructive, and healthy to deal with the infrequent problems as counseling rather than punishment occasions. The ambience and milieu of our community, it is felt, make it quite clear that sex among students is inappropriate on our campus, and that all students are aware of that...[193]

The faculty has diverse opinions about the "inappropriateness" of student sex at Andover, and the school prefers to avoid standardized policies in preference to offering individual counseling.

Counseling students about relationships, sexual or not, is done most often by friends, parents, house counselors, and Graham House counselors. Yet the school has provided in recent years a thoughtful group discussion program about human relationships and sexuality which emphasizes counseling and personal choice. Associate Dean of Residence for Health Issues 'Cilla Bonney-Smith first works with faculty volunteers to provide up-to-date information and to talk about ways of facilitating small group discussions. The format for the groups varies. Topics range from the physiology of reproduction to commitment, marriage, morals, trust, perceptions of the opposite sex, dating mores, and friendships. About twenty faculty members work individually with small sex-balanced student groups. The ground rule is confidentiality; the goals include honesty and building better communication between the sexes. Because the program is voluntary and it competes with class work, sports, and extracurriculars for students' time, about a quarter of the student body participates in it each year. Even so, many participants believe that these discussion groups affect the community more extensively because students bring back new insights to share with their friends in the dorm.[194]

In addition to the human relationships and sexuality program that Bonney-Smith sponsors, peer counseling groups are run on the cluster level by students with help from adults. Most clusters rarely have as many as fifty students involved in peer counseling at one time, but in some years Graham House has trained as many as seventy students to do peer counseling. In the past a small number of student and faculty-student women's groups enjoyed some success on campus, and an informal Human Relationships Group led by Father Richard Gross in Abbot Cluster and a Moral Decisions Group started by Nancy Sizer in West Quad North are still thriving. The longevity of such groups depends almost entirely on student interest and initiative, as well as adult support. Regardless of the numbers of participants or the duration of the efforts, Bonney-Smith's program, peer counseling and other groups are attempts to promote understanding of relationships of all kinds. They help students of both sexes with the developmental task of building new affiliative bonds, and they are indications that the school actively seeks to support better interpersonal relationships on campus.

STUDENT ATTITUDES TOWARD PARIETALS

Although Andover promotes discussion and offers counseling about male-female relationships, students often perceive the enforcement of the parietals rule as an attempt to prohibit male-female friendships and to police sexuality. Termed by some students the "absurd invention of adult paranoia," the parietals rule is the most unpopular school rule among students. In fact, students rarely criticize the school for being anti-affiliation except in the area of parietal policies and in adult attitudes toward student romances. Only 21% of the boys and 20% of the girls said they were satisfied with the parietal system, and 52% of the boys and 49% of the girls registered dissatisfaction with it.

In the open-ended responses to the student questionnaire, students were outspoken in their dislike of parietals. Many students resent in particular the implication by faculty—imagined or real—that opposite sex room visiting means that sexual intercourse will occur. Complaining that parietals were too limited to allow friendships to grow, one girl wrote that during parietals: "It's insulting that faculty insinuate SEX because this is not always true. It is a way to spend time together. Missing out on these important friendships deprives students of a critical part of personal development." Claiming that Andover was not "too coeducational," another student wrote that the association of parietals with sex restricted the mixing of boys and girls: "Let's wake up folks! High school students can have best friends who are members of the opposite sex, but not here."

Because parietals are associated in some minds with sexuality, on rare occasions remarks are written on sign-in sheets in boys' dorms about the morals of girls who have parietals there. Students are still influenced somewhat by the old double standard that penalizes females who have premarital sex without alloting any stigma to the male partner. Therefore, girls are more likely than boys to suffer social disapproval for having parietals. One student complained about the unfairness of the "uncomfortable stigma in the dorm towards girls who have frequent parietals or contact with 'members of the opposite sex'."

One girl wrote that the thing she liked least about Andover was the parietal rules:

> It makes you feel like guys are different animals! . . . Be serious, how are we to have respect for each other if you never get to know them? Parietal rules really backfire on the school–respect for females especially.

Students have also pointed out that the school has been hypocritical in justifying its room visiting policies as a matter of fire safety—requiring parietal visitors but no other guests to sign in so the school can know who is in the dorm in case of a fire.

Even among students who praise the "aura of equality among the sexes" at Andover and the "support" given to "male-female friendships," coeducation on occasion has been seen as having a "negative effect" on students' emotional growth. Because, according to one student, "girls have to take on qualities of (competitiveness, etc.) that are usually attributed to guys," the "male-female intermingling is mostly based on academic and athletic competitiveness." The student added that, as a result, P.A. boys and girls are "sexually retarded."

The major complaint about the parietals system and the school's attitude toward boy-girl romances hinges on some students' insistence that Andover inhibits them from forming attachments to other students. In fact, discontent is so widespread that only 43% of the boys and 46% of the girls reported being satisfied with boy-girl relationships at P.A. Asserting that "friendships among teenagers are tremendously important to their personal development," one student said the school "down-played" "the importance of these" relationships. Another student wrote that:

Now that it is prom time, I can see how the early sign-in hours and the difficulty of having parietals have prevented many students from getting to know their classmates better, especially males-fe-males. I know if given more of an opportunity, I'm sure they could find that members of the opposite sex can be worthy friends as well as just classmates.

Parietals, limited social life, and boy-girl relationships were listed second most often among things students liked least about P.A.

WHAT STUDENTS LIKE *LEAST* ABOUT P.A.:
VOLUNTARY RESPONSES TO OPEN-ENDED QUESTIONS

M	F		
69	100	1.	Pace of Life/Pressure/Lack of Time for Relaxing, Building of Relationships or Thinking
52	42	2.	Parietals/Boy-Girl Relationships/Limited Social Life
42	28	3.	Rules + Discipline System/Lack of Consistency between Clusters + Dorms/Too Moralistic
34	36	4.	Elite Preppiness, Social Climbing, Snobbiness, Cliqueishness, Materialism
41	26	5.	Food/Quality, Starchiness, Taste, Unfairness of Distribution
21	41	6.	Too much Competitive Spirit/Grade Consciousness
35	36	7.	Faculty Relations with Students/Lack of Respect/Not Taking Them Seriously in School Governance, Hypocrisy in Way They Carry Out Rules, Lack of Interest in Students
16	17	8.	Impersonality/Size of School/Lack of Spirit of Cohesiveness/Sense of Loneliness

---

Related to complaints about student social life were references to elite preppiness, social climbing, snobbishness, and cliquishness which also made the list of the top eight things students like least about Phillips Academy. Though faculty and administration value diversity highly, it does not necessarily follow that complete egalitarianism will automatically sprout throughout student peer culture. Students who commit overt discrimination, such as taking anti-semitic or racist actions, have sometimes been dealt with through the disciplinary system with dismissal as a possible consequence. The school considers overt discrimination a serious rule violation.

Most cases of snobbishness, sexism, or ethnic or racial intolerance that are brought to adults' attention, however, are dealt with as counseling problems and as educational issues. Of course, most instances of social tensions or cliquishness among students would never be brought to adults' attention, even if they interfere with the basically healthy and egalitarian student social environment. A few minority students reported on the student questionnaire that they felt excluded from the mainstream of student social life, but they have not called on adults to solve the problem. Students keep most peer social tensions to themselves.

Though student discontent with parietals and male-female relationships is heartfelt and worthy of further attention, the tendency among some students to blame parietals and adult supervision for the lack of satisfactory male-female relationships is not totally fair. The school has put considerable effort and resources into providing social and recreational options for all students. The school offers dances, a recreation room, and freedom for students to interact socially, especially on weekends. In 1985 the school invested money and energy in an elegant but low-priced prom on the Abbot campus, a gesture which was supportive of making social life available to all students regardless of their finances. Student initiatives, such as AfLatAm Society dances and overnights, trips to restaurants by the Asian Cultural Society, and dorm slumber parties, have improved the quality of many students' social lives at Andover, especially minority students. But adult efforts to provide recreational and social opportunities to students do not necessarily predetermine the quality of male-female relationships at Andover.

The fact that boys and girls often attend weekend dances in same-sex groups sometimes makes mixing socially difficult.[195] No school policy can be blamed for the discomfort students feel mixing at dances. That discomfort seems to be built into adolescent social life, and many adults in the community lived through it when they were teenagers, too. Andover's student social life is different from the average high school for one main reason: students came to this school because they wanted to devote themselves to gaining an excellent education. By comparison with many high school students elsewhere, Andover students are more preoccupied with academic, athletic, and extracurricular activities than they are with dating and social life. Studies have shown that females' urge to achieve can be dampened permanently by an excess of concern with popularity and peer social approval during adolescence, so Andover's emphasis on achievement may have a special benefit for girls. It is true that adults at Andover reinforce students' choice to make achievement take precedence over socializing. Most students would have chosen to attend other schools if social concerns were a higher priority for them than achievement. Because of the atmosphere at Andover, relatively little social pressure is exerted within the student peer culture to have steady dating relationships, but some flourish anyway. The prevalence of male-female friendships on campus is a sign that coeducation can succeed in the realm of student social life.

DOES ANDOVER PROVIDE A "CHILLY CLIMATE" FOR EITHER SEX IN THE AREA OF STUDENT SOCIAL LIFE?

As we look at the texture of student social life at Andover do we see pervasive equity or do we see a "chilly climate" limiting the personal and educational growth of either sex? When the Project on the Status and Education of Women of the Association of American Colleges described typical college-level student social life they found that for women and minorities the climate outside the classroom was as "chilly" as it was inside.

—Women students may be less likely to be encouraged to seek leadership positions than men...

—Women who do hold such positions may find that their credentials are systematically doubted while men's tend to be presumed adequate...

—Women may receive less mentoring, help and information so that they function less effectively.

—Student leaders may be chosen on the basis of gender stereotypes, as, for example, when men are customarily considered for positions requiring budgeting skills, women for those geared to social events.[196]

In addition to these problems, student social life has been marred on some college campuses in more overtly hostile ways. When coeducation began at one college, male students expressed their hostility toward the newly arrived female students by calling them "cohogs" and posting unwelcoming sexist signs around campus. Sadie Hawkins dances, wet T-shirt contests, X-rated movies, and fraternity party "gross-outs" aimed at insulting women have also demeaned women on many college campuses.[197] Gang rapes as well as date and acquaintance rapes have also occurred on college campuses in recent years. The equity earthquake has not yet shaken college students' social lives much because many college authorities have not made equity an issue.

On the high school level students' young age demands adult guidance. Yet equity in students' high school social life remains a neglected issue. At Andover, however, since coeducation began, adult guidance has been used to create a more equitable student social life. Overt anti-female actions have very rarely characterized coeducation at Andover, a fact for which students as well as faculty and administration deserve credit. Coeducation began in 1973 in a state of uneasy tension rather than open hostility, and since then the school's leadership has, with very few exceptions, stopped any overt public sexism before it started. Yet—except where adults intervene—Andover is very much like other educational institutions in the more subtle ways that a chilly climate can be created for women. We have seen examples of this in the predominance of males in certain extracurriculars and student government.

The Andover environment is, however, both coeducational and healthy in its encouragement of students' autonomy and individual development. Both boys and girls thrive on the freedom offered by the school, and both have access to adult support as they make their autonomous choices. The school's support for affiliation is more ambiguous. Day student boys' lack of dorm affiliation may be the most telling example of an "affiliation gap." The myth of the self-sufficient boys' dorms and demanding girls' dorms may not create a chilly climate for either sex, even though it may suggest inaccurate gender-typing. Our evidence shows that dedicated house counselors spend a lot of time working with students, regardless of their gender or the students' gender.

If there is an "affiliation gap" in the school, it may isolate boys more. It may also be a natural outgrowth of the emphasis placed on achievement at the school. Faculty and students have been discussing the issue of adult guidance already. Concern with affiliation issues, especially increasing students' access to adult guidance in dorms and providing support and relief for busy house counselors, caused the faculty to vote in 1985 for a system of complementary house counselors who could come into dorms to work with students. Thus, students would have even more chances to build bonds with and receive support from adults. In addition, to emphasize the importance of faculty family life as well as the need for faculty to have time reserved for house counseling, the faculty voted in 1985 to prohibit most meetings from occurring after 8 P.M. As a result, house counselors and students could have more time in the evening set aside for informal talks, and faculty could also be guaranteed that no committee meetings would interfere with their personal lives and dormitory work after 8 P.M.

Parietals clearly irritate many students of both sexes, and they may deserve further community-wide discussions. Yet, if those discussions occur at all, students will need to understand why adults can legitimately ask questions about the consequences of relaxing the parietals rule. Given the sex-bias evident when extracurriculars lack direct adult guidance, more student freedom in controlling their own room visiting could follow the same pattern. If room visiting rules were liberalized and student romance and sexuality were permitted to increase, would male dominance, sexism, deemphasis on achievement, or complications in adult-student relationships occur? While the sexual stigma attached to room visiting is troubling and possibly preventable, adult guidance of student social life remains vital at Andover if sex equity is to be achieved.[198]

Chapter Six:
TEACHERS, COACHES, HOUSE COUNSELORS, and DEANS

Has the school recruited and hired faculty and defined their workload expectations so that good teachers of both sexes will gladly build their careers at P.A.?

ROLE MODELS FOR STUDENTS

Who determines whether an educational environment offers a chilly climate for boys or girls? Obviously, student attitudes, peer culture, and student behavior can shape the environment a great deal. But students leave and the adults of the community stay. Together faculty, administrators, trustees, and other adults with decision-making power at Andover affect the long-term values and policies which can thwart or facilitate the growth of sex equity within the school environment.

Trustees can choose to hire a Headmaster who makes sex equity a priority, as well as allocating budgetary resources to promote an equitable form of coeducation. The Headmaster can decide whether students will see both sexes—or only one sex—in positions of authority on campus. Furthermore, the Headmaster, in consultation with Trustees and others, can set employment policies which may or may not encourage faculty of both sexes to build their careers at Andover. The Dean of Faculty in partnership with department chairs can decide the gender composition of the faculty and the degree to which students have contact with role models of either sex. The faculty can collectively determine whether students are instructed using a curriculum that leaves out or includes women and minorities. Individually teachers can control the level of equity and encouragement for both sexes that characterize their classroom interactions. Thus, adults at Andover have immense power to create a positive environment in which both boys and girls are respected and treated fairly.

It would be naive to assume that every policy decision ever made at Andover was fully conscious or that when the policy was made its impact on each gender was anticipated. Furthermore, as we will see in the final chapter, community values and educational environments are also molded by forces outside the conscious control of any single faculty member or administrator.[199] As we saw in the chapters on athletics and student social life, official policies have not yet solved many equity problems that originate with deeply ingrained attitudes or previous socialization.

Throughout this study we have explored many of the choices that have been made over the years at Andover to create an equitable climate for students, and we have also found problems that have not yet been solved. Within the faculty itself and the policies governing faculty life at P.A. another set of choices for and against equity has been made. Though a school exists to educate students, equity in the treatment of faculty affects the overall equity climate of the school.

Several studies show, for example, that the gender composition of the faculty makes a big difference to students.[200] A faculty made up of one sex limits the experiences students have working with authority figures and learning about varied teaching styles. Though many students might not admit it, adolescents often look up to and identify with their teachers. In this way teachers serve their students as examples—even ideals—of behavior and belief. Students' need to work with same-sex role models has been documented as one of the basic requirements of good education.[201] Mentoring, serving as a model and a guide, can be done well by teachers of the opposite sex. Yet working with same-sex role models helps students realize what they may become as adults. Sociologists have found that "the lack of female faculty models with whom thay can identify and discuss problems, anxieties, and future plans" can affect female students' willingness to venture into new academic fields, as well as their ability to build confidence in their own potentials.[202]

Students often recognize how important adult role models are to them. In 1981 a student representative wrote a short essay about coeducation, and the school included her comments in its official response to the New England Association of Schools and Colleges Visiting Committee's "androgyny report." The student essay was based on information she gathered talking to about fifteen other girls. She recorded that the group had only one complaint: "the lack of women role models on the faculty." From their perspective:

> Few, if any, *women* on the faculty display the same wit, wisdom, vitality, and charisma with which numerous (or at least, *several*) *men* on the faculty have won the respect and hearts of men and women, students and faculty. There are many *fine, fine* women teachers and administrators, yet the rarity of true women leaders on campus is disturbing.[203]

It might be hurtful for women faculty to read that students on occasion have viewed them as less wise and charismatic than their more numerous male counterparts. Yet the students' concern with the lack of adult female role models and their tendency to judge all teachers by comparison with a charismatic male model should not be entirely surprising.

The average Andover student still interacts with more male role models each day, so it is natural for them to see males as the norm against which "others" should be compared. Furthermore, as we saw in the chapter on academic life, students were more likely to view male teachers as challenging and demanding, while they saw no positive or negative teaching characteristic as uniquely female. As noted before, studies of other educational settings show that students find so-called "masculine" teaching styles of authoritative, charismatic performance more impressive than so-called "feminine" styles of nurturant interaction.[204]

In keeping with these trends, institutional recognition for greatness in teaching thoughout American education has historically been awarded at a higher rate to men than women. At Andover no tenure exists except for honorary teaching chairs which are given to a few senior teachers in recognition of outstanding teaching and service to the school. Only two out of 22 teachers with teaching foundation chairs are women, a fact that can be partially explained by the underrepresentation of women in the over-40 faculty age group. If the tendency to value female teachers less highly than male teachers —which has been noted by educational researchers elsewhere—exists at Andover, it would diminish the status of female teachers and the esteem in which they are held.[205] Nevertheless, many students at Andover recognize how important faculty of both sexes are to them, as role models and mentors, and both sexes miss vital educational experiences if too few female role models are available to them.

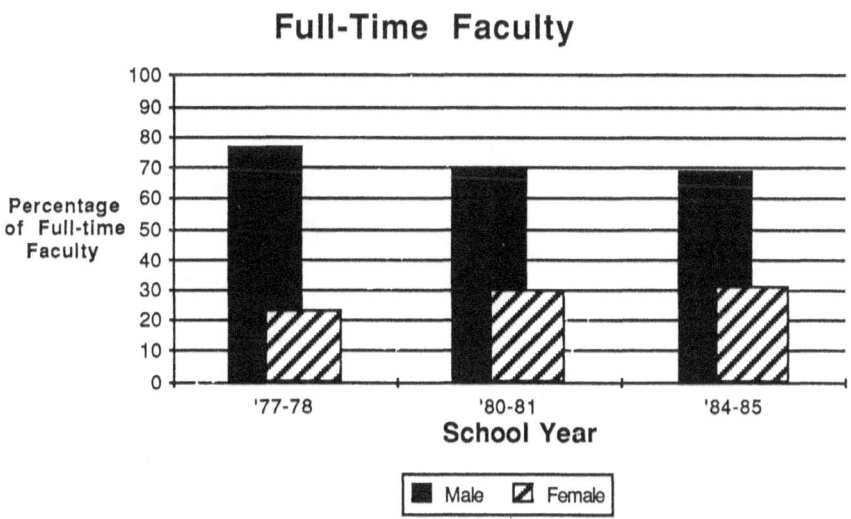

Full-Time Faculty

Total Faculty

(including part time faculty)

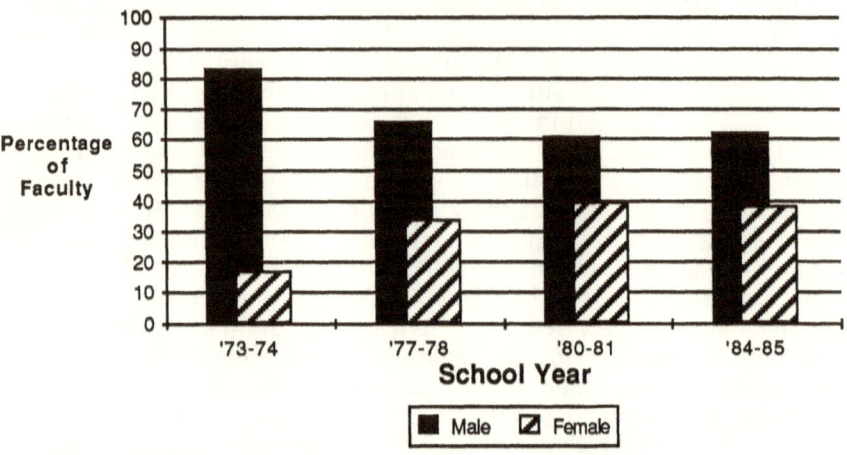

The lack of female role models on the faculty was most dire at the beginning of coeducation, when women made up less than 20% of the faculty. Today women make up 28% of the full-time faculty, though they make up 77% of the part-time faculty. Because of the gender agreement rule, almost all boarding students live in a dorm supervised by a house counselor of the same sex, so almost every boarding student has at least one same-sex role model, a house counselor, with whom s/he has frequent contact. On the other hand, day students are more likely to have males than females as day student counselors. Even today students are more likely to be taught, academically advised, and coached by men.

Almost 3/4 of the academic advisors are men, as are the coaches and full-time classroom teachers. Academic advisors are a more heavily male group than house counselors because of generation factors. All non-music and art faculty (with a few exceptions) are required to spend a minimum of 10-12 years as house counselors at the beginning of their P.A. careers. After completing their dorm service, usually in their forties or fifties, they move into non-dorm housing and serve instead as academic advisors. Although the number of female academic advisors has increased from nine to 13 in the past three years, the vast majority of the senior faculty since the merger have been male, and academic advisors tend to be senior male faculty members who have already finished their dorm service. Andover's academic advising system is based on the assumption that senior faculty have sufficient experience with the curriculum to provide the requisite academic advice to students. Although 9th and 10th grade advisors have met to discuss equity issues, including gender and racial issues, no special counseling training has been offered advisors. Nor has the school explored the implications of the current system for offering varied role models and guidance to both sexes.[206]

Men tend to predominate among full-time classroom teachers due in part to the fact that many women opt to be part-time teachers. Although the option of being a part-time teacher with reduced workload and compensation is available to all faculty members, women have been much more likely to choose to work part-time. Women make up three quarters of the part-time faculty, including in 1984-85 two married couples who were job sharers. Certainly part-time faculty serve as role models just as full-time teachers do, but students are prone to have less contact with them because they teach fewer sections. Coaches are predominantly male because the ratio of female coaches reflects the proportion of full-time women faculty who are expected to perform the triple threat of dorm counseling, teaching, and coaching.

When Sizer was Headmaster he decided to change the definition of faculty from strictly classroom teachers and top administrators to include a greater portion of the Andover community: the school doctor, librarians, College and Graham House counselors, additional administrators, part-time spouse house counselors, athletic trainers, and the food service manager. By redefining the faculty, he not only opened up voting in faculty meetings to a new group of employees, but, more significantly, he transmitted a feeling of membership in the community to a great many people who had not been included before. If part-time and full-time classroom teachers, as well as many non-teachers who have faculty status, are combined as "total faculty," then in 1984-85 women made up 38% and men 62%. As a result, there is an important female presence on campus.

Part-time women faculty, including spouse house counselors, have a higher status within the Andover community than they would have at many other schools and colleges. Part-time faculty have served as administrators, committee chairs, and as Faculty Advisory Committee representatives elected by the faculty to advise the Headmaster. Unlike some institutions in which junior faculty and part-timers are never allowed to attend department meetings, at Andover few, if any, distinctions are made among part and full-time or junior and senior faculty when community-wide or departmental decision-making occurs.[207] Thus, Sizer's expansion of faculty status helped create a more egalitarian atmosphere which welcomed new men and women into full community membership. But, regardless of the presence and acceptance of part-time faculty at P.A., a student's direct daily contact with important role models such as housecounselors, teachers, coaches, and academic advisors is still much more likely to occur with men. As the chart on student contact with male and female teachers shows, the school has recently made progress in increasing the percentage of female faculty who work with students in the classroom.

STUDENT CONTACT WITH MALE AND FEMALE TEACHERS

	SPRING '77-78	SPRING '82-83	FALL '85-86
%TAUGHT BY MALE TEACHERS	72%	70%	64%
% TAUGHT BY FEMALE TEACHERS	28%	30%	36%

*based on Registrar's Office data on total number of student enrollments (e.g. in Fall '85 there are 5860)

RECRUITING THE FACULTY

The overriding reason that the majority of adult contact that students have is with males is that the faculty which resulted from the merger of P.A. and Abbot was overwhelmingly male, and since then hiring efforts have not completely altered the imbalance. Both Abbot and Phillips Academies began in eras when few schools and colleges welcomed diverse faculties or student bodies. *The Constitution of Phillips Academy*, revised in 1828 from the original 1778 version, describes the qualifications required of Andover faculty:

> No person shall be chosen, as a principal Instructor, unless a professor of the Christian Religion, of exemplary manners, of good natural abilities and literary acquirements, of a good acquaintance with human nature, of a natural aptitude for instruction and government; and, in the appointment of any Instructor, regard shall be had to qualifications only, without preference of kindred or friend, place of birth, education, or residence ... Protestants only shall even be concerned in the Trust or Instruction of this Seminary.[208]

It was taken for granted that all faculty would be white, Caucasian, and male. In the Abbot Academy *Constitution* written in 1828 no qualifications for teachers were listed, other than that the Principal Instructor "whether male or female" was required to be a "professor of the Christian religion, of exemplary piety."[209]

Diversity came slowly to the Abbot and P.A. faculties. P.A. Headmaster Claude Fuess commented about a student denied admission to P.A. in 1935 that it was "just too bad about the little Jewish boy, but I can't very well blame Dean Lynde for trying to keep our school as predominantly Aryan as possible."[210] It took Abbot about 125 years to hire its first full-time male teacher, and it took Phillips Academy almost two hundred years to hire its first full-time female teacher.[211] Abbot and P.A. changed at the same time as most private institutions: diversity suddenly became more attractive in the mid-sixties. The hiring of Catholics, Jews, and middle-class teachers pre-dated coeducation, and coeducation coincided with an ever increasing concern with diversity in hiring. The days are long since past when a new student or a new faculty member at P.A. or Abbot would be introduced—as at least one was in 1968—as being "from a fine old New York family."[212]

For many years after it had made an explicit commitment to building a more varied faculty, P.A. took a passive approach to hiring women and minorities. Because of the school's reputation and the attractiveness of the teaching jobs, the school has always had an abundance of job applicants. No official search procedures or policies existed. Gradually, the practice of hiring through personal contact—using the "old boy network"—was questioned, for it had proven to be an ineffective way to bring diversity to the faculty.[213]

Serving as Dean of Faculty in the early eighties, History instructor John Richards II described the faculty recruiting process as being in a "state of evolution," moving from "a passive policy to a more active one." More advertising in newspapers, professional newsletters, and education publications was being done, and Richards personally wrote to a great number of black colleges and encouraged others to utilize women's placement networks in order to attract candidates who might not otherwise apply. Richards recruited at NAIS and professional conventions, and he made travel funds available to department chairs and search committees to allow them to recruit.

While the Dean of Faculty facilitated the search for job candidates, most of the recruiting was done by the individual department chairs and, in some cases, by search committees. In recent years the Dean of Faculty usually has accepted the recruitment and hiring recommendations of the department involved. As a result, hiring policy at Andover is decentralized. The schoolwide goal of seeking diversity occasionally has been neglected in the fragmented departmental search process; nevertheless, an affirmative action review policy is on record as official school policy. In the *Faculty Handbook* it is clearly spelled out that Andover is:

> committed to a policy of Equal Employment Opportunity and non-discrimination in the treatment of employees or applicants for employment without consideration for race, color, religion, sex, age, or national origin. To this end, a program has been established to review all employment policies and practices and to increase the numbers and job levels of women and of members of minority groups in those areas in which numbers may be low in relation to the available supply of qualified individuals.[214]

Unlike many schools and colleges that have been forced by federal regulators or civil suits to establish affirmative action goals, Andover adopted the policy in 1974 because of the school's commitment to diversity.[215] However, despite the official affirmative action policy and efforts being made to recruit women and minority faculty, in 1985 some members of the faculty were registering "deep concern over the continuing underrepresentation of Blacks, Hispanics and women on our faculty."[216]

A letter to the Headmaster from two faculty members urged the school to "clarify the goals and process of affirmative action" and to adopt a hiring policy that stated "if several qualified candidates apply for the same position, the one from a previously excluded group should be hired over the one from the previously included group."[217] While the letter acknowledged that real progress had been made since 1973, it also pointed out that the teaching faculty still had fewer than 6% Black and Hispanic members and fewer than 30% women members. Forty-nine percent of all high school teachers in America are women; thus Andover's full-time rate of 28% and total faculty rate of 38% women are both below national averages.[218] Yet Andover has a higher percentage of minority and women on its faculty than a great many private schools and colleges. Less than 10% of the full professors in major universities are women, and in 1981 only 27% of the full-time university faculty were women.[219]

Recent recruiting and hiring records show that a higher percentage of women applicants than men have been invited to be interviewed for teaching jobs at Andover. In most years, for each person finally offered a job at P.A., there are more than 40 unsuccessful applicants. In fact, in the strict sense of probability, only a very small percentage of the applicants for faculty jobs are actually hired. In some years a higher percentage of women applicants have been hired, but that pattern varies from year to year. Clearly the school is trying to hire more women.

The most pressing problem in faculty hiring remains recruitment—making the initial positive contact with women and minority teachers who might not otherwise apply. Even after the "old boy network" has been replaced by national advertising and large, open searches, the yield turns up mostly white male applicants. Andover may have inadvertently discouraged some women from applying, by persisting for many years in advertising for teachers who can coach. The school may have

Faculty Hiring

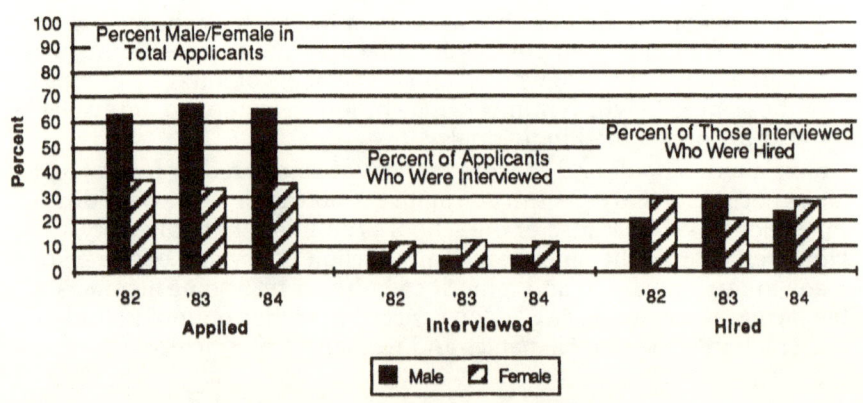

alienated some prospective female applicants who do not see themselves as potential coaches. Other schools have found that "adding coaching to a job description eliminates most women applicants."[220] These schools have decided that it is better to advertise for teachers who can coach *or* supervise recreational programs. Due to a suggestion by the Dean of Studies, some Andover job advertisements now mention the availability of day care facilities on campus which, it is hoped, will encourage female applicants.

Did male and female faculty have different reasons for coming to Andover in the first place? On one level, no; both male and female faculty were attracted to P.A. because of the teaching opportunities, which 83% of the males and 75% of the females answering the faculty questionnaire described as being "important" or "very important" in their decision to come to P.A. For men, coaching, housing, and job security were more important than they were for women. Very few (8%) women came to P.A. because of coaching, and 70% of the women rated coaching as "unimportant" or "very unimportant" to their decision to come to P.A. For women counseling opportunities influenced their choice of P.A. more than they did men. More than one-third of the females cited counseling opportunities as "very important" or "important" compared to 12% of the males.

In addition, a larger percentage of female respondents than male respondents considered their family situation a "very important" factor in deciding to come to P.A. Family situation could mean geographic proximity to their husbands' jobs, close relatives, the desire for children to attend P.A., or many other family factors. P.A.'s location was also a more important factor for women. Women were also more likely to view administrative opportunities as a reason to come to P.A. Forty-four percent of the women viewed administrative opportunities as "important" or "very important" while 56% of the men viewed them as "unimportant" or "very unimportant."

NEPOTISM

Because of its efforts to hire based on the goal of increasing faculty diversity, P.A. has reexamined the original nepotism policy it adopted in the early years of coeducation. Nepotism has become a women's issue in some affirmative action cases because schools and colleges have often refused to hire qualified women because they were married to employees—often faculty members.[221] When coeducation began Andover had not yet hired enough women teachers to staff all the new girls' dorms. So, as noted in the chapter on the roots of coeducation, the school often hired the wives of male teachers to run these dorms. In order to make this arrangement attractive, the school continued to pay the male teacher a full-time triple threat (dorm-coaching-teaching) salary at the same time that a part-time salary was paid to his wife. In addition, she was granted faculty status.

In the early years of coeducation the school also had to set a policy about the hiring of close relatives. In general it became a common and acceptable practice for both members of the family to be employed at P.A. Out of 219 faculty and faculty associates listed in 1984-85, between 90 and 100 had benefitted at some time during their career from the flexible nepotism policy which allowed the Academy to employ two close relatives at once. But by the early eighties the nepotism policy was suffering from its own success. It became much more complicated in a closely entwined residential community to decide *not* to hire a close relative of a faculty member after it had been such a commonplace practice. Spouse-hiring began to look like almost a job benefit or perquisite. As the school moved toward nationally advertised job searches and self-conscious recruiting for diversity, could it continue to hire so often from "inside" the community?

Therefore, a new nepotism and spouse hiring policy was announced in 1984. Portions of the policy were familiar:

> members of one family may be hired, promoted, and compensated strictly on the grounds of their individual merit without consideration of their relationship with other employees or marital status except that the Academy will not hire, transfer, or promote an individual to work directly under a family-related supervisor. This means that spouses will not normally be hired in the same academic department. Family-related shall mean the members of the immediate family (parents, children, siblings, and their spouses) of the supervisor, or the supervisor's spouse.[222]

In addition, co-house counselors would not be hired in the future. If part-time spouse house counselors were hired in the future they would not be paid extra to supervise dorms. Instead, for salary purposes, they would be considered to be job sharing with their spouses. Though the hiring of spouse house counselors was still permitted at the convenience of the Academy, the job sharing status decreased its attractiveness as an employment option. A number of faculty members regretted the shift in policy, but others viewed it as one equitable solution to a thorny employment problem. While hiring qualified relatives, especially spouses, would certainly continue in a modified form, the Academy had made it clear that the employment of relatives was neither an expected benefit nor a practice that could occur outside the regular competitive hiring process.

FACULTY SALARIES

One of the reasons that P.A. has had such a large pool of job applicants in recent years (besides the excellent teaching opportunities, the proximity to Boston, and the lack of comparable high school and college options) is that the school offers attractive salary and benefits. Headmaster McNemar and the Trustees have set as a central school goal for the eighties "recruiting and supporting" a first-rate faculty of "outstanding teachers" and in the process making sure that they are "among the best compensated teachers in independent schools."[223]

"Teaching at Andover," a faculty recruiting flier, explains that the workload for P.A. faculty is demanding but the compensation is excellent, equivalent to if not better than salaries paid to teachers in many small colleges.[224] When the faculty was asked how they found the salary offered by the school, 66% of the men and 60% of the women viewed the salary as excellent or very good.

Are salaries given out fairly to both sexes? Earlier in this century P.A. faculty salaries were decided subjectively by the Headmaster without reference to a salary scale.[225] Single men had been doing the same work but were paid less than their married colleagues who were presumed to need more money until Headmaster Kemper finally evened out the discrepencies that existed between married and single men's salaries.[226] Both P.A. and Abbot eventually adopted salary scales to reward all faculty by an objective standard. At the time of the merger the median Abbot salary was about $3,000 less than the median P.A. salary, but after coeducation, adjustments were made to bring the former Abbot teachers' salaries closer to P.A. pay scales. [227]

Although "The Equal Pay Act of 1963, the Civil Rights Act of 1964, and Title IX of the Education Amendment Act of 1972 have made salary discrimination due to race or sex illegal," salary discrimination is still widespread in American education.[228] In fact, recent National Center for Education statistics show that the average male college professor earns $29,527 compared to $22,105 earned by the average female college professor.[229] Many people have assumed that Andover pays women faculty less. But records show that (for the age groups studied) no faculty salary discrimination exists today at Andover.[230] As the following information on salaries shows, men and women in the same age cohorts are paid approximately the same salaries. Salaries were not listed for the most senior age groups because the administration did not want to release information on age groups with small numbers (1 and 4 women in the two groups which could make the data traceable to specific individuals).

How are salaries determined at Andover? The *Faculty Handbook* for 1985-86 states that "The 1985-86 range for full-time teaching salaries is from $11,500 to $35,000 plus. Experience, responsibilities, and merit are all considered by the Headmaster, Associate Headmaster, and Dean of Faculty in recommending specific salaries to the Trustees."[231] Assistant Business Manager Susan Stott did a multiple regression analysis of salaries and found that age proved to be the most significant influence on a person's salary. Merit evaluations were of lesser importance, and sex was not a determining factor of any significance. Merit is judged by taking into consideration a variety of factors: formal and informal evaluations by Cluster Deans, the Athletic Director, and Department Chairs, an overall assessment of the faculty's contribution to the community, and the relative value of the tasks s/he performs. No information is available on whether higher merit rating is given jobs, like coaching varsity sports, that men fulfill more than women. Grievance procedures are available for any employment problem, but faculty usually talk directly to the Dean of Faculty if they have questions about their salaries.

FACULTY SALARIES
FULL-TIME TEACHERS–COMPENSATION COMPARISON 1983–84
10-YEAR AGE GROUPS

Age	Number of Males	Average Male Salary	Number of Females	Average Female Salary	Difference
21-30	8	$ 14256	11	$ 13823	+ $433 male + 3.1%
31-40	31	$ 19579	11	$ 19991	+ $412 female + 2.1%
41-50	21	$ 27036	5	$ 27450	+ $414 female + 1.5%
51-60	18	—	4	—	
61 +	7	—	1	—	
Total	85	—	32	—	= 27% female

Part-time salaries were not studied in depth, but evidence suggests that Andover pays its part-timers at a higher rate than many other schools and colleges. A point system has been used at times to determine salary: 10/10 means a full load, 5/10 a half-time load, and 2/10 a part-time load which includes coaching or house counseling. Faculty appointed at less than a 5/10 load are normally not eligible for sick leave, disability insurance, retirement plans, an annual physical exam, educational leaves of absence, tuition grants for faculty children, or reduced P.A. tuition for their children. But under certain circumstances they can be eligible for some health insurance, worker's compensation, maternity leave, housing, professional development, Kenan and Abbot Academy Association grants, and Andover credit union memberships. All full and part-time faculty are eligible to take their families to eat at Commons during the school year, a significant benefit added by Sizer in 1981 in hope of encouraging faculty-student interaction. Part and full-time faculty and staff are given priority in enrollment and the option of flexible schedules at Andover Community Child Care Center. In general, part-time faculty at Andover receive better salary and benefits than they would as part-time employees in many other schools and colleges.

Our evidence suggests that no sex discrimination exists in determining salaries, or in the way employment policies are applied to both sexes. But a few reported incidents suggest that the school's informal attitudes toward its female employees may not always be equitable. One former faculty member wrote to the Coeducation Committee that:

> When I was hired, my husband's salary was cited as a reason that I should be "happy" with what I was being offered. Once on campus, I was often referred to as "X's wife," even though he was not on the faculty and some of those men did not bother to learn my name for a while . . . When I questioned a financial matter . . . I was told to "ask your husband to explain it to you."

In another case a woman's employment at P.A. was assumed to be ending because her husband's employment was about to end, and on one occasion the revision of a woman's workload was discussed with another faculty member—her husband— before she was notified. These examples may be rare exceptions to the normally fair dealings with women faculty at P.A., but they may also reflect the fact that a few faculty and administrators may still make assumptions about female faculty that they would never make about male faculty.

FACULTY BENEFITS

Faculty benefits have expanded in recent years, and all benefits are available to men and women alike. Applause and enthusiastic thanks have been the faculty response almost every time Don McNemar has announced a new benefit at a faculty meeting. In 1985 he and the Trustees approved a real estate financing plan to provide mortgage money to faculty and a personal computer financing plan which provides a loan for

---

BENEFITS WHICH PORTIONS OF THE FACULTY BELIEVE ARE EXCELLENT OR VERY GOOD
1. Salary 72%
2. Health Insurance 59%
3. Faculty Housing 61%
4. Retirement Plan 51%
5. Tuition Plan for Faculty Dependents 50% *
6. Life Insurance 29%
7. Child Care 25% **
8. Personal Counseling and Support 25% **
9. Opportunities for Spouse Employment 23%
10. Maternity Leave 21%
11. Paternity Leave 12%

* 10% + more men than women believe this benefit is excellent or very good
** 10% + more women than men believe this benefit is excellent or very good

---

to 2/3 of the purchase price of a computer.[232] A faculty member can now be eligible to receive, in addition to computer and mortgage loans, greatly reduced tuition for their children who attend P.A., research and professional development grants, fully paid year-long sabbaticals, and emergency financial assistance in times of crisis. In order to offer recognition and support to house counseling, McNemar proposed to the Trustees, and they accepted, that an additional stipend be paid to faculty supervising dorms. No detailed study of the faculty benefits was conducted by the Coeducation Committee. But Susan Stott reviewed non-housing benefits and found that all such benefits were distributed equally with respect to sex.

Overall, the faculty holds positive attitudes toward the benefits they receive. Ironically, some of the things faculty indicate as excellent or very good benefits are not official benefits at all but informal opportunities that they may gain but cannot expect as a condition of employment. The Coeducation Committee listed them along with official benefits because they are features of faculty life that are *sometimes* beneficial to faculty, though they are not all real benefits. For example, faculty have sometimes benefited from opportunities for spouse employment and from personal counseling and support, but these are clearly *not* official benefits. On occasion Cluster Deans have covered child care expenses or even offered work duty students to cover job-related faculty child care needs. Yet no official child care benefit exists, except for access to the day care center, which is currently too full to accommodate all faculty and staff needs. Similarly, paternity leave does not exist though it could be worked out informally. The 12% of the faculty who responded that paternity leave was an excellent or very good benefit may have been misinformed or they may have incorrectly assumed that the flexible schedules or part-time workloads that some fathers of young children have arranged are related to some sort of paternity leave.

BENEFITS WHICH PORTIONS OF THE FACULTY BELIEVE NEED
IMPROVEMENT
1. Life Insurance 28%
2. Personal Counseling and Support 25% **
3. Paternity Leave 21%
4. Health Insurance 18% *
5. Salary 17%
6. Child Care 15%
7. Maternity Leave 14% **
8. Tuition plan for Faculty Dependents 14% *
9. Opportunity for Spouse Employment 12%
10. Faculty Housing 12%
11. Retirement plan 9%

* 10% more men than women believe this benefit needs improving
** 10% more women than men believe this benefit needs improving

---

Most of the faculty who answered the question about benefits on the survey did not indicate that any benefit needed improving. Women were more likely than men to answer that personal counseling and support and maternity leave needed improvement, while men were noticeably more likely than women to look for improvement in the tuition plan for faculty dependents and health insurance. Some of the reasons for these gender differences are obvious. P.A. male faculty are more likely than their female colleagues to be in the age group which has children who could use the tuition plan. Also, they are more likely to be married and therefore to object to the fact that family health plans are paid for only up to the amount that is covered for single faculty.

Maternity leave is a greater concern of women faculty. Andover now offers an unpaid maternity leave of up to a trimester without loss of seniority. Paid sick leave accumulated according to length of service can be used if medical complications occur. Though a few other schools offer somewhat better maternity leave policies, the school has been flexible in arranging part-time workloads and flexible teaching schedules to suit the needs of parents.[233] Some women report being hesitant to take maternity leave during the school year because the school rarely hires substitutes, but instead asks colleagues to cover the classes in addition to their normal load. Sixty-two percent of the male and 52% of the females who answered the faculty questionnaire either did not answer the question about maternity leave or they indicated that they considered it an unimportant benefit. A majority of the faculty of both sexes indicated that paternity leave was unimportant, too.

FACULTY HOUSING

Housing is the most troublesome "benefit" of all in residential schools, for no system or arbitrary method of distribution of dorm apartments or houses can satisfy all parties. Some schools find it is the most divisive community issue of all. In fact, because Andover *requires* every one of its full-time faculty to live on or near campus so they can work with students more conveniently and more often, housing—especially doing dorm service—may not really classify as a benefit. But when faculty look at the whole Andover "package," they must consider free housing, free maintenance, free heating, and free utilities as financial advantages in their employment by the Academy.

Housing was not distributed by an objective points system at either Abbot or P.A. for most of their pre-coeducation existences.[234] Headmaster Fuess handled housing as subjectively as he did salaries. One year he promised the same house to three different faculty families.[235] Divisiveness over housing has been avoided at Andover in recent years primarily because a points system which awards points for age and dorm and teaching service was devised in the first year of coeducation. When dormitory housing opened up, faculty could bid for it by totalling their years of teaching and years of house counseling. The faculty bidding with the most points moved into the dorm. Non-dormitory houses were bid for in the same way except that age was added to teaching and dorm years for points.

Housing distribution has been linked to gender since coeducation began at Andover. The 1974 version of the housing points system—established when the faculty was made up largely of married men—favored married couples over single people by allowing a faculty family to bid for more desirable housing using either spouse's points. In recognition of the fact that many wives volunteered to help out with their husband's dorm responsibilities, the 1974 system gave the same number of dorm service points to spouses as to the designated house counselor.

In 1984 Don McNemar proposed to change the housing system to allow faculty to bid on dorms that they would supervise based *only* on their own points. No longer could people outbid more experienced faculty by using their spouse's points. The Ad-Hoc Faculty Housing Committee set up to review this proposal and to reexamine the entire housing system decided to change the system to respond to a more diverse faculty;

> make-up of the faculty has significantly changed in a number of ways that bear on issues related to faculty housing: the faculty has grown in size; more faculty work part-time; there are more dormitories housing females and fewer dormitories housing males, the number of female faculty members has increased; the number of single faculty members has increased; and the proportion of faculty members who are house counselors has gone down. As the faculty has become more diverse, it has become increasingly clear that different types of people have different needs and desires with respect to their housing.[236]

For a while the Ad-Hoc Housing Committee considered abolishing all points for the spouses of house counselors, though some members favored the retention of the old system whereby spouses were given the same points as house counselors. Finally, they compromised and spouses were given half the housing points of the designated house counselor.

This change was significant for women. Before coeducation began the school habitually expected free labor from faculty wives in support of their husbands' house counseling roles. The Ad-Hoc Housing Committee's report pointed out that:

> In an earlier era, Headmaster John Kemper addressed a meeting of Benevie by telling his audience that their main contribution to the school was to provide the kind of support for their teaching husbands that would free them to do their best possible work for the school. The faculty wives' help with the dormitory was seen as an important form of support.[237]

In that era giving faculty wives points for living in the dorm had been a way to compensate and recognize them for the valuable services they gave the school. But times had changed. Today almost 40% of the house

counselors are single and many faculty spouses have other jobs. Therefore, the Housing Committee's report insisted that within the dorm "active spouse support can no longer be taken for granted." By decreasing
the housing points given to faculty spouses for living in a dorm, the
school recognized that it no longer expected spouses to be assistant
house counselors—unless they wanted to. By decreasing the spouse
points the committee was saying that running a dorm was deserving of
more points than living in one. However, by maintaining half points for
spouses the committee recognized that "living in a dormitory requires
sacrifices and makes demands" on the house counselor's family.[238] As
one letter to the committee signed by eight faculty members stated,
"Equal access to housing could be a new symbol of the growing acceptance of women faculty members on campus . . . this is a powerful symbolic issue!"[239]

Other signs that the new housing points system was responding to a
more coeducational faculty was the addition of points for maternity or
paternity leave. In addition, the committee reaffirmed the Headmaster's
plan to have people bid to house counsel a particular dorm based on
their own and not their spouse's points. Not only did some committee
members feel that to do otherwise would give married people an unfair
advantage over single people who had no spouse's points to aid them,
but it was also in the school's interest to have a dormitory bidding system that would reward points earned by previous job experience over
points earned by marital status. The committee also proposed that a
time-out from the expected 10-12 year minimum dorm service be granted to any interested faculty member for a period of up to five years,
which offered new flexibility to faculty who might want to take a break
from dorm service. The faculty approved all of the committee's recommendations in a faculty meeting that was outstanding for its reasonable
tone and unified spirit.

When the housing points system was adapted to the changing roles of
women and the increasing presence of single faculty at P.A., did all campus housing get distributed equally on the basis of sex? Both sexes have
access to equivalent dorm housing, but non-dorm housing is still distributed unequally. The main reason that the best non-dorm housing has
gone to male faculty is simple: non-dorm housing was and is awarded to
faculty on the basis of age, as well as years of dorm and teaching service,
and most of the senior faculty is male. Of 66 non-dormitory houses studied 43 were occupied by male faculty, 8 by female faculty, and 13 by
faculty couples. Property values published by the Town of Andover for
these non-dorm houses also differed: the women's houses were valued
at less than the couples' or men's houses. The average valuation of the
women's houses was $98,725 compared to an average of $131,350 for
couples' houses and $130,281 for men's houses.[240]

Furthermore, among women holding administrative positions, housing values are less than among men holding equivalent positions. The
dilemma for the Academy is providing housing for women administra-

133

tors who are hired from outside the community and for women administrators whose age or years of service may not allow them to compete within the housing points system for suitable houses. Should the school intervene in the faculty-voted housing system by taking houses off the market to award them to women administrators? Because the points system favors senior men, should the school try to equalize this "benefit?" In general the administration has tried to strike a balance by providing suitable housing for women administrators without taking houses off the housing market (although it has the perogative to remove houses from the market). Women are more likely than men to live in off-campus housing which is not paid for by the school, and there have also been more instances of women administrators being hired with the expectation that faculty housing would not be available to them.

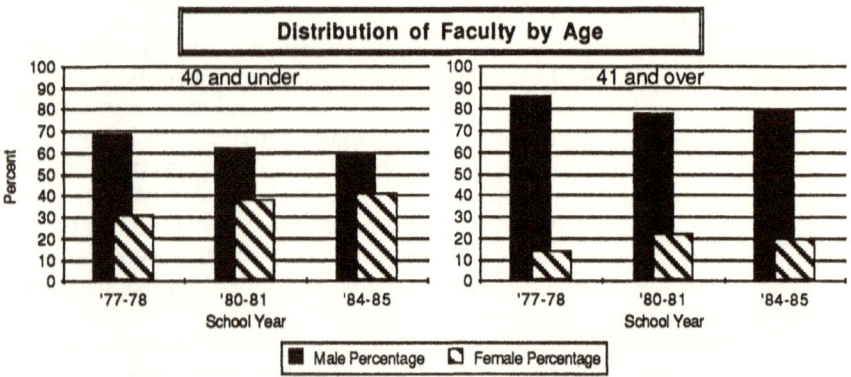

THE TRIPLE THREAT MODEL

Have workload expectations changed since coeducation began? Institutional flexibility about workload and support for families under stress has been increasingly characteristic of administrative dealings with the faculty since the merger. P.A. families with new children, ailing parents, alcoholism, other health problems, or impending divorces have been offered support from the administration, including occasional relief from triple threat expectations. For P.A. faculty who are not necessarily under stress, but prefer not to work full-time, flexible working arrangements have been negotiated. Job sharing arrangements and teachers moving from full to part-time work have been signs of increasing willingness to respond to individual needs.

When women faculty members began to take the part-time option in increasing numbers, and when some Abbot teachers were hired as double threats, not everyone applauded the administration's flexibility. Some resentment was felt among the full-time former boys' school faculty because they felt that special favors were being granted women. After

134

all, the triple threat standard had not been relaxed for them. In 1971, before the merger a P.A. faculty workload committee had described the triple threat lifestyle lived by house masters as difficult and hectic, but even after the report no adjustment in faculty workloads was made.[241] Therefore, it may have seemed like a cruel irony to P.A. teachers in 1973 to see their new colleagues from Abbot being given what some of them hoped for: a different array of job expectations.

But the triple threat, despite exceptions, survived the transition to co-education because enough faculty were willing to do it. The Merger Study showed in 1974 a trend that has held true in the Coeducation Study of '83-85: triple threat workload demands have been more familiar and acceptable to P.A. male faculty hired before coeducation than they have been to former Abbot faculty or faculty of either sex hired in recent years. Fred Peterson wrote in 1974 that:

> Phillips Academy's concept of the teacher-coach-counselor-adminis-trator called for a total and wholly engrossing commitment to the school. A number of faculty members, not all from Abbot, now be-lieve that such an arrangement causes confusion and increases anxi-eties in the interrelations of administrators, teachers, counselors, and students. The younger P.A. faculty members and others new to the staff are questioning the kind of total personal commitment to P.A. required by such a multiplicity of roles. A differing conception of faculty roles and commitment to P.A. between the older and younger faculty members was an issue.[242]

The triple threat remained an issue in 1985: was the triple threat an ap-propriate job definition for the newly diverse faculty?

One senior male faculty member in the early seventies said that he believed women faculty were not "tough enough" to live up to the rigor-ous work expectations at P.A. Yet female triple-threaters like Mary Min-ard and Nancy Sizer proved him wrong, and by the eighties "toughness" no longer seemed to be an issue. Certainly full-time and part-time wom-en from Abbot and from post-1973 hiring *could* work as hard as any of the dedicated P.A. men who coached, taught, house counseled, and took on myriad additional responsibilities. But women were less likely than men to seek that type of workload.

Distributing workloads fairly and meeting the needs of the school and each individual faculty member was no small assignment. The policy followed by Dean Richards was a modified heir to the triple threat. He wrote that:

> With an increasing number of working spouses and single parents on the faculty, the traditional "triple-threat" model, in which a facul-ty member teaches, coaches, and runs a dormitory, is less feasible. We continue to explore ways in which adjustments can be made to the system which will make the working environment at the Acade-my more suited to faculty members with widely differing circum-stances and needs, while at the same time maintaining a basic qual-ity of instruction and equity of workload.[243]

The most common adjustment to the triple-threat remained part-time work for part-time pay. Most inter-faculty resentments over workload abated after the faculty accepted the fact that many colleagues could be dedicated without being triple threaters, and strong collegial cooperation became the norm. Eventually it even became more acceptable for a few men to take the part-time option.

Yet, the triple threat remained the only ideal faculty workload and the work ethic still predominated at Andover. As a result, some women who chose not to do the triple threat were made to feel guilty on occasion. One woman faculty member wrote to the Faculty Advisory Committee in 1984, pointing out that "the male institution that Andover is sees these women as not pulling their oar because they are not living up to the 'Triple Threat expectation.'" She added that many Andover women were doing the "Quadruple Threat"—the triple threat plus caring for children—the personal demands of which the institution viewed as an "unacknowledged and somehow illegitimate threat."[244] Despite social pressure and internalized guilt, the school still offered flexible workloads to all faculty. Many faculty with small children easily arranged part-time work or class schedules that made it possible for them to manage both their work and family lives. However, where a family's economic needs prevented faculty from taking the part-time option, the triple-threat expectation could weigh heavily.

The triple threat expectation was viewed as "stressful" or "very stressful" by 61% of the women and 47% of the men. Male respondents were twice as likely as females to find the triple threat "not stressful" (32% to 15%). Marital status appears not to have a definite effect on one's attitude toward the triple threat, but age is a big influence. Younger faculty find the triple threat more stressful. In the 45 and under age group, only 22% of the males who responded to the question found the triple threat expectation "not stressful," compared to 15% of the females. Faculty over 45, including many who had already done their dorm service and some who no longer coached, were less likely than other groups to view the triple threat as stressful. Three times more men under 45 viewed it as stressful than did the men in the over 45 group.

Despite the fact that a majority of the faculty does not do the triple threat throughout their careers, a degree of social and administrative pressure still exists for full-time faculty to live up to the triple threat model. The triple threat model remains appealing as a way of providing adult guidance in every aspect of student life. By working with students in athletics, academics, and residential life a teacher can be concerned with the growth of the whole student. For athletic Renaissance Men (or Women) the triple threat is the perfect way to avoid over-specialization of tasks. And no one denies that the triple threat is economically advantageous to residential schools like Andover. Faculty workload committees have been proposed regularly over the years to examine the issue of overwork and task distribution among the faculty, but in general, the faculty by the mid-eighties was not in enough agreement about the nature of the workload problem to propose possible cures for it.[245]

WORKLOAD AND JOB-RELATED STRESS

Did workload and job-related stress affect one sex more than the other? Male faculty respondents were more likely than female respondents to rate their overall workload as "very heavy" (21% to 13%). When those answering that their workloads were "heavy" or "very heavy" are lumped together, no sex difference exists. Sixty-two percent of the men and 61% of the women perceived their workloads as "heavy" or "very heavy."

When Estelle Ramey spoke to the faculty about stress in 1983, she stated that, compared to most people in the world—factory or agricultural workers, for instance—the P.A. faculty did not live under significant stress. For the most part, the faculty disagreed with her: 83%, when asked whether they found their workload stressful, answered "very stressful" (12%), "stressful" (41%), or "somewhat stressful" (30%). Men registered a higher level of stress than women: 62% of male respondents described their workload as "stressful" or "very stressful" while 44% of female respondents described it in the same way. Why should almost two-thirds of the male faculty report such stress? Because men are much less likely than women to take the part-time option, they typically work full-time, often doing the "triple threat." Because no open-ended responses to the faculty questionnaire shed light on the problem of male stress, we do not know if any relationship exists between male stress and insufficient time for leisure, socializing, or building friendships. Because excess stress can have serious health consequences, this issue may require further study.[246]

House counselors in particular may view their workload as stressful because of the need to be available at all hours for dorm emergencies. Many of the students' needs inevitably interrupt them during class preparation and family time—even during sleep time. Among respondents who answered a question about the stress of house counseling, 64% of the males found it "stressful" or "very stressful" and 48% of the females found it so. As noted in the earlier discussion of the myth of the self-sufficient boys dorm and the demanding girls dorm, men's expectations about the time required by boys' dorms may affect their attitudes toward hours they spend in house counseling, as well as the stress involved. Both sexes were satisfied with the basic physical attributes of their dorms (size, location, quality of room), and the only undertone of dissatisfaction came from one quarter of the female faculty who do not like the quality of the rooms in their dorms. House counselors of both sexes reported high levels of satisfaction with their relationships with students. Sixty-four percent of the females and 59% of the males considered their relationships with students in their dorm "excellent" or "very satisfactory."

Even though most faculty enjoy house counseling, a majority of each sex reports dissatisfaction with the effect of their dorm work on family and/or personal life. In fact, this is the *only* aspect of the dorm situation

Stressful Aspects of Faculty Life

FQ#43. What aspects of life here do you find stressful?

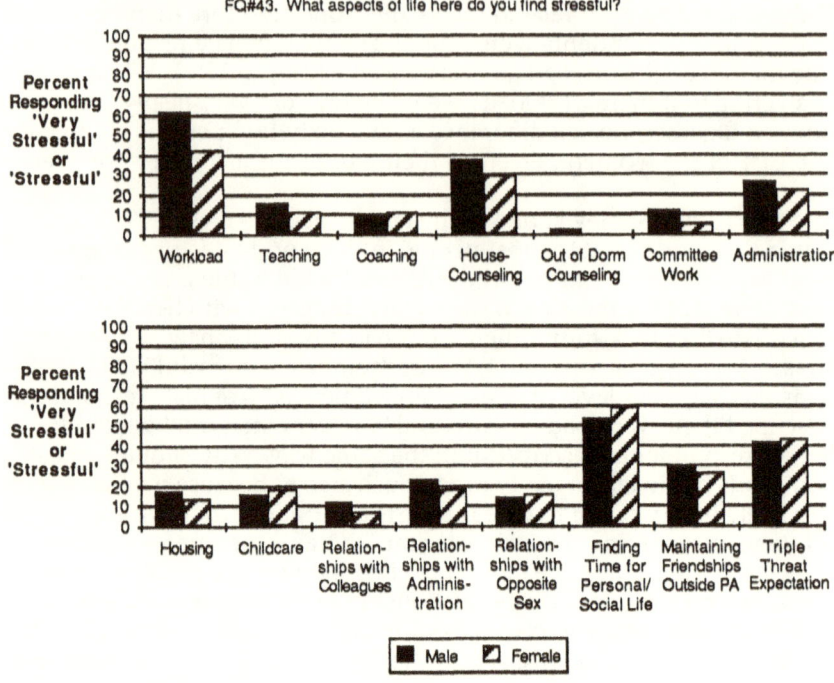

with which a majority (52%) of male respondents reported dissatisfaction. And yet this is also an area of notable gender difference, since an even higher rate (64%) of female respondents expressed dissatisfaction with the impact of the dorm on family and/or personal life. Dorm life was perceived more often by single respondents than by married respondents to have an unsatisfactory effect on family and/or personal life. Sixty-five percent of all single respondents said the dorm had a "somewhat unsatisfactory" or "totally unsatisfactory" effect on family and/or personal life, while 51% of the married respondents answered in the same way. However, 84% of all single women respondents said that the dorm had an unsatisfactory effect on family and/or personal life, compared to 48% of the single men. Single women are by far the group most likely to find that being a house counselor has a negative impact on their personal lives.

Among those responding to a question about the stress of child care as part of faculty life at P.A., 53% of the women found child care "stressful" or "very stressful," while only 36% of the men found it so. Other aspects of faculty life were rarely perceived as stressful: housing, coaching, teaching, committee work, relationships with colleagues, and relationships with the opposite sex at P.A. Of those who responded to a question about the stress involved in doing administrative work, 30% of the

138

females found it "very stressful" and 13% of the males found it so. However, when the "stressful" responses are added to the "very stressful," the gender differences narrow a great deal. Forty-five percent of the females and 40% of the males who did administrative work found it "stressful" or "very stressful."

Men found many areas of faculty life more stressful than women did, but they also found teaching, coaching and administration more rewarding than women did. Men had much more positive feelings about coaching than they did about many other aspects of their job. Eighty percent of all male respondents (compared to 67% of the females) found coaching "rewarding" or "very rewarding."

Women, on the other hand, found greater rewards in a number of other basic tasks. For instance, nearly two-thirds of the women who responded to a question about academic advising found it "rewarding" or "very rewarding," compared to 35% of the men. Sixty percent of the women who responded to a question about committee work found that area of work "rewarding," compared to 47% of the men. Similarly, women found house counseling more rewarding than men did. Male faculty may find more rewards in coaching and teaching roles in which they serve as individual authority figures, and female faculty may be more comfortable with cooperative committee work, as well as nurturant counseling roles.

FACULTY LIVES

Wives of faculty members are still more likely to assist their husbands with their jobs than are husbands of faculty members likely to aid their wives. Forty-four percent of the male respondents said their wives were "very involved" in working with the dorm, compared to thirty-one percent of the female respondents to the same question who said their husbands were "very involved in the dorm." Twenty-two percent of the male respondents said their wives were "very involved" in student extracurriculars, compared to 8% of the female respondents. Wives of faculty members were also twice as likely to be involved in the social life of the P.A. community as husbands of faculty members were.

In addition to family assistance with faculty workload, there are many other ways that faculty gain support within the Andover community. Early in the twentieth century radical feminist Charlotte Perkins Gilman argued that women's lot in life could be improved—and their domestic workload be lessened —if large apartment buildings were constructed with shared kitchens and nurseries.[247] In an odd sense the Andover faculty, especially working mothers and fathers, are sometimes offered support opportunities that are not too distant from Gilman's feminist utopian model. Faculty are provided free housing, utilities, repairs, and heat, and their homes and dormitory apartments are within a short walk of the school dining hall where they can feed their families three meals a day during the school year. Excellent day care, opportunities for establishing play groups, exchanging child care with neighbors, and hiring responsible students to do cleaning and additional child care help faculty members of both sexes combine work with family responsibilities.

Family life is supported informally within the community in myriad ways. Children's clothes and baby equipment are passed on from generation to generation. When a family has a time of need, the Andover neighbors of both sexes usually rally around. Faculty families sometimes share a faculty children's Christmas pageant, Easter egg hunt, and Halloween party, as well as Passover seders. Faculty children are welcome on campus, especially at the new playgrounds funded by the Abbot Academy Association. While some mothers who stay home to care for their families full-time have felt left out of the bustle of campus life, they are rarely as socially isolated as they would be in many suburban neighborhoods across the country. Privacy and finding leisure time are often bigger problems at Andover than social isolation, for the sense of community and interconnectedness is quite strong.

As a result, the Andover faculty has been criticized by some for being excessively family-oriented. With 42 being the median age of the faculty and the majority being married, young single people sometimes feel left out socially. However, teaching fellows and younger faculty often create their own networks of support. Most tensions between married and single faculty seem to have faded over time. Several years ago a teacher brought her new baby to a committee meeting, and an unmarried faculty member complained. But today faculty parents bring their children to occasional meetings and in emergency situations to class without any negative reaction from colleagues.

Besides not benefiting much from the family side of community life, single people's personal lives fit less conveniently into dorm counseling expectations. Families with children and married couples without children are often home a lot at Andover, and their home is the best place for students in the dorm to find them. But single faculty, who often must go to friends' or family's houses or to parties to have a social life, are less likely than other faculty to be able to blend their own social needs with the needs of the dorm. Often staying home with the dorm means single people will have no adult company at all. Time is also a problem that hits single people harder. Finding time for personal life is reported far more often to be stressful by single respondents: 72% reported it was stressful compared to 47% of the married respondents. The resulting lack of a private life may be one of the several reasons single faculty quit their jobs at Andover at a higher rate than do married faculty.

ATTRITION OF WOMEN FACULTY

Though much of our examination of faculty life at P.A.—salaries, benefits, workload, stress, lifestyles—show only a few differences between men and women on the faculty, one profound gender difference exists which dwarfs all others in significance. Women faculty do not stay at

Andover as long as men do. A Coeducation Committee study of the faculty who have left voluntarily (excluding retirement, firing, time-limited appointments, and leaves) in the last six years showed that a larger number of women left the faculty than men. And among the faculty who left, younger people outnumbered older people.

Attrition of Faculty 1979-85
Faculty Who Left of Their Own Free Will

(excludes time-limited appointments,
firings, deaths, and retirements)

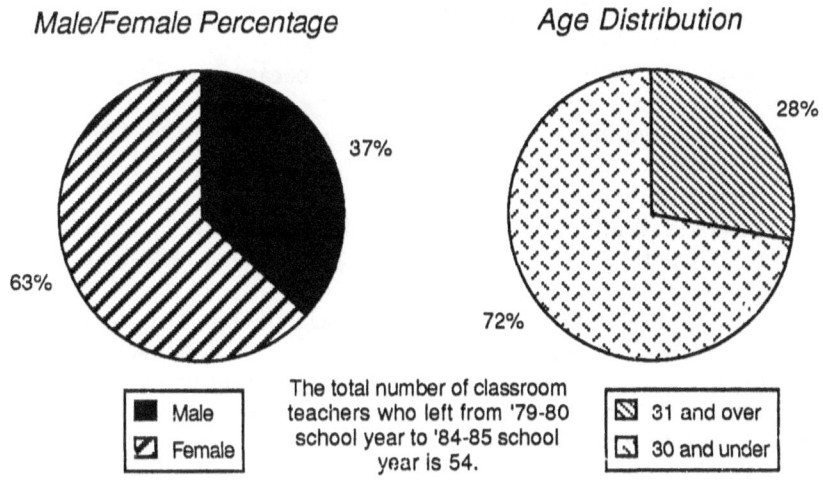

Male/Female Percentage   *Age Distribution*

37%

28%

63%

72%

| Male | The total number of classroom teachers who left from '79-80 school year to '84-85 school year is 54. | 31 and over |
| Female | | 30 and under |

Most departures occurred within the first few years of employment. In addition, when the faculty was asked on the questionnaire how long they intended to stay at P.A., over half the men replied that they intended to stay forever or more than 15 years. In contrast, more than half the women were planning to leave within one to ten years. Younger people are also less likely to stay: 73% of the faculty under 35 indicated they planned to stay at P.A. ten years or less. But sex remains the most important factor. Eighty-four percent of the under 35 females intend to stay less than 10 years compared to 64% of the males under 35.

Why are women less likely to want to build careers at P.A.? When respondents were asked to rank six factors as reasons that would make them consider leaving P.A., a higher percentage of females than males ranked "pace of life" first, second, or third. More nearly equal proportions of male and female faculty viewed other reasons for leaving at the same level of significance: a new career outside teaching, demands of dorm supervision, and lack of privacy. Men, however, were more likely to rank insufficient pay first, second, or third, and women were twice as likely as men to rank "limits of social life" first.

Very few open-ended responses to the questionnaire shed light on the higher attrition rates among women faculty, especially younger faculty. Only one comment seemed to have been written from the viewpoint of the group most likely to leave, young women house counselors:

> It strikes me that house counseling here is hardest for those who have most difficulty drawing lines in their lives. While I do think that girls' dorms take more time to run than a boys', I see a strong difference between the way women and men house counsel. Single women particularly, but women generally more than men, invest themselves, their souls, emotions, energies, . . . in their dorms more than men. They are, for example, more motivated by guilt and a sense that they should
>
> —go back to their dorm after dinner "because I feel badly that I wasn't there for parietals last night."
> —feed their students
> —cook or bake what their students eat
> —-act more as surrogate parent
>
> The result is higher burn-out for young single women, and a feeling on their part that they are constrained here more than single males in particular.

Recognizing the stress and limitations on social life faced by single house counselors and the unique and demanding role that all house counselors were expected to play, the House Counselors Committee and Pace of Life group proposed, and the faculty voted, to establish a system of complementary house counselors to help alleviate the stress on regular house counselors. The system implemented in the fall of 1985 would bring faculty who had served less than 15 years in dorms into "an active role of supervision and interaction" with students one night a week with the possibility of supervising the dorm for one weekend a month. If this system relieved the stress on house counselors, it might also lessen the female faculty attrition rate. No matter how hard the faculty and administration tries to recruit and hire women faculty, their efforts will be wasted if more women do not feel comfortable staying and building their careers at Andover.

COMMUNITY LEADERSHIP ROLES

As we have seen, the gender-balance in the faculty can affect students' educational experience by providing them with same sex mentors and role models. The gender-balance in the administration and other leadership posts also has educational significance for students. If students perceive decision-making as the province only of one sex or they are comfortable dealing only with authority figures of one sex, their educational experience will be limited. Furthermore, their future ability to deal with decisions made by authority figures of both sexes—even when they begin their work careers—may be handicapped.[248]

Limiting community leadership roles to one sex may also have a negative effect on adults in the community. When women with strong administrative qualifications have been turned down for promotions to leadership positions in public school districts, for example, they have felt that their professional growth has been stymied because of their gender. Public school teachers have also complained that school administration too often has been defined solely as male turf.[249] When one sex is excluded from community leadership positions it may have an overall "chilling effect" on all members of that sex. The feeling of exclusion from influence may "trickle down," and all members of the non-leadership sex may feel less comfortable participating in community decision-making.[250] Thus, letting both sexes into the ranks of the community leaders has a profound impact on the equity environment in a school.

Community Leadership Roles 1984-85

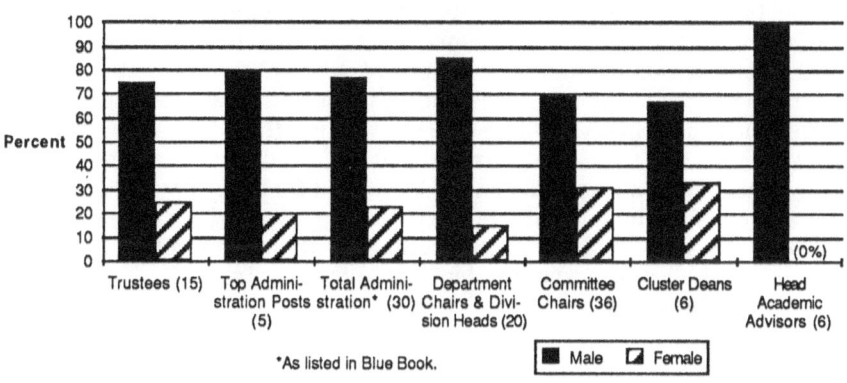

*As listed in Blue Book. ■ Male ▨ Female

At Phillips Academy significant progress has been made in welcoming women into the ranks of top administrators, cluster deans, committee chairs, and department heads. Because of the rotation system started by Ted Sizer, many administrators are appointed only for five year terms. As a result, many faculty members hold a leadership post during their careers at Andover. When we look at the proportion of the faculty in a given year who have had administrative experience in the past or who currently hold a post, men still outnumber women by about four to one. Although an increasing number of women are chosen to serve as leaders each year, more might have been chosen if the ranks of senior women were not so small. In the 41 and older age group from which administrators have often been chosen there were only ten full-time women in 1983-84, compared to 46 men. A number of these senior women have

143

served as leaders in the school, but Andover still suffers from a "missing generation" of women leadership candidates.

Despite significant progress women are still outnumbered in most leadership posts by two to one or three to one. Of the five most visible administrative positions, Headmaster, Associate Headmaster, Dean of Faculty, Dean of Studies, and Dean of Residence, only one is filled by a woman. In 1984-85 only three out of 20 department chairs and division heads were women, though two additional women chairs were appointed at the end of the 1984-85 school year. In the ten years since coeducation began only three women have served as head academic advisors. Though women are more likely than men to come to Andover because of administrative opportunities, since coeducation began fewer women than men have been chosen to take on leadership responsibilities. However, with the appointment of a female school doctor, a female Dean of Admissions, and more female department chairs in recent years, the administration has shown a commitment to achieving a more complete gender-balance in community leadership positions. In recent years only two women sat at the Wednesday Lunch Group of top administrators which included nine men. But with each new female appointment the school has come closer to gender-balance. The Wednesday Lunch Group had more than a 25% female membership rate in 1985.

Male and female faculty members have different opinions about the appropriate gender-balance in the administration, however. Females were much more likely (73% to 46%) to say that there are "a few too many males" or "far too many males" in the administration. The difference is also stark among those who answered that there were "far too many males" in the administration: 27% females and 8% males chose this answer. Only a very small percentage of the male faculty (1%) replied that there were too many females in the administration.

Faculty View of Male/Female Ratio in Administration

FQ#36. How do you feel about the present composition of the adminstration?

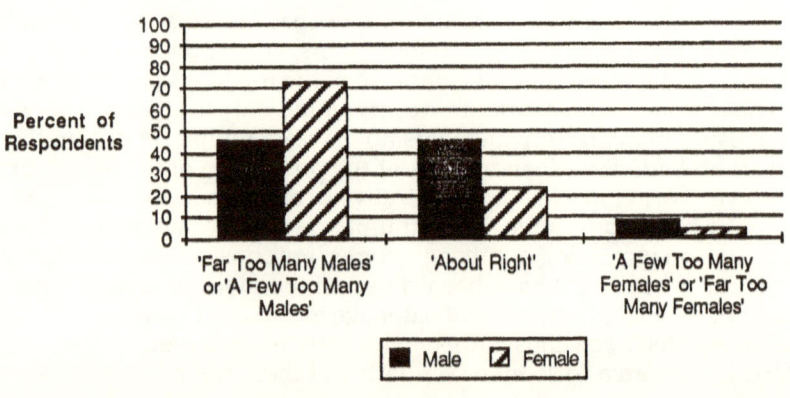

Percent of Respondents

'Far Too Many Males' or 'A Few Too Many Males' — 'About Right' — 'A Few Too Many Females' or 'Far Too Many Females'

■ Male ▨ Female

Are men and women faculty equally willing to seek administrative jobs? In general, men expressed a slightly greater interest in assuming a position in leadership in the central administration. About a third of the men compared with about a quarter of the women were interested in such jobs. Nearly two-thirds of the men expressed interest in academic leadership jobs, compared to less than half the women. Very few women were interested in athletic administration, but that type of job appealed to about a third of the men. In keeping with their tendency to find greater rewards in counseling, women showed more interest than men in seeking leadership jobs in residential life. Women were also more interested in becoming leaders in the Office of Academy Resources, College Counseling, or Admissions.

When faculty were asked about their chances of success if they sought an administrative job, 20% of the females and 18% of the males rated their chances of success as "excellent." However, males rated their chances "very good" more often than females (38% to 24%), while females were more likely to see their chances as "good" or "fair." Many factors may be at work in these answers— perceptions of their own actual chances, estimates of the previous chances their sex had gaining administrative jobs in the past, and personal self-confidence. If very few women had perceived their chances of success as "excellent" or "very good" it would have been a sign of a closed administrative hirin gsystem. But it is evident that leadership positions are open to both sexes at Andover. Significant percentages of both sexes believe they have a chance to be leaders.

Faculty View of Chances of Success in Seeking an Administrative Position

FQ#21. Whether or not your are actually interested in assuming administrative responsibility, how would you rate your chances for success if you sought it?

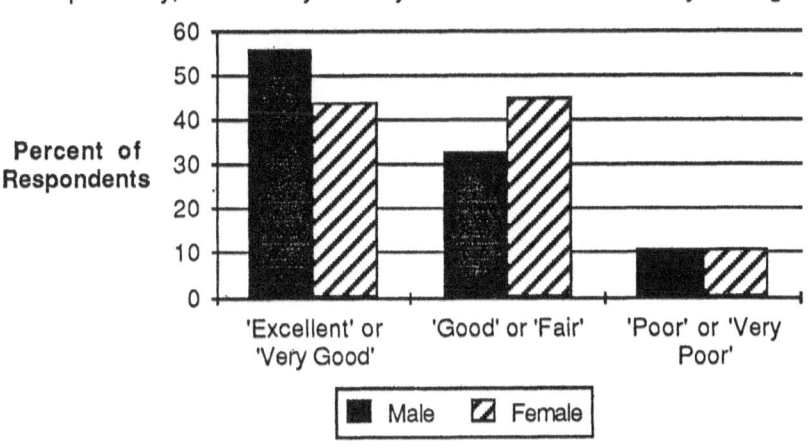

DO BOTH SEXES EXERT AN EQUAL INFLUENCE IN COMMUNITY DECISION-MAKING?

Most day-to-day administrative decisions and many policy issues have to be made by the people who are full-time administrators. Yet at Andover the expectation of faculty participation in curricular and other decision-making derives from strong pre-coeducation traditions of faculty participation at Abbot and P.A. As noted earlier, faculty votes have shaped the housing policy, the 8 P.M. limitation on meetings, the amount of work assigned in class, the new complementary house counselor system, and many other policies. Such faculty votes are taken during faculty meetings after nearly 200 faculty members are given a chance to participate in the open discussion of the issue to be voted. Committee membership is now optional for faculty members, but faculty often volunteer to serve on committees in order to share in the decision-making process. The faculty elects representatives to the Faculty Advisory Committee which meets with the Headmaster and Associate Headmaster weekly so that faculty opinion can be heard regularly. Faculty also have a voice in department meetings and cluster meetings, and they also speak directly to administrators about policy questions with some regularity. In these ways, faculty members play an important role in influencing community decision-making.

Are both sexes equally comfortable exercising this potential influence? In general, men and women are equally comfortable stating their views about school policy at department meetings, cluster meetings, and committee meetings. They also report they are equally comfortable bringing their concerns to the attention of Faculty Advisory Committee members.

Men, however, are more comfortable stating their views in formal meetings with administrators and at faculty meetings. Male faculty over age 35 were the group that reported at the highest rate feeling comfortable talking about their views with administrators. The group that was least likely to feel comfortable stating their views in formal meetings with administrators was women faculty under age 35. Only half felt comfortable in such situations. Furthermore, women twice as often as men reported that they would be "not at all" likely to turn to administrators for help or guidance.

At faculty meetings women are less likely to speak up than men. For example, in an open discussion of the housing points system, more than twice as many comments were made by men than women on the floor of the meeting. And, according to the faculty survey, 60% of the women faculty reported feeling "uncomfortable" about speaking up at faculty meetings, compared to 36% of the men. One former faculty member wrote the Coeducation Committee, stating that she "felt that faculty meetings were run with a specifically male gestalt; when women talked they were intimidated." She also observed that:

> I often heard women I know well adopting a different talking style, a more masculine one . . . a toning down of affect and an accommodation to a certain protocol [that was] . . . part of the P.A. male style.

As a secondary result, women in faculty meetings often giggled with neighbors . . . and most important did not feel free or confident to share their thoughts.

While many faculty would disagree with this description of gender dynamics at faculty meetings, the fact remains that one sex speaks less, feels less comfortable speaking, and as a result, probably has less influence over faculty meetings. Women are not alone, however, in their discomfort. Seventy-one percent of all faculty members aged 35 and under reported feeling uncomfortable stating their views in faculty meetings. But even within the younger group women report feeling uncomfortable speaking up at faculty meetings at a higher rate than men.

When men and women faculty were asked how satisfied they were with their influence on certain administrative decisions, men were more likely to be satisfied with their influence over salary and benefits. Men and women were equally satisfied with their ability to influence decisions affecting their own general workload, courses which they taught, their methods of teaching, and housing. Men were much more likely to be satisfied with their influence over the sports they coached.

Faculty Satisfaction With Influence On Administrative Decisions

FQ#37. How satisfied are you with your present influence on administrative decisions in the following areas?

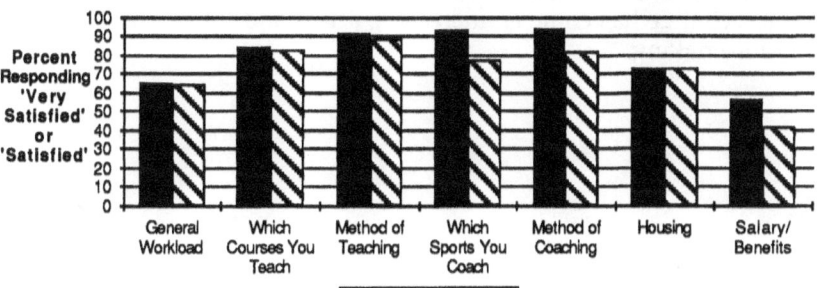

At the heart of the community influence issue are two factors—previous female and male socialization and the school's willingness to make room for gender-balance in community decision-making. Countless studies have shown that even many professionally accomplished women have trouble moving beyond their previous socialization, socialization that inhibits their ability to speak out, to assert their interests, to invite conflict if necessary.[251] Women on the Andover faculty shrink from exerting their influence in the community whenever they do not speak up at faculty meetings or when they feel discomfort asserting themselves in a formal meeting with an administrator. Men, too, may be held back by previous socialization if they ever take for granted that power and influence are still primarily male concerns.

Evaluating the school's willingness to make room for gender-balance in community decision-making is more complicated than counting male and female administrators. In appointing administrators the school has shown an increasing commitment to including women in important decision-making roles. Yet, when asked to elect three faculty representatives to the Faculty Advisory Committee in 1984, the faculty elected three men. And men are chosen to be committee chairs much more often than women. The habit of thinking of leadership as a male activity is so widespread that it affects the selection process and it inhibits women from aspiring to leadership positions. But then, Andover's leadership is more gender-balanced than many schools, for 90% of all college students in America attend institutions in which the top three administrative posts are held by men.[252]

Clear progress has been made in bringing equality into Andover's adult community. In salary and benefits the school has been fair-minded. In recruiting and hiring the school has pursued its goal of achieving a better gender-balance on the faculty, but the high female attrition rate has diminished some of its accomplishments.

Coeducation has added flexibility to the triple threat model, but the ideal faculty workload still seems to be best suited to men's work expectations. Power and influence in the community is not shared equally, but the number of women administrators increases each year. With that significant change has come an increasing acceptance of gender-balance in decision-making.

Chapter Seven:
COMMUNITY VALUES, THE EDUCATIONAL ENVIRONMENT, AND THE EFFECTS OF THE EQUITY EARTHQUAKE AT ANDOVER TODAY

COMMUNITY VALUES AND GENDER AT ANDOVER

Though this study has explored a multitude of questions about Phillips Academy today, one essential question has been postponed : "Does the school educate both sexes well?" Perhaps it seems too basic to ask or too profound to answer. But our reply is yes. Andover, despite the gender differences outlined earlier, offers an excellent education to both sexes. It is a school that works well, that engages its faculty and students in the excitement of learning. Students come to Andover knowing of the high academic standards and the immense athletic and extracurricular opportunities, and the school sustains their spirits and motivation well—even to the point of exhaustion at times. Boys and girls both benefit from attending a school that works.

But in the school's plan to guide students' education its ambitions transcend book learning. The faculty and administration explicitly hope to promote "moral education", to make students even better people, to encourage them to honor good values. What are the dominant values of the school, and how do they influence the educational environment at Andover? The long-standing "non-sibi" tradition of living not for oneself alone has deep historical roots in the two parent schools' Protestant origins. But today it is nourished more directly by an increasingly ecumenical expression of faith.[253] During the past decade the presence of an ecumenical ministry of rabbi, priest, and minister has strengthened a broad-based spirit of self-giving in the community. In addition, a "non-sibi" award given at graduation recognizes the importance Andover places upon service to others. Coeducation (and coordination) have coincided with a renaissance of the "non-sibi" tradition. Since the late sixties student leaders have made community service a high priority for segments of the student body. A strong belief in affiliation, responsibility to others, social concern, and a commitment to unselfishness is evident throughout the school's value system. When adults speak about school goals at convocation, senior dinners, or all-school meetings they often focus on concern for others as a theme. And when adults talk about "moral education" at Andover they usually mean "non-sibi."

Of course, self-consciously stated faculty values are different from the working, day-to-day values faculty convey to students. When asked what they thought their teachers valued most in students, academic achievement and motivation rated higher than "non-sibi" attributes. Yet students also perceived their teachers valuing supportiveness of others more than competitiveness.

VALUED TRAITS

SQ #27. What describes the qualities you think teachers value most in students? Responses listed below include percentages of students who responded "highly valued" or "valued."

Male	Female	
93%	98%	1. Motivation
89	93	2. Ability to speak in class
87	89	3. Mastery of material
84	91	4. Ability to listen
82	89	5. Thoroughness
77	83	6. Analytic ability
75	75	7. Assertiveness
71	76	8. Imagination
66	73	9. Independence
61	61	10. Supportiveness of others
50	56	11. Willingness to take risks
46	51	12. Eagerness to please
42	35	13. Competitiveness
16	17	14. Physical attractiveness

But educational environments—including the values they inculcate best— are not always created by the conscious design of the faculty. Outside influences and pressures and student values also contribute to a school's educational environment—often more than teachers' plans for "moral education." As Alexander Astin pointed out in his book on *The College Environment*, educational institutions vary greatly in offering co-operative or competitive environments. He added that "certain environmental characteristics are highly dependent on the sex ratio of the student body."[254] He found that college environments are "largely dependent on the characteristics of the entering students" and that the percentage of males in the student body directly affected the degree of competitiveness in the environment.[255] Astin's research on cooperative and competitive environments was conducted before the equity earthquake. Yet his conclusion that environments are influenced by students' characteristics is probably true today—and true at Andover.

Today competitiveness and the achievement of success appear to be valued by both sexes, though not equally, and recent studies about the possible consequences of the drive to succeed have shown that a generation gap exists between the "pressured generation" and their elders. In a Stanford Research Institute study respondents were asked : "Do you believe success comes only at the expense of others?"[256] People under 34 were twice as likely as those over 34 to answer "yes." Fifty percent more of the younger group "agreed that success requires giving up some friends." A psychologist who counsels affluent teenagers of the "pressured generation" in California explained that she was witnessing "tremendous pressure on kids to be successful. The kids have to step on one another to get ahead. There's a feeling that there's not enough to go around."[257] Competitiveness, an extreme version of achievement-orientation, looks like a historical necessity to many members of the "pressured generation" as they grow up with high aspirations coupled with the suspicion that there will be less room at the top. As noted earlier, competitiveness can have implications for students' ability to form close relationships, as well as undermining "non-sibi" values.

How influential are such competitive values at Andover today? Despite the school's firm commitment to teaching "non-sibi" values, Andover's educational environment is also affected by the presence of competitive and even rivalrous individualism, caricatured by one student journalist as the "pro-sibi" tradition. Even though the faculty is not perceived as valuing competitiveness very highly, over 90% of the faculty over age 45 reported that they value competitiveness in students. Almost three-quarters of this same faculty age group reported that they value competitiveness as a trait in administrators. Men more than women and senior faculty more than junior faculty believe in the value of competitiveness. Similarly, competitiveness is valued by students as a desirable trait. Sixty-four percent of the boys and 46% of the girls describe themselves as competitive. Competitiveness was valued in student leaders by 68% of the boys and 54% of the girls. Without a doubt, competitiveness is valued positively in large segments of the Andover community.

Does the presence of competitiveness within the school's value system create problems for either sex? Anyone who has heard the slogans "no pain-no gain," "what doesn't kill you improves you," "play the game to win," or "if it doesn't hurt you're not trying hard enough," quoted on the P.A. campus today is most likely to be listening to a boy who believes in competition. Among faculty and students males are more likely than females to value competitiveness. As noted in the section on teacher evaluations of students, without being competitive some students, most often girls, may not be able to do as well academically or to win their teacher's approval. The lack of competitiveness in male students may also be perceived as "sex-inappropriate" by teachers who expect all boys to be competitive. Despite modifications in the competitive athletic tradition, a student's lack of competitiveness can also be seen as a problem in the athletic program where competitiveness is still valued. Because a majority of P.A. students value competitiveness in their leaders, candidates who are not competitive—again, more often girls—may be at a disadvantage in getting elected or appointed by their peers. A cross-cultural study showed that more than many other cultures American culture values male competitiveness highly, and in competitive situations "intrinsic motivation" decreases most often for women.[258] When competition is valued in an academic environment, females, who often have been socialized to avoid competition, are sometimes affected negatively.[259]

SOURCES OF SELF-CONFIDENCE AND THE EDUCATIONAL ENVIRONMENT

Competitiveness as an Andover value takes its most serious toll on female self-confidence. The frog pond effect—feeling intimidated and less capable when surrounded by a great number of outstanding peers—has been shown to affect girls more often than boys.[260] The personalities that seem to thrive best in competitive academic environments are, not surprisingly, personalities that see themselves as competitive, assertive, independent, and willing to take risks. And, because girls are still less likely than boys to be socialized to possess these traits, girls are less likely to thrive in competitive academic environments.

As we have seen throughout the study, female students have shown less self-confidence than their male peers. They rated their intelligence lower, their success at athletics lower, and their success at leadership and popularity lower. Andover boys were more likely than girls to have a high self-concept, and girls were more likely than boys to have a low self-concept.

	Self-Concept*	
	Male	Female
High	37%	25%
Average	33%	38%
Low	30%	37%

*All differences between genders here are statistically significant.

Recognizing that female students studied elsewhere also have lower self-concepts than their male counterparts, we have identified what may be three of the main reasons for this trend to be so notable at Andover: the unequal sex-ratio in the student body exacerbates females' "fear of success;" their sense of marginality may be worsened by being outnumbered in sex-imbalanced classes; and their lack of contact with sufficient numbers of admired adult female role models, especially in traditionally male fields like math, may be a deficit which diminishes their chances of receiving needed mentoring.[261] But an additional factor contributing to low female (and some male) self-concept at Andover was discovered by Brandeis University researchers Janet Giele, Peter Dunn, and Mary Gilfus. When these scholars explored the student survey data for correlations (degrees of relationship or association) they found strong connections between students with high self-concept and students with what we call the Type I personality traits (assertiveness, competitiveness, independence, willingness to take risks.) In addition, Type I personalities were also associated with personal success in athletics, leadership, and being male. Often, therefore, a student who sees him/herself as assertive, competitive, independent and risk-taking feels successful at Andover.

High Self-Concept in Relation to Other Factors: Stepwise Regression Method

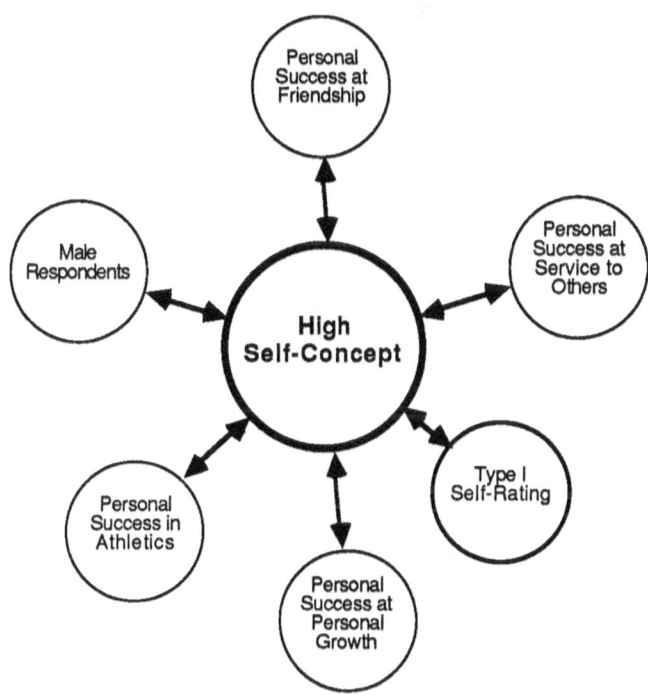

.45(High Self-Concept) = .32 x Type I + .24 x Personal Success at Friendship + .20 x Personal Success at Athletics + .14 x Personal Success at Service to Others + .16 x Male Respondents + .12 x Personal Success at Teacher Approval + .09 x Personal Success at Personal Growth

Why should the Andover educational environment encourage the growth of high self-concept in Type I personalities more than other personality types? Evidently the achievement-oriented and competitive values within the school culture reward Type I students' assertive, competitive, independent, and risk-taking behaviors.[262] Students who are Mixed Type or Type II personalities are less likely to fit as well into the dominant values of the school.

"Incongruence" or lack of fit between some female students and P.A.'s environment was described in an essay response to the faculty questionnaire written by a former faculty member. She described Andover as an environment in which:

> the image of the 'ideal student' as an independent, aggressive, go-getter type is gender-biased toward a pattern of development and a style of interaction toward which males are socialized from infancy. Girls are not rewarded for their interpersonal skills . . . to the same extent that they are rewarded for their independence. Both skills should be equally valued in each sex. Simultaneously, boys who are not as assertive or aggressive are often not viewed as favorably by faculty. Listen to the values that are rampant in the end of the term cluster and all school faculty meetings.

From this viewpoint the Andover environment rewards and respects most highly students who are "independent, aggressive, go-getters," and boys are socialized to fit this pattern more often than girls are.

PERSONALITY TRAITS

		Male	Female
TYPE I*		38%	28%
	(rated higher on assertiveness, competitiveness, independence, willingness to take risks than on Type II traits)		
MIXED TYPE		34%	34%
	(identifies self as having a mixture of I + II traits)		
TYPE II*		28%	39%
	(rated higher on gentleness, sensitivity to others, sympathy, understanding than on Type I traits)		

*Difference between groups are statistically significant. Typing of personality traits is based on students' answers to SQ question #41 and the Bem scale. A fuller explanation of Type scale appears in the Appendix.

What happens to students who don't fit into the Type I pattern? A majority of females did not fit into the Type I pattern. Thirty-nine percent of the females described themselves as possessing Type II traits:

being gentle, sensitive to others, sympathetic, and understanding—traits consistent with the "non-sibi" tradition. Among the Type II girls 44% had low self-concept and 40% had average self-concept, while only 16% had high self-concept. Of course, 28% of the boys also see themselves as Type II. Over a third of the Type II boys also had low self-concept, which suggests that gender is not the only factor related to low self-concept. In general, Type II students, i.e., those who describe themselves as being directed toward the needs of others, are less likely than Type I students to have high self-concept.

An alternative route to high self-concept at Andover was discovered by our Brandeis consultants. High self-concept was found to be strongly

Significantly Correlated Variables*

By Mary Gilfus & Peter Dunn

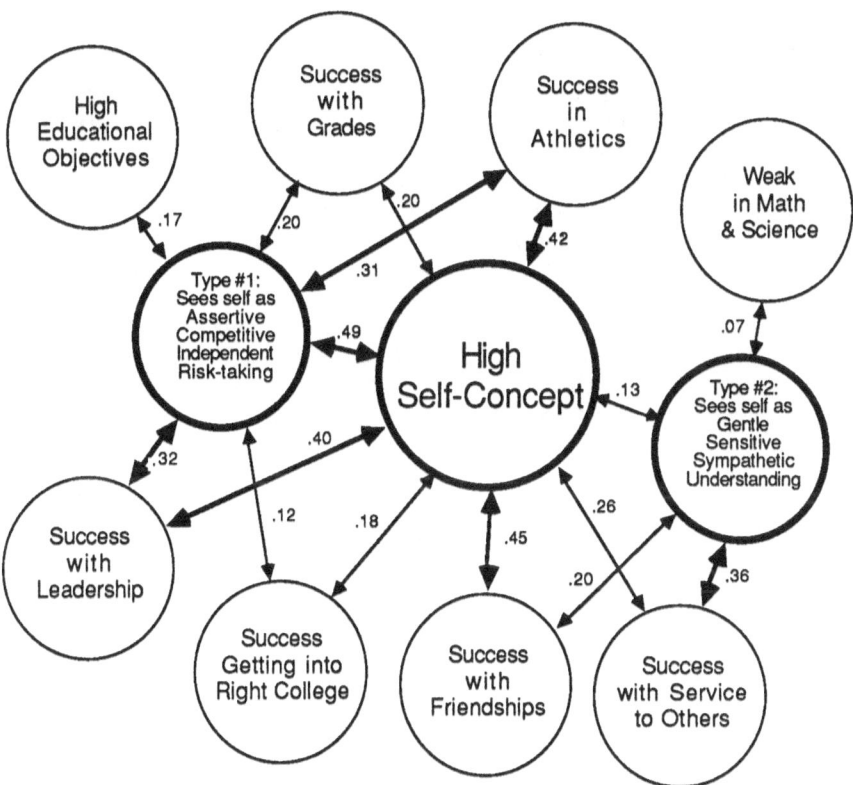

* The number above each arrow represents a Pearson's correlation coefficient. Higher coefficients indicate stronger relationships between the variables.

connected with students who viewed themselves as successful at friendships. In addition, some connection was found between high self-concept and Type II students. Janet Giele and Mary Gilfus believe this represents an affiliative path to high self-concept at Andover, a way in which the "non-sibi" values of the community encourage students to build positive feelings about themselves by caring for others. Thus, both competitive and nurturant personalities have felt at home at Andover. The school community's value system still emphasizes individual achievement, independence, autonomy, and competition somewhat more than affiliation, sensitivity to others, and nurturance. Females more often than males appear to be at odds with the competitive side of Andover's value system, and the strength of the competitive and Type I values may suggest to some observers that traditionally male values still predominate at Andover. But both Type I and Type II values and personality traits are available to both sexes, and a variety of personalities can thrive within the Andover environment.

THE EQUITY EARTHQUAKE AND PERSONAL CHANGE

The lack of historical data on Type I and Type II personalities at Andover limits greatly what we can conclude about the effects of the equity earthquake and institutional changes on student personalities. However, we do know that, compared to the early years of coeducation, boys and girls at Andover today are more alike in aptitudes and performance, life goals, educational aspirations and career orientation. The increased similarity between the sexes is in itself an equalizing influence on the Andover community.

We do not know for sure what percentage of males or females would have defined themselves as Type I, Mixed Type, or Type II in 1973. We may assume, based on the Merger Study and records of O.R.E., that more boys saw themselves as strictly Type I in the early seventies than do so today and that fewer boys would have been comfortable defining themselves as Type II then. Girls may have been less likely to be comfortable viewing themselves as competitive and risk-taking in 1972 than they are now. But we cannot be sure without more perfectly comparable data.

In the 1984 Coeducation Study the 34% of the boys and girls who defined themselves as Mixed Type are significant. Evidently about a third of the boys and girls at Andover are comfortable mixing sensitivity with competition, gentleness with assertiveness, sympathy and understanding with independence. If about a third of both sexes have Mixed Type traits, the school's "non-sibi" teachings and competitive values may find compatible homes within the personalities of both sexes. The 28% of the boys who classify themselves as Type II and 28% of the girls who classify themselves as Type I, also provide evidence that the Andover environment does not force rigid or archaic sex-stereotypes on its students. Perhaps some Andover boys can now see themselves as sensitive and gentle and some girls can see themselves as competitive and assertive without anyone assuming those traits are inappropriate to their sex. Without perfectly comparable data from 1973 we do not know for sure that this is a new trend. However, we suspect that throughout American education today boys and girls have more encouragement for combining Mixed Type traits than they did before the equity earthquake. Increased pressure for girls to fit Type I traits may also be a result of recent cultural emphasis on girls becoming "superwoman" achievers. Despite the new pressures on girls, by 1985 American society appears to be less likely to view achievement-orientation and competitiveness as "unfeminine" traits.

COEDUCATION'S SUCCESS AND THE EDUCATIONAL ENVIRONMENT

Throughout the report we have referred to the Hall and Sandler "chilly climate" studies which show how women are devalued or undermined by overt discrimination and subtle put-downs throughout their college educations. Assessing the chilliness or warmth of the educational environment for girls at Andover is a complex task. According to Hall and Sandler, even rare instances of stereotyping can create a "chilly climate." The only straightforward data we have on the topic is student and faculty rating of the success of coeducation and the relations between the sexes at Andover.

Although students were not asked about coeducation, faculty were asked to rate how successful coeducation was at Andover. Sixty-five percent rated it as very successful, 30% as moderately successful, and only 1% as unsuccessful (3% neutral, 2% had no opinion). Again, women were more likely than men to perceive it as moderately successful.

	SUCCESS OF COEDUCATION	
	Male	Female
Very successful	73%	55%
Moderately successful	23%	36%
Neutral	2%	3%
Unsuccessful	0%	2%
No opinion	1%	3%

When students were asked to rate the relations between the sexes at P.A., most saw them as egalitarian or tending toward egalitarianism. Twenty-eight percent of the girls perceived the relationships between the sexes at Andover as sexist or tending toward sexism, but only 15% of the boys agreed with them.

Faculty members were asked to rate the relations between the sexes: a) among faculty, b) between faculty and administration, c) among students, and d) between faculty and students. Females were more inclined to see tendencies toward sexism where males saw egalitarianism. Faculty of both sexes saw sexism most often in relations between the sexes among students and least often between faculty and administration, but in each category the faculty's response clearly indicates that women perceive a tendency toward sexism throughout the school at a much higher rate than men.

Though most faculty agree with the Ten-Year Coeducation Committee's assessment that coeducation at Andover is successful, their reservations are worth noting. Some members of the Andover community probably view the educational environment as a "chilly climate" for women—others clearly do not.

PERCENTAGE OF FACULTY WHO PERCEIVE THE RELATIONS BETWEEN THE SEXES AS SEXIST OR TENDING TOWARD SEXISM

	Faculty Overall	*Male*	*Female*
1. Sexism Among Students	39%	32%	47%
2. Sexism Among Faculty	31%	23%	44%
3. Sexism Between Faculty and Student	29%	21%	40%
4. Sexism Between Faculty and Administration	27%	20%	40%

Students Who View Relations Between Sexes at PA as 'Sexist' or 'Tending Toward Sexism'

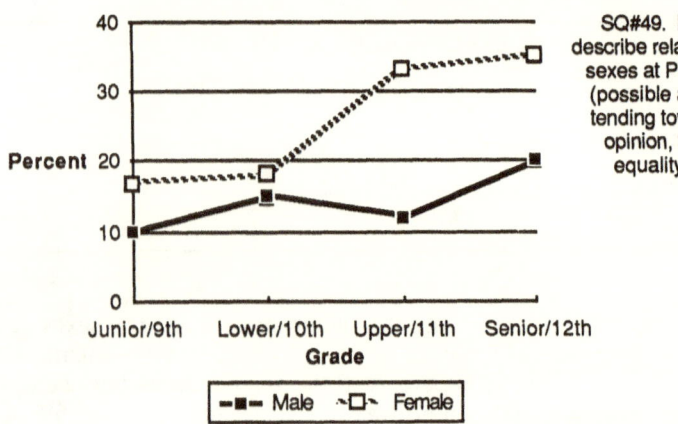

SQ#49. How would you describe relations between the sexes at Phillips Academy? (possible answers: sexist, tending toward sexism, no opinion, tending toward equality, egalitarian)

AMERICA'S EQUITY EARTHQUAKE AT ANDOVER

In 1970 the Women's Equity Action League filed a class action complaint with the Department of Labor against all universities and colleges in America charging an "industry-wide pattern" of discrimination against women—including sex-based admission quotas, unequal financial aid, payment of lower salaries to women, and less promoting and hiring of women.[263] By 1978, 130,000 individual complaints about sex discrimination in employment awaited investigation by the Equal Employment Opportunity Commission, a sign that the problem of sex discrimination had not been solved by the end of the seventies.[264] Yet these actions served as catalysts for change, as well as proof that expectations about sex equity were already changing.

The equity earthquake's effects are not yet fully understood, but they are nonetheless profound. In 1965 no one seemed to question the rationale behind paying women lower salaries. In 1985 sex discrimination in salaries is illegal. In 1965 few women held administrative positions in education and few questioned why they were absent. Today gender-balance and fair hiring standards, though still unachieved ideals, are much more common goals among educators. In 1965 the right to commit sexual harassment was viewed by some college professors as a job perquisite. By 1985 colleges have been sued and their harassing employees fired. In 1965 few people realized women were treated differently from men in schools and colleges. Today extensive research has documented overt and subtle forms of discrimination against women in education. In 1985 a wide range of educational, lobbying, legal, and counseling networks exist to create more equality in education.[265]

Andover has changed with the times, and it has done its changing well. In 1965 Abbot and P.A. were single-sex schools. In 1985 Andover has become a fully coeducational school committed to the idea of sex equity. The equity earthquake has shaken every part of school life—from athletics to student social life, from teacher-student relationships to faculty hiring policies, from the number of women serving as deans to the number of girls graduating with honors. If we recall the early "marriage" of Abbot Academy and Phillips Academy, especially the P.A. teacher with doubts about finding enough qualified girls to allow coeducation to begin, we see today a transformed school. Andover has combined the best of its parent schools to become a truly fine coeducational environment.

Progress in achieving sex equity is evident everywhere at Andover. From the girls' ice hockey team to boys in the dance program, we see an athletic program that has adapted the old P.A. competitive athletic tradition to the new coeducational student body. In classrooms, in the debate society, in student government, in Trustees' meetings, in administrative discussions, and on the floor of faculty meetings, female voices are heard—and listened to—more than anyone ever dreamed possible in 1973. Women and girls have made a place for themselves in the new school.

As we review the issues raised throughout this study we must finally wonder: how many gender differences exist because of the way the school is and how many do students and faculty bring with them? How many gender differences at Andover come from previous socialization and how many are produced by the school's environment? Because no social scientist has ever answered these questions definitively we cannot hope to do so here. Yet some boundaries between the influence of education and previous socialization can be drawn.

Gender identity emerges not long after small children learn to walk and talk.[266] Years before children see the inside of a classroom they have already incorporated—in unconscious ways—appropriate sex-socialization into their personalities. Lesser female self-confidence, the assumption of male superiority, and male competitiveness are three powerful products of early sex-role socialization that schools cannot reverse easily. For example, if a boy has been raised not to take female athletes seriously, school policies at Andover and coaches' efforts may not be able to change his mind. He may continue to believe in male superiority even in the face of massive evidence of equality. If a girl has been raised to think of herself as merely "average" in intelligence despite high scores in math, a school counselor may not be able to convince her that her abilities warrant applying to the most selective engineering schools. At Andover even if the male/female ratio in the student body were 50-50, some girls, because of previous socialization, might still feel intimidated in class with boys. Even if Andover worked harder to convey "non-sibi" values, competitive students of both sexes, but especially boys, might prefer to test their abilities against others by defining academic and athletic success as a contest between rivals. Schools cannot have the power to overcome all previous socialization.

A school's policies may be helpless to alter many aspects of previous sex-role socialization that hold students back from receiving the fullest benefits of a fine education. However, policies clearly make a difference in equalizing an educational environment. For example, the institutional policy of recruiting minorities has brought welcome diversity to the Andover campus, just as the policy decision to increase the percentage of girls in the student body to 43% has created a more coeducational school. The institutional commitment to sex equity in athletics was embodied in a new Abbot wing to the gym, new female coaches, and new athletic opportunities for female athletes. Out of this came a conscious policy decision to modify the competitive athletic tradition to suit the needs of a more varied coeducational student body.

In student social life adult guidance has also brought students closer to equity than ever before. The school has insisted—in many but not all areas—that students be given equal treatment and equal chances to grow and learn. In academics the school has mandated—in almost all areas—that achievement by both sexes be recognized. By now, thousands of Andover boys and girls have had more equal educational experiences because of those policy decisions.

Policy changes have also made faculty life more equitable. The school developed an affirmative action policy, and it has hired an increasing number of women faculty over the years. More women served as department chairs and as deans in 1985 than at any time since coeducation began. A clear policy against the sexual harassment of employees and students may have reduced the frequency of such incidents. Furthermore, the harassment policy may also have the potential to empower females on campus to assert their rights to object to overt gender-bias. Policy-makers at Andover, from Headmasters and deans to teachers, have chosen the path of equality many times since 1973.

Of course, not all changes have occurred because of formal policies. Outside the scope of this study are the multitude of efforts by students, their parents, faculty, administrators, trustees, faculty families, alumnae/alumni, staff, and others to make coeducation work. A variety of grass-roots efforts have made the Andover community a better place to live for both sexes: for example, parents organizing an Ad Hoc Child Care Committee that brought up the idea of having a day care center on campus, and Benevie's integrative efforts to foster friendships among all women on campus and a community spirit that is inclusive rather than exclusive. Coeducation has been supported further by teachers who have taken the initiative to bring speakers on campus to raise gender and career issues for students and by students who spontaneously held discussion groups about gender-related topics. Furthermore, academic advisors and teachers have worked extra hours with students of both sexes to help them overcome the educational burdens of math-anxiety or writing problems. Donors have given funds earmarked to support coeducational programs. House counselors have also promoted the success of coeducation by helping their students sort out their relationships with the opposite sex.

No one forced the grass-roots to respond graciously to coeducation by offering such extra initiatives. It was in the nature of the Andover community to innovate in a new situation. Coeducation's success has been as dependent on these volunteers as it has been on formal policy change. And coeducation could never have evolved as it has without the dedication and flexibility of those people whose attitudes about gender changed over the years. Without widespread cooperation from all generations, both sexes, and all members of the extended Abbot, P.A., and merged school communities, coeducation would never have turned out so well.

During its first decade of change and adjustment, coeducation and the equity earthquake became sources of new life for the school. Similarly, new coeducational agendas could also provide fresh direction for Andover in the future. The purpose of the Coeducation Study Project is to help the school focus on areas of needed change in its second decade of coeducation. Many changes are already taking place throughout the school—curriculum revision, gender-balancing enrollments in some courses, and the appointment of more women leaders are just a few examples. Because of the healthy diversity of opinion within the school, an approximate consensus will have to be reached about which concerns lend themselves best to practical solutions. Among the concerns raised in this study the most prominent issues are:

1) how to define admissions policies for both sexes equitably;
2) how to make the classroom atmosphere more comfortable and equal for both sexes;
3) how to find sensitive and long-lasting ways to encourage the growth of male and female self-confidence;
4) how to support the educational aspirations and career ambitions of both sexes;
5) how to encourage more equal student recognition of athletes and a program that serves both sexes equally well;
6) how to guide students' extracurriculars and peer culture toward a spirit of inclusion and respect for both sexes;
7) how to aid students of both sexes in looking toward their future, including the possible blending of career achievement with fulfilling personal lives;
8) how to move beyond male "great teacher" norms to offer more numerous adult female role models;
9) how to provide an equitable faculty workload that does not create excess stress for either sex;
10) how to recruit and hire women and minorities on the faculty;
11) how to reduce the female faculty attrition rate;
12) how to make participation in community decision-making available to both sexes;
13) how to seek a balance in community values between achievement and affiliation as well as between competition, concern for others, and cooperation;
14) how to put an end to sexism and sex discrimination;
15) how to make gender-balance, full coeducation, and sex equity more self-conscious goals for the whole community.

Some of these issues may never be faced by the Andover community because they may seem too elusive or solutions may not be easy to find. But, given the school's past record of responding to coeducation, we have reason to believe that the school will embrace the challenge with enthusiasm. As Andover grapples with these issues, learning from the experiences of other schools and colleges and sharing our insights together will be vital to solving the remaining gender inequity problems that exist throughout American education.

The equity earthquake has shaken Andover in the past decade, rear-ranging roles, policies, and patterns of behavior. After ten years of co-education the Andover community has demonstrated institutional flexi-bility, wisdom, strength, and an innovative spirit in its response to the challenges posed by coeducation. In the second decade those qualities will be needed if the school is to make further progress.

Footnotes to Preface

[1]Bernice Resnick Sandler, "The Quiet Revolution," in Karen Bogart, ed., *Toward Equity: An Action Manual for Women in Academe*, report of the Project on the Status and Education of Women (Washington, D.C.: Association of American Colleges, 1984); Bernice R. Sandler, "A Little Help from Our Government: WEAL and Contract Compliance," and Jo Freeman, "Women on the Move: Roots of Revolt," in Alice S. Rossi and Ann Calderwood, *Academic Women on the Move*, (N.Y.: Russell Sage Foundation, 1973); Constantina Safilios-Rothschild, *Sex Role Socialization and Sex Discrimination: A Synthesis and Critique of the Literature* (Washington, D.C.: U. S. Department of Health, Education, and Welfare and the National Institute of Education, October 1979); Roberta M Hall and Bernice R Sandler, "The Classroom Climate: A Chilly One for Women?" report of the Project on the Status and Education of Women, (Washington, D C : Association of American Colleges, 1982); Roberta M Hall and Bernice R. Sandler, "Out of the Classroom: A Chilly Campus Climate for Women?," report of the Project on the Status and Education of Women, (Washington, D.C.: Association of American Colleges, 1985); Marlaine E. Lockheed, with Susan S. Klein, "Sex Equity in Classroom Organization and Climate," and Susan S. Klein, Lillian N. Russo, Patricia B. Campbell, and Glen Harvey, "Examining the Achievement of Sex Equity in and through Education," in Susan S. Klein, *Handbook for Achieving Sex Equity* (Baltimore, Md: The Johns Hopkins University Press, 1985); Patricia A Schmuck, "Context of Change: The Women's Movement as a Political Process," and Ken Kempner, "A Social-Psychological Analysis of the Context for Change," in Jean Stockard, Patricia A Schmuck, Ken Kempner, Peg Williams, Sakre K. Edson, Mary Ann Smith, *Sex Equity in Education* (N.Y.: Academic Press, 1980); Judith Hole and Ellen Levine, eds., *Rebirth of Feminism* (N Y.: Quadrangle Books, 1971); Gene P. Agre, Barbara Finkelstein, "Feminism and School Reform: The Last Fifteen Years," *Teachers College Record*, Dec. 1978, Vol. 80, #2, pp 307-315.

[2]Alexander W. Astin, *The College Environment* (Washington, D C : American Council on Education, 1968), pp. 128-130.

[3]Esther Manning Westervelt, "The Higher Education of Women: A Carnegie Study," in *Women's Experience and Education*, Harvard Educational Review Reprint Series #17,(Cambridge, Mass: Harvard Educational Review, 1985); Susan McIntosh Lloyd, *A Singular School: Abbot Academy, 1828-1973* (Hanover, N.H.: University Press of New England, 1979), pp. 336-337.

[4]Sara Evans, *Personal Politics: The Roots of Women's Liberation in the Civil Rights Movement and the New Left* (N.Y.: Vintage Books, 1980), p. 4.

[5]James Gilbert, *Another Chance: Postwar America, 1945-1968* (Philadelphia, Pa : Temple University Press, 1981), pp.63-75; Barbara Ehrenreich and Deirdre English, *For Her Own Good: 150 Years of the Experts' Advice to Women* (Garden City, N.Y.: Anchor Press, 1979), pp. 230-240; Joseph Rheingold, M D , *The Fear of Being a Woman: A Theory of Maternal Destructiveness* (N.Y.: Grune and Stratton, 1964); an interesting contrast to the earlier negative portrayal of working mothers is Anita Shreve, "The Working Mother As Role Model," *The New York Times Magazine*, September 9, 1984, pp. 39-43, 50, 52, 54.

[6]Gloria Steinem, *Outrageous Acts and Everyday Rebellions* (N.Y.: Holt, Rinehart and Winston, 1983), p. 149

[7]Steinem, *Acts*, p. 149

[8]Steinem, *Acts*, p. 150

[9]E. Anthony Rotundo, "American Fatherhood: A Historical Perspective", *American Behavioral Scientist*, Vol. 29, No. 1, September/ October 1985, pp. 7-25; Joseph H. Pleck, "Men's New Roles in the Family: Housework and Childcare," (Wellesley, Mass.: Working Papers, Wellesley College Center for Research on Women, 1976); Peter Gabriel Filene, *Him/Her Self Sex Roles in Modern America* (N.Y.: New American Library, 1976), p. 213-218; Joseph H.Pleck and Jack Sawyer, eds. *Men and Masculinity* (Englewood Cliffs, N.J : Prentice-Hall, Inc., 1974); Warren Farrell, *The Liberated Man*,(N.Y.: Bantam Books, 1975); Donald H. Bell, *Being A Man: The Paradox of Masculinity* (Brattleboro, Vt.: The Lewis Publishing Company, 1982).

[10]Alex Karras, "The Real Men on TV—And the Wimps," *TV Guide*, Aug. 17, 1985, pp. 4-8.

[11]Safilios-Rothschild, *Sex Role*, p. 127-129; Klein, *Handbook*.

[12]Hall & Sandler, "Chilly . . . Classroom" and "Chilly . . . Out of the Classroom "

[13]*Men and Women Learning Together: A Study of College Students in the Late 70's*, Office of the Provost, Brown University, April 1980, hereafter cited as Brown Project.

[14]Brown Project, pp. 156-157.

[15]See the sources cited throughout the footnotes.

[16]Governor's Commission on the Status of Women, Commonwealth of Massachusetts, *Report of Task Force on Education*, 1973, in Janice Pottker and Andrew Fishel, *Sex Bias in the Schools*, (Teaneck, N.J.: Fairleigh Dickinson University Press, 1977), p. 465; see also Andrew Fishel and Janice Pottker, "Sex Bias in Secondary School: The Impact of Title IX," in Pottker and Fishel, *Sex Bias*, pp. 92-104.

[17]Mary Kay Tetreault and Patricia A. Schmuck, "Equity, Educational Reform, and Gender," manuscript in press for 1985 issue of *Issues in Education*

[18]"Proposal: A Study of the First Ten Years of Women Students At Andover," by anonymous donors, included in Memo to the Coed Committee by Marion Finbury, September 15, 1983.

[19]Carol Gilligan, *In a Different Voice: Psychological Theory and Women's Development*, (Cambridge, Mass.: Harvard University Press, 1982); Carol Gilligan, "Woman's Place in Man's Life Cycle," in *Women's Experience and Education*; references to other studies can be found in Lynn Olson "The Emma Willard School Questions Old Assumptions," *Education Week*, March 27, 1985, p. 12.

[20]Sandra L. Bem, "Probing the Promise of Androgyny," in A. G. Kaplan and J. P. Bean, *Beyond Sex-Role Stereotypes: Readings Toward a Psychology of Androgyny* (Boston, Mass.: Little, Brown, 1976), pp. 48-62; Sandra L. Bem, "Beyond Androgyny: Some Presumptuous Prescriptions for a Liberated Sexual Identity," in J. Sherman and F. Denmark, eds , *Psychology of Women: Future Directions of Research*, (N.Y.: Psychological Dimensions, 1978); among the many recent critiques of the Bem approach is Peter B. Zeldow, "The Androgynous Vision: A Critical Examination," *Bulletin of the Menninger Clinic*, Vol. 46, September 1982, No. 5, pp. 401-413.; see also Candace Garrett Schau with Carol Kehr Tittle, "Educational Equity and Sex Role Development," in Klein, *Handbook*; Joseph H. Pleck, *The Myth of Masculinity* (Cambridge, Mass.: The M.I T. Press, 1981); to understand other theoretical assumptions and typing see Janet Giele's theoretical appendix and Mary Gilfus' essay, and Giele's idea of the "crossover motif" in Janet Zollinger Giele, "Adulthood as Transcendence of Age and Sex" in Neil J. Smelser and Erik H. Erikson, eds., *Themes of Work and Love in Adulthood* (Cambridge, Mass.: Harvard University Press, 1980).

[21]Anyone interested in the legal sex equity literature can check the legal references listed in the footnotes here, and can write to the Project on the Status and Education of Women for its Title IX packet and other legal information (PSEW, Association of American Colleges, 1818 R St. N.W., Washington, D.C. 20009); in addition, the Project on Equal Education Rights offers information about the impact of the Grove City case and other legal issues (PEER, 1413 K St , N.W., Washington, D.C. 20005); the National Women's Law Center and the National Leadership Conference on Civil Rights can be contacted for up-to-date legal and legislative information about sex discrimination in education; "Discrimination Laws and the Independent School," Memo to School Heads and Board Chairman, from Cary Pottér, President, N.A.I.S.; Kathleen M. Dalton, "Legal Sex Equity in Independent Schools," manuscript draft.

Footnotes to Chapter One:
ROOTS OF COEDUCATION AT ANDOVER

[22]"The Constitution of Phillips Academy," in Frederick S. Allis, Jr., *Youth from Every Quarter: A Bicentennial History of Phillips Academy, Andover* (Hanover, N.H.: University Press of New England, 1979), p. 688; "Constitution of Abbot Academy," in Lloyd, *Singular*, p. 453. For a more detailed history of coeducation than we can offer here, please refer to Lloyd and Allis; all sources not specifically cited in footnotes are official school records.

[23]Lloyd, *Singular*, pp. 411-413.

[24]Lloyd, *Singular*, p. 124.

[25]Lloyd, *Singular*, p.125.

[26]Allis, *Youth*, p.671.

[27]Lloyd, *Singular*, p.412.

[28]Lloyd, *Singular*, p.366.

[29]Lloyd, *Singular*, p. 370; Simeon Hyde, "Memorandum to the Trustees: The Coeducation Issue and the Development of Collaboration with Abbot Academy, History and Current Status," p. 1.

[30]Hyde, "Memo," p. 10.

[31]Hyde, "Memo," pp. 2-3, 8-9, 16

[32]Hyde, "Memo," p. 14.

[33]Lloyd, *Singular*, pp. 425, 427.

[34]Lloyd, *Singular*, p. 413.

[35]Lloyd, *Singular*, p. 423; Esther Hamilton, "Phillips Academy/Abbot Academy Merger Case," research paper, Harvard Graduate School of Education, January 1977, p 26

[36]Lloyd, *Singular*, p.430.

[37]Allis, *Youth*, p. 674.

[38]Lloyd, *Singular*, p. 430.

[39]Lloyd, *Singular*, pp 427-428.

[40]Frederick A. Peterson, Office of Research and Evaluation, Edward F. Iwanicki, Maida A. Broadbent, Michael Cauley, Center for Field Research and School Services, *The Phillips Academy Merger Study*, Commissioned by the Abbot Academy Association, (Andover, Mass.: Phillips Academy, 1974).

[41]Lloyd, *Singular*, pp 372-374; Allis, *Youth* p 670

[42]Allis, *Youth*, pp 665-666.

[43]Allis, *Youth*, pp. 666-669.

[44]Lloyd, *Singular*, pp. 432-439; Allis, *Youth*, pp. 677-678.

[45]Donald H. McLean, Jr. to the Alumni of Andover, quoted in Julie Owen, "Phillips and Abbot Academies: A Case for Coeducation," research paper, Harvard Graduate School of Education, March, 1977, p.49; "Speculations on Andover II: The Issue of Coeducation," Memorandum to the Trustees from Theodore Sizer, Sept. 11, 1972.

[46]Lloyd, *Singular*, p. 440.

[47]Lloyd, *Singular*, p. 409.

[48]Lloyd, *Singular*, pp. 439-442

[49]Allis, *Youth*, pp. 680-682

[50]Frederick A. Peterson, Office of Research and Evaluation, "Characteristics of Abbot and Phillips Entering Students as seen in their Responses to Questa I," administered in September 1972, hereafter cited as Questa Study.

[51]Emily Bernstein, "The Long Arduous Road to PA Coeducation," in the Coeducation Supplement to the *Phillipian*, June 3, 1984, p 2

[52]Lloyd, *Singular*, p 444.

[53]Lloyd, *Singular*, p. 445.

[54]Alumni and Alumnae Reunion Weekend, June, 1985, Panel on Coeducation, comments made during the open discussion following the presentations; at the reunion session after one alumna talked about feeling "on trial" at P.A. during the first year, 1973-'74, a male alumnus from the twenties responded by saying that he could understand her feelings because he had felt that way during his Andover years, too. Clearly men and women almuni/nae have shared many of the same experiences. Personal memories of men of pre-

coeducation Andover are recorded in a fascinating collection, Claude M Fuess, ed., *In My Time: A Medley of Andover Reminiscences* (Andover, Mass., Phillips Academy, 1959); for further information on the merger see Frederick A Peterson, Jr., '34, "First the Good News—then the Bad," *Andover Bulletin*, Vol. 68, #3, Winter 1975, pp. 103.

[55]Helen Eccles, "If I only had a wife . . ," *Andover Bulletin*, Vol. 68, #3, Winter 1975, pp. 4-10.

[56]Lloyd, *Singular*, p. 410.

[57]Harriet Beecher Stowe, who is buried in the P.A. cemetery near her husband Calvin, pursued her literary career while residing in Stowe House, currently a girls' dorm and Cluster Dean's residence. Barbara M Cross, "Harriet Beecher Stowe," in Edward T James, Janet Wilson James, and Paul S. Boyer, eds , *Notable American Women*, (Cambridge, Mass : The Belknap Press of Harvard University Press, 1971), Vol III, pp. 393-402. Andover Theological Seminary faculty daughter Elizabeth Stuart Phelps (Ward), while living in the current P.A. Headmaster's House, captured nineteenth century readers' hearts by depicting the wonders of heaven in her famous novel *The Gates Ajar* Phelps attended Abbot and studied theology with a private tutor from the Andover Theological Seminary of which her father was president. Beatrice K. Hofstadter, "Elizabeth Stuart Phelps Ward," in James, *Notable Women*, Vol. III, pp 538-539.

[58]Eccles "If."

[59]Eccles, "If;" the inadvertent "denigration" of traditionally female nurturant roles, especially housewife, has resulted from the strong emphasis the Women's Liberation Movement has placed on career achievement and bringing women into the economic market place, according to Agre, Finkelstein, "Feminism;" a similar concern with American culture's and many feminists' deemphasis on nurturance and affliation is evident in Betty Friedan, *The Second Stage* (N.Y.: Summit Books, 1981)

[60]Peterson, *Merger Study*.

[61]Peterson, *Merger Study*.

[62]Kelly Smith, "Girls' Sports Improve with Merger," Coeducation Supplement, *Phillipian*, June 3, 1984, p. 9.

[63]Fred H. Harrison, *Athletics For All: Physical Education and Athletics at Phillips Academy, Andover 1778-1978*, (Andover, Mass.: Phillips Academy, 1983), p. 439

[64]Letter from Joe Wennik to Ted Sizer, January 31, 1978; earlier Athletic Director Ted Harrison had also stated that the locker room situation was "deplorable" but that such "discrimination is beyond our control until the new facilities come," Harrison, *Athletics*, p 439.

[65]Elizabeth Parker Powell, Abbot '56, "Some Facts on the Role of Women and the Use of Abbot's Assets at Andover," a revised version of her 1977 Convocation Speech

[66]Powell, "Facts."

[67]"Report of the Visiting Committee of the New England Association of Schools and Colleges," 1979.

[68]"Interim Report to the New England Association of Schools and Colleges," 1981.

[69]"Interim Report."

[70]Letter to the Quality of Life Committee, Karl Roehrig, Chairman, from Mary Chivers, Natalie Schorr, Rebecca Sheldon, Shirley Veenema, Barbara Wicks, December 18, 1979.

[71]Minutes of Ad Hoc Day Care Study Committee, Tuesday, May 11, [1982], Stimson House East by Cilla Bonney-Smith (Members Vincent Avery, Jeanne Bussiere-Stephens, Cilla Bonney-Smith, Jenny Cline, Jon Stableford, Sandy Thorpe, Kathy Dalton, Alexandra Kubler-Merrill, Britta McNemar, Phyllis Powell); another form of stock taking came from a report put together by Jenny Cline and Susan Lloyd for Women Educators in Boarding Schools, November 1983.

Footnotes for Chapter Two:
ADMISSIONS AFTER A DECADE OF CHANGE

[72]Digby Baltzell, *The Protestant Establishment* (N.Y: Vintage Edition, 1966), p. 127.

[73]Andover's emphasis on diversity is shared by other independent schools; see the portrait of Milton Academy in Sara Lawrence Lightfoot, *The Good High School: Portraits of Char-*

acter and Culture (N.Y.: Basic Books, Inc 1983), pp. 295-302

[74]*Andover Catalog,*(Andover, Mass.: Phillips Academy, 1984-85), p 6.

[75]Bernice R Sandler, "Admissions and the Law" in *Graduate and Professional Education of Women,* Proceedings of May, 1974; Margaret C. Dunkle and Bernice R. Sandler, "Sex Discrimination Against Students: Implications of Title IX of the Education Amendments of 1972," pamphlet distributed by the Project on the Status and Education of Women, originally published in *Inequality in Education,* October, 1974; Dunkle and Sandler state that "an admissions policy based on the number or percentage of applicants from each sex would violate Title IX. For example, admitting 30 percent of female applicants and 30 percent of male applicants would tie admission to sex and could result in admitting members of one sex who were less qualified than some of the students of the other sex who were rejected. Also, ranking or evaluating applicants separately on the basis of sex would be a Title IX violation," (p.6); see also Bernice R Sandler, "Sex Discrimination, Educational Institutions, and the Law: A New Issue on Campus," in Elga Wasserman, Arie Y Lewin, Linda H Bleiweis, eds , *Women in Academia: Evolving Policies Toward Equal Opportunities* (N.Y: Praeger Publishers, 1977); also Letter, John H Lawson, Massachusetts' Commissioner of Education, to Kathleen M. Dalton, August 1, 1985.

[76]Letter from I.R.S to Kathleen M. Dalton, September 14, 1985; the National Association of Independent Schools "filed an amicus brief with the U.S. Supreme Court supporting the Treasury Department's position in the Bob Jones University/Goldsboro Christian Schools Case," Letter, John E. Bachman, Vice President, N.A.I.S., to Kathleen M. Dalton, August 27, 1985. Memo to School Heads and Board Chairman, from John W Sanders, Director of Government Relations, N.A.I.S., April 10, 1979

[77]Nancy Duff Campbell, Marcia D. Greenberger, Margaret A. Kohn, Shirley Wilcher, National Women's Law Center Attorneys, *Sex Discrimination in Education : Legal Rights and Remedies,* (Washington, D.C.: National Women's Law Center, 1983), p. 4-1, "higher admissions criteria" were challenged in Berkelman v. San Francisco Unified School District, 2-4; it should be noted that, unlike Title IX admissions standards, the Fourteenth Amendment certainly does apply to private secondary schools' admissions policies, as do state Equal Rights Amendments; Dalton, "Legal . . Independent Schools."

[78]Title IX Regulations, 34 C.F. R. 106 issued by the Department of Education, in Campbell, *Legal Rights,* Vol. II, p. 30959

[79]College Counseling Office records.

[80]"Admissions Data," a memo from Susan Stott.

[81]Brown Project, p. 22.

[82]Martha Scott Hennessey, "Female Adolescence as a Function of Educational Context: Coeducational and Single-Sex Schooling," A Dissertation in Interdisciplinary Studies in Human Development, University of Pennsylvania, 1985, pp. 23-24; M. E. Lockheed, "Female Motive to Avoid Success: A Psychological Barrier or a Response to Deviancy?," *Sex Roles,* Vol. 1, 1975, pp 41-50; Georgia Sassen, "Success Anxiety in Women: A Constructivist Interpretation of Its Source and its Significance," in *Women's Experience and Education;* Sassen redefines Matina Horner's original concept of "fear of success" as "anxiety regarding competitive success," p 178.

[83]Brown Project, pp 247.

[84]Klein, *Handbook,* pp. 199-207.

[85]Brown Project, pp. 248-249

Footnotes to Chapter Three:
ACADEMIC ATMOSPHERE AND ACADEMIC CHOICES

[86]Kathleen M. Dalton, "Report on Evaluations of Students by Teachers, House Counselors, College Counselors, and Coaches," based on random samples and coding of 1400 items. Samples of the 1985 Senior Class were taken in the College Counselling office and samples of the 1974 Senior Class were taken in the P.A. Archives in the basement of Oliver Wendell Holmes Library

[87]Dalton, "Evaluations."

[88]James Coleman, "The Adolescent Culture," in Pottker and Fishel, *Sex Bias,* pp. 73-75.

[89]Hall and Sandler, "Chilly . . . Classroom."

[90]Brown Project, pp. 17-18.

[91]Hall and Sandler, "Chilly . . . Classroom," p. 6.

[92]Dalton, "Evaluations."

[93]*Webster's New World Dictionary of the American Language* (N.Y.: The World Publishing Co., 1960), p. 298.

[94]Marlaine E. Lockheed, with Susan S. Klein, "Sex Equity in Classroom Organization and Climate," in Klein, *Handbook*.

[95]Susan A. Basow and Nancy T. Silberg, "Student Evaluations of College Professors: Are Males Prejudiced Against Women Professors?" paper presented to the meeting of the Eastern Psychological Association, Boston, March 1985.

[96]Lockheed, "Classroom," in Klein, *Handbook*, pp. 196, 205.

[97]Basow and Silberg, "Professors."

[98]Basow and Silberg, "Professors "

[99]Basow and Silberg, "Professors."

[100]Gilligan, *Voice*; Carol Gilligan, "In a Different Voice: Women's Conceptions of Self and of Morality," in *Women's Experience and Education*; Nancy Chodorow, *The Reproduction of Mothering: Psychoanalysis and the Sociology of Gender* (Berkeley, Ca : University of California Press, 1978); Nancy Chodorow, "Family Structure and Feminine Personality," in M Rosaldo and L. Lamphere, eds., *Women, Culture and Society* (Stanford, Ca.: Stanford University Press, 1974.)

[101]Olson, "Willard."

[102]Lockheed, "Classroom," in Klein, *Handbook*, pp. 198-199; also Candace Garrett Schau, with Carol Kehr Tittle, "Educational Equity and Sex Role Development," in Klein, *Handbook*, p. 87.

[103]Lockheed, "Classroom," in Klein, Handbook, pp. 199; Hall and Sandler, "Chilly . . Classroom."

[104]Ellen Furlough, "Sexual Harassment," *Perspectives: American Historical Association Newsletter*, Vol. 23, #3, March 1985, p. 18-19; Liz McMillan, "Despite New Laws and Colleges' Policies, Women Say Sexism Lingers on Campuses," *The Chronicle of Higher Education*, February 6, 1985.

[105]Furlough, "Harassment," and Campbell, *Legal Rights*, p. 4-45 to 4-53.

[106]Furlough, "Harassment;" "The Importance of Preventing Sexual Harassment Cases," in *The CEO Management Letter Update*, Vol. IV, #8, 1985, pp. 1-6.

[107]Sidney Verba, with Joseph DiNunzio and Christina Spaulding, "Unwanted Attention: Report on a Sexual Harassment Survey," Report to the Faculty Council of the Faculty of Arts and Sciences, Harvard University, September 1983; Patricia A. Vigderman, "Harvard Men and Harvard Women: Sexual Harassment Comes Out from the Ivy," *The Boston Phoenix*, Section One, December 13, 1983, pp. 6-7, 46.

[108]Hall and Sandler, "Chilly . . . Classroom."

[109] *Faculty Handbook*, p. 5-6

[110]Brown Project, p. 295

[111]Campbell, *Legal Rights*, Vol. II, Appendices, Title IX Regulations, "Where a recipient finds that a particular class contains a substantially disproportionate number of individuals of one sex, the recipient shall take such action as is necessary to assure itself that such disproportion is not the result of discrimination on the basis of sex in counseling or appraisal materials or by counselors," p. 30961.

[112]Natalie Schorr, Abbot Grant proposal—French Department.

[113]Dale Spender, ed. *The Impact of Feminism on the Academic Disciplines* (N.Y.: Permagon Press, 1981.); Marilyn Schuster and Susan Van Dyne, "Feminist Transformation of the Curriculum: The Changing Classroom, Changing the Institution;" Peggy McIntosh, "The Study of Women: Implications for Reconstructing the Liberal Arts Disciplines," in *Forum: The Forum for Liberal Education*, October 1981, Vol. IV, #1, p 1-3; Peggy McIntosh, "Interactive Phases of Curricular Re-Vision: A Feminist Perspective," October, 1983, Wellesley College Center for Research on Women Working Paper.

[114]Olson, "Willard."

[115]Olson, "Willard."

[116]Lockheed, "Classroom," in Klein, *Handbook*, p. 212

[117]Kathryn P. Scott and Candace Garrett Schau, "Sex Equity and Sex Bias in Instructional Materials," in Klein, *Handbook*; M. Federbush, "The Sex Problems of School Math Books," J. Stacey, S. Bereand and J. Daniels, eds., *And Jill Came Tumbling After: Sexism in American Education* (N.Y.: Dell Publishing Co., Inc., 1974), pp. 178-184; Beatrice Dupont, *Unequal Education: A Study of Sex Differences in Secondary School Curriculum* (Paris, France: United Nations Educational, Scientific, and Cultural Organization, 1981), p. 118.

[119]Rosalind Rosenberg, *Beyond Separate Spheres: Intellectual Roots of Modern Feminism* (New Haven, Conn.: Yale University Press, 1982), p. 1-12.

[120]"National Report in College-Bound Seniors, 1984," (Princeton, N.J.: College Entrance Examination Board, 1984.)

[121]Jen Swihart and Aimee Vincent, "Speakers Discuss Lack of Females," *Phillipian*, April 12, 1985, p. 2

[122]Lynn H. Fox, *The Problem of Women and Mathematics: A Report to the Ford Foundation* (N.Y.: Ford Foundation, 1980); Sheila Tobias, *Overcoming Math Anxiety* (N.Y.: W.W. Norton, 1978); Lynn H. Fox and Sanford J. Cohn, "Sex Differences in the Development of Precocious Mathematical Talent," in Lynn H. Fox, Linda Brody, and Dianne Tobin, *Women and the Mathematical Mystique* (Baltimore, Md: Johns Hopkins University Press, 1980); J.M Armstrong, *A National Assessment of Achievement and Participation of Women in Mathematics* (Denver, Co.: Education Commission of the States, 1979); G.L. Fox, "Some Observations and Data on the Availability of Same-Sex Models as a Factor in Undergraduate Career Choice," *Sociological Focus*, 1974, 7, pp 15-30.

[123]E.W. Haven, "Factors Associated with the Selection of Advanced Academic Mathematics Course by Girls in High School," *Research Bulletin*, 72:12 (Princeton, N.J.: Educational Testing Service, 1972); Judith Berman Brandenburg, "Women and Men in Yale College: Majors and Educational Aspirations," Yale University, revised November 1982

[124]Swihart and Vincent, "Speakers."

[125]Alice S. Rossi, "Barriers to the Career Choice of Engineering, Medicine or Science Among American Women," In J Mattfeld and C Van Aken, eds., *Women and the Scientific Professions* (Cambridge, Mass: M.I.T. Press, 1965), pp. 51-127; Laraine T. Zappert and Kendyll Stansbury, "In the Pipeline: A Comparative Analysis of Men and Women in Graduate Programs in Science, Engineering and Medicine at Stanford University" pamphlet, Stanford Women's Research Center; they note that though women enter graduate school with excellent records of achievement and ability they have lower self-confidence and their classmates may be "significantly underestimating" women's competence (p. 17).

[126]Peterson, *Merger Study*.

[127]Robert Cope and William Hannah, *Revolving College Doors: The Causes and Consequences of Dropping Out, Stopping Out, and Transferring* (N.Y.: John Wiley and Sons, 1975); Cope and Hannah point out that few educational institutions know why students drop-out. They cite studies by Alexander Astin which connect the generally higher female drop-out rate to environmental factors such as "a high level of student competitiveness." (pp. 28-29) In addition, the authors cite the possible lack of the individual's "congruence" with the institutional environment as another factor which may increase the likelihood of dropping out. (p. 29)

[128]See Mary Gilfus' essay in the Appendix for an explanation of the self-concept scale used; M.B. Fink, "Self-Concept as it Relates to Academic Underachievement," *California Journal of Educational Research* 13:57-61, 1969; H. Leviton, "The Implications of the Relationship between Self-concept and Academic Achievement," *Child Study Journal* 5:25-36, 1975.

[129]Alexander W. Astin, *Four Critical Years: The Effects of College on Beliefs, Attitudes and Knowledge* (San Francisco: Jossey-Bass Publishers, 1977), p. 132; Brown Project, pp 7-11; Beatrice Dupont writes that "educational decisions are career decisions" in *Unequal Education*, p. 22; Brandenburg, "Yale," p. 10.

[130]P.A. College Counseling Office Records

[131]Brown Project, p. 7-8

[132]Brown Project, p. 9-11; see also Astin, *Four Critical Years*.

[133]Girls have often been excluded from vocational education and other courses simply because of their gender, according to the United States Commission on Civil Rights, *The Equal Rights Amendment: Guaranteeing Equal Rights for Women Under the Constitution*, June 1981, p. 18.

Footnotes to Chapter Four:
THE COMPETITIVE ATHLETIC TRADITION UPDATED

[134]Questa Study

[135]Frederick H. Harrison, *Athletics for All*, p. 358.

[136]Bruce Haley, *The Healthy Body and Victorian Culture* (Cambridge, Mass.: Harvard University Press, 1978), p. 166, 129; "Edward Bowen of Harrow, tried to infuse the whole life of the school with the spirit of the game   " (p. 259).

[137]James McLachlan, *American Boarding Schools: A Historical Study* (N.Y.: Charles Scribner's Sons, 1970), pp. 284-285.

[138]McLachlan, *Boarding Schools*, p. 284.

[139]Harrison, *Athletics*, p. 230.

[140]Harrison, *Athletics*, p. 32-33.

[141]Harrison, *Athletics*, p. 358.

[142]Patricia L. Geadelman, with Judy Bischoff, Mary Hoferek, and Dorothy B McKnight, "Sex Equity in Physical Education and Athletics," in Klein, *Handbook*, p. 321; Barbara Ehrenreich and Deidre English, *For Her Own Good: 150 Years of the Experts' Advice to Women* (Garden City, N Y.: Anchor Press/Doubleday, 1979), pp. 270-276; Dr. Hendrick Ruitenbeck, *Psychoanalysis and Female Sexuality* (New Haven: College and University Press, 1966), p. 11; Ferdinand Lundberg and Marynia Farnham, "Some Aspects of Women's Psyche," in Elaine Showalter (ed) *Women's Liberation and Literature* (N.Y.: Harcourt Brace Jovanovich, 1971), pp. 233-248; women may have been discouraged from showing their competitive urges in athletics and career achievement, but obviously, the social pressure did not sanction against social competition among women and it has been socially permissable for women to exhibit some competitive feelings about appearance, popularity, and certain kinds of affiliative achievement.

[143]Harrison, *Athletics*, p. 436

[144]Peterson, *Merger Study*.

[145]Peterson, *Merger Study*.

[146]Joe Wennik note to Kathleen M. Dalton.

[147]Exerpted from "Long Range Planning Group Report: Athletics."

[148]*Blue Book* '84-85, p. 33.

[149]The Athletic Department, "Objectives and Philosophy."

[150]Lydia Goetze, verbally to author

[151]Jon Stableford, "Some Notes on the Athletic Section of the Co-Ed Investigation," May 29, 1984.

[152]Kathleen M. Dalton, Interview with Paul Kalkstein, May 30, 1985

[153]A member of the community described the Andover-Exeter week as a "male ritual" or "male tradition" at an open Faculty Advisory Committee meeting, and he is quoted here with his permission.

[154]Kalkstein interview.

[155]"Long Range Planning."

[156]Marion Finbury, "Athletic Awards Report to Coed Committee," June, 1985

[157]Stableford, "Notes."

[158]Paul Kalkstein, Note to Kathleen M. Dalton.

[159]Kalkstein interview; also interviews with women athletes

[160]Joe Wennik, "Report of the Athletic Director," April 1983

[161]Hall and Sandler, "Chilly. . . Out," p 10; in addition, another study noted that "by not playing in team sports, girls forfeit an excellent opportunity to learn complex rules, to increase their mastery of the skills of teamwork, to receive mentoring from older children, and to be trained in settling disputes;" Lockheed, "Classroom," in Klein, *Handbook*, p 193.

[162]Hennessey, "Female Adolescence," p. 59

Footnotes for Chapter Five:
EQUALITY, AUTONOMY, AND AFFILIATION IN STUDENT SOCIAL LIFE

[163]See Appendix for a brief sociological profile of students at Andover

[164]Questa Study

[165]Philip Blumstein and Pepper Schwartz, *American Couples* (N.Y: William Morrow and Co., Inc., 1983), pp. 34-35. The assumption that marriage is a desirable goal is widely held today despite many alterations in courtship, dating, and sexual patterns, according to Ellen K Rothman, *Hands and Hearts: A History of Courtship in America* (N.Y: Basic Books, Inc., 1984), pp. 310-311

[166]Brown Project, p. 86

[167]*Catalogue,* p. 6

[168]*Catalogue,* p. 7; *Blue Book,* p. 4.

[169]Andrew McNaught, "Coeducation Committee Submits Accumulated Report to Faculty," *The Phillipian,* June 2, 1985, p. A2

[170]Letter, Everett Gendler to the Coeducation Committee, January 3, 1985

[171]Susan Glasser and Noel Wanner, "Sexism: An Andover Dilemma?" *The Phillipian,* January 11, 1985, p. 3

[172]Gendler letter; Memorandum to Everett Gendler from Tom Lyons, January 5, 1985

[173]Glasser, "Sexism."

[174]Glasser, "Sexism "

[175]"A Vicious Cycle," *The Phillipian,* January 11, 1985, p. 2

[176]Kathleen M Dalton, Interview with female *Phillipian* staff members, July 18, 1985

[177]Brown Project, p. 13

[178]Dean of Residence Office, "Report on Disciplinary Action, 1984 "

[179]*Blue Book*

[180]Milton F. Shore and Joseph L Massimo, "Contributions of an Innovative Psychoanalytic Therapeutic Program with Adolescent Delinquents to Developmental Psychology," in Stanley I. Greenspan and George H Pollock, eds , *The Course of Life: Psychoanalytic Contributions Toward Understanding Personality Development* Vol II (Adelphi, Md : Mental Health Study Center, NIMH, 1980), pp. 445-462; Daniel Offer, *The Psychological World of the Teenager: A Study of Normal Adolescent Boys* (N.Y: Basic Books, 1969)

[181]Compare Offer, *Psychological World* with Erik H Erikson, *Identity: Youth and Crisis* (N Y: W W Norton, Inc , 1968)

[182]Gilligan, *Voice*; Gilligan, "Woman's Place," in Women's Experience and Education; Chodorow, *Mothering*; Jean Baker Miller, *Toward a New Psychology of Women* (Boston, Mass.: Beacon Press, 1976)

[183]Miller, Chodorow, and Gilligan have offered important new insights on the developmental needs of both sexes, but the significance of affiliation, as well as separation-individuation, in human development has long been recognized by scholars. Erik Erikson, the most widely read spokesman for the developmental stages viewpoint, writes about the separation-individuation process as identity formation, but he also places emphasis on affiliation as a central developmental issue. Erikson's concept of "generativity"—the achievement of maturity by establishing a giving role, often "regenerating" oneself in the aging process through nurturance of younger people—is a concept that applies to both sexes. Affiliative development has been emphasized by other ego psychologists as well, including Sullivanians and object relations theorists; see Harry Stack Sullivan, *The Interpersonal Theory of Psychiatry* (N Y: W W. Norton, Inc , 1953); Harry Stack Sullivan, "The Illusion of Personal Individuality," in *The Fusion of Psychiatry and Social Science* (N Y.: W.W Norton & Co , Inc , 1971); Robert G. Kvarnes and Gloria Parloff, eds. *A Harry Stack Sullivan Case Seminar: Treatment of a Young Male Schizophrenic* (N.Y.: W W. Norton Co , Inc. 1976); for references to object relations theory which emphasizes affiliative development see note #7, Kathleen M Dalton, "Why America Loved Teddy Roosevelt: or, Charisma Is in the Eyes of the Beholders," in Robert J. Brugger, ed *Our Selves/Our Past: Psychological Approaches to American History* (Baltimore, Md.: The John Hopkins University Press, 1981); see also Giele, "Adulthood as Transcendence," in Smelser and Erikson, *Themes*

[184]Daniel J. Levinson, *The Seasons of a Man's Life* (N.Y.: Alfred A. Knopf, 1978); Pleck, *Myth*; George E Vaillant, *Adaptation to Life* (Boston, Mass.: Little, Brown, 1977); David McClelland, *The Achieving Society* (N.Y.: VanNostrand, 1961).

[185]Andover's *Catalogue* (p. 14) states that "The school encourages independence and personal responsibility: there are study hours but no study halls, and decisions about the use of one's time are largely left to the judgement of the individual;" the emphasis on autonomy over affiliation in the independent school world is indirectly documented by Peter S. Prescott, *A World of Our Own: Notes on Life and Learning in a Boys' Preparatory School* (N.Y.: Coward-McCann, Inc., 1970) and McLachlan, *Boarding Schools*; Lightfoot's description of nurturance within the Milton environment in *The Good High School* is also true of Andover The "affiliation gap" at Andover may come not from an absence of teachers' nurturance toward students, but from the emphasis on achievement

[186]Levinson, *Seasons*; Pleck, *Myth*.

[187]Jonathan Marlowe to the Coeducation Committee on use of Graham House by students. Students also go to the school's doctor and nurses for help

[188]"Notes on Use of the Infirmary" show that little difference exists in the infirmary visiting rates of girls and boys.

[189]*Catalogue*, p. 16.

[190]Pleck, *Myth*.

[191]Gilligan, *Voice*, p. 17; see also Chodorow, *Mothering*.

[192]Lloyd, *Singular*, p. 419.

[193]Letter, David Cobb to Faculty Advisory Committee, 1985.

[194]Kathleen M. Dalton interview with 'Cilla Bonney-Smith.

[195]Hall and Sandler, "Chilly: Out.".

[196]Hall and Sandler, "Chilly: Out."

[197]Hall and Sandler, "Chilly: Out."

[198]Hall and Sandler, "Chilly: Out."

Footnotes to Chapter Six:
TEACHERS, COACHES, HOUSE COUSELORS, and DEANS

[199]The varied sources of educational change are not always easy to locate, but Bogart, *Toward Equity* is an excellent starting point for understanding the many ways colleges are trying to implement policy and personnel changes as well as to effect the most difficult transformation of all, attitude changes.

[200]Safilios-Rothschild, *Sex Role Socialization*, p. 79; and Lucy W. Sells, *Sex Differences in Graduate School Survival*, paper presented at the American Sociological Association Annual Meeting, New York, August 28, 1973.

[201]J.E. Stake and C.R. Granger, "Same-Sex Opposite-Sex Teacher Model Influences on Science Career Commitment Among High School Students," *Journal of Educational Psychology*, 1978, 70(2), pp. 180-186.

[202]Safilios-Rothschild, *Sex Role Socialization*, p. 80.

[203]"Interim Report."

[204]Basow and Silberg, "Professors."

[205]Basow and Silberg, "Professors."

[206]Michele Harway and Helen S. Astin in *Sex Discrimination in Career Counseling and Education* (N.Y.: Praeger Publishers, 1977), p. 104, state that "Although the picture of sex discrimination in guidance and counseling at the secondary and postsecondary level is bleak, the view is not without relief " Harway and Astin are concerned with counselors guiding students into "sex-appropriate" careers or in the case of girls, into no careers at all. In addition, they suggest that counselors should develop programs and strategies to respond effectively to some girls' lack of future-orientation, some girls' more limited educational aspirations, and sex role stereotypes such as "sex-appropriate" course selection which may hold girls back from realizing their potential (pp 104-126).

[207]Only 25% of the colleges surveyed nationwide permit part-timers to vote in faculty meetings, according to Judith M. Guppa, "Employing Part-time Faculty: Thoughtful Approaches to Continuing Problems," *American Association for Higher Education Bulletin*, Vol. 37, #2, October 1984, pp. 3-7

[208]*The Constitution of Phillips Academy*, Andover, p. 7, 10

[209]"Constitution of Abbot Academy," in Lloyd, *Singular*, p. 452.

[210]Allis, *Youth*, p. 616.

[211]Lloyd, *Singular*, p.315.

[212]Lloyd, *Singular*, p.360; Lloyd personally overheard the 1968 incident.

[213]Kathleen M. Dalton and Marion Finbury, Interview with John Richards.

[214]*Faculty Handbook*, '84-85, p. 2.

[215]Sandler, "Help from Our Government," in Rossi, *Academic Women*.

[216]Letter from Leslie Ballard and Ann Harper to Don McNemar, March 4, 1985; letter to the Faculty of Phillips Academy, from the Black Seniors, Christopher Patrick, Sidney R. Smith, III, Lori Kathryn James, Ayo Heinegg, Uzoma Ugochilawa, Kim Edmunds, Rosanne Adderly, Cheryl Nelson, Mary Hill, Amenyu Makuku, Nicole S. Gray, May 2, 1985

[217]Ballard/Harper letter

[218]Tetreault and Schmuck, "Equity."

[219]Sandler, "Quiet Revolution," in Bogart, *Toward Equity*, p. 1; "Women Faculty and Administrators—A Matter of Fact," *On Campus With Women* Vol. 15, No. 1, Summer 1985, p. 1; 11% of the full-time teachers in public high schools are minorities (p 94) according to "The Condition of Education," National Center for Education Statistics.

[220]Middlesex document, Coeducation file.

[221]Lenore J Weitzman, "Affirmative Action Plans for Eliminating Sex Discrimination in Academe," in Rossi, *Academic Women*, p. 486; federal affirmative action regulations prohibit anti-nepotism in hiring practices, except for family supervisors

[222]*Faculty Handbook*, p. 12.

[223]Donald W McNemar, *Annual Report*, p. 3

[224]"Teaching at Andover" is included in the Appendix

[225]Allis, *Youth*, p. 498.

[226]Allis, *Youth*, p. 542.

[227]Lloyd, *Singular*, p. 426.

[228]Thomas R. Pezzullo and Barbara E. Brittingham, *Salary Equity: Detecting Sex Bias in Salaries among College and University Professors* (Lexington, Mass : D C Heath & Co , p. 69)

[229]National Center for Education Statistics, Washington, D C

[230]Memo to Donald W McNemar from Susan Garth Stott, "Male/Female Faculty Comparison Roles and Compensations," November 6, 1984.

[231]*Faculty Handbook*, p. 5.

[232]Memo from Don McNemar to faculty, January 30, 1985

[233]Janice Pottker and Andrew Fishel, "Sex Discrimination as Public Policy: The Case of Maternity Leave Policies for Teachers" p 320 in Pottker and Fishel, *Sex Bias in the Schools*

[234]Allis, *Youth*, p. 498.

[235]Allis, *Youth*, p. 698

[236]"Report of the Ad-Hoc Committee on Faculty Housing," January 3, 1985

[237]"Ad-Hoc "

[238]"Ad-Hoc."

[239]Letter from Kathy Dalton, Mary Mulligan, Frances Taylor, Mary Minard, Susan Lloyd, Tony Rotundo, Maggie Jackson, and Pamela Brown to Skip Eccles, October, 1984.

[240]Housing values compiled from published valuations in *Andover Townsman* by Marion Finbury, August, 1985

[241]Report of the Committee on Organization, June 1971, Peterson, Merger Study

[242]Peterson, Merger Study.

[243]John Richards II, "Report of the Dean of Faculty," *Annual Report*, 1984-85, p. 7

[244]Letter, from Lydia Goetze to the Faculty Advisory Committee, April 6, 1984

[245]Minutes of the Advisory Committee, April 25, 1985, *Andover Gazette*, Vol X, #27, p. 5

[246]Loretta McLaughlin, "Stress, Isolation Called Fatal Risks," *The Boston Globe*, August 30, 1984, p 4; for employment issues faced by other teachers see Dan C Lortie, *Schoolteacher: A Sociological Study* (Chicago: University of Chicago Press, 1977)

[247]Carl N. Degler, "Charlotte Anna Perkins Stetson Gilman," in James, *Notable Women*, Vol. II, pp. 39-42
[248]Safilios-Rothschild, *Sex Role Socialization."*
[249]"Consent decree in Szewiola v Los Angeles Unified School District," in Campbell, *Legal Rights*, Vol. II; also see Campbell, *Legal Rights*, Vol I, p. 5-14; for a discussion of reasons for the lack of female administrators in educational institutions see Tetreault and Schmuck, "Equity," and Charol Shakeshaft, "Strategies for Overcoming the Barriers to Women in Educational Administration," in Klein, *Handbook.*
[250]Safilios-Rothschild, *Sex Role Socialization*, pp. 109-111.
[251]Safilios-Rothschild, *Sex Role Socialization*; Tetreault and Schmuck, "Equity;" Vigderman, "Harvard Men　," p. 46
[252]Sandler, "Quiet Revolution," p. 1

Footnotes to Chapter Seven: COMMUNITY VALUES, THE EDUCATIONAL ENVIRONMENT, AND THE EFFECTS OF THE EQUITY EARTHQUAKE AT ANDOVER TODAY

[253]McLachlan, *Boarding Schools*, offers an extensive analysis of the cultural roots of the idea of teaching social responsibility or concern for others as a central value in independent schools; part of the tradition is Victorian, part is connected with the ideal of a gentleman and "noblesse oblige," part comes out of the Social Gospel of the late nineteenth and early twentieth century; although McLachlan did not trace it, at Andover the "non-sibi" ideal was revived by the reformist idealism of the 1960s
[254]Astin, *College Environment*, p. 135.
[255]Astin, *College Environment*, p. 131, 135.
[256]Stanford Research Institute study quoted in Randall Sullivan, "Death of a Cheerleader," *Rolling Stone*, July 18, August 1, 1985, #452/453, p. 121
[257]Stanford Research Institute.
[258]Jennifer Levin, "When Winning Takes All," *Ms. Magazine*, May 1983, p. 93; Astin, *College Environment*, p. 17
[259]Brown Project, pp. 8-11; Pezzullo, *Salary*
[260]Brown Project, pp. 8-11
[261]Alexander W Astin, "The Undergraduate Woman," in Helen S. Astin and Werner Z. Hirsch, eds., *The Higher Education of Women: Essays in Honor of Rosemary Park* (N Y.: Praeger Publishers, 1978).
[262]Letter from Mary Gilfus to Kathleen M Dalton, July 3, 1985
[263]Bernice Sandler, "Help from our Government," in Rossi, *Academic Women*, pp 440-441
[264]Sheila Rothman, *Woman's Proper Place: A History of Changing Ideals and Practices, 1870 to the Present* (N.Y.: Basic Books, Inc., 1978), p. 264.
[265]See extensive network listings in the Appendix of Myra Pollack Sadker and David Miller Sadker, *Sex Equity Handbook for Schools* (N Y: Longman, 1982).
[266]Chodorow, *Mothering*, pp. 150-151; Robert Stoller, "A Contribution to the Study of Gender Identity," *International Journal of Psychoanalysis*, 45, 1964, pp. 220-226; see a differing view on how society teaches gender identity in Pleck, *Myth*; Pleck does not believe gender identity is "internalized," nor does he accept the Chodorow psychoanalytic framework

Afterword
by Marion Finbury

Obviously no project of this kind is the work of only a few. In order to accomplish this prodigious task our network extended across the campus and beyond.

Because coeducation pervades the lives of Andover's 1200 students and 200 faculty in so many different ways, and because the quality of its coeducation could not be evaluated without some analysis of many of the community's structures, policies, attitudes, traditions, and behaviors, a simple study seemed impossible. The Committee decided that it would be useful to look at coeducation in wide-ranging terms, and therefore divided its complex task into three stages. In the first two stages the committee gathered information: initially through the collection of descriptive material from departments of the school and second, through surveying attitudes and experiences using a student and a faculty questionnaire. In the final stage the data was analyzed and written up.

The information gathering phase of the study required the Coeducation Committee to decide what questions it wanted to ask. After a preliminary open-ended questionnaire to the faculty, the Committee compiled sets of questions. I coordinated the process, refining the questions, and working with appropriate department heads to explore whether the requested information was available. It was necessary to work out individualized methods with each department for data collection. In most cases three target years were studied ('77-78, '79-80, '82-83) and then brought up to present. In some cases paid researchers were brought in to survey records and in other cases staff found time to research the answers to the committee's questions.

Members of the Coeducation Committee concentrated their research on specialized aspects of coeducation. Sue Lloyd gathered statistics from the Admissions Office and served as our historical consultant and editor. David Cobb analyzed information of student residential life such as housing patterns, discipline and leadership. Nat Smith focused on the curriculum, working with the Registrar and Recorder in the Dean of Studies' office, and Jonathan Stableford carefully went through the Athletic Department's files. Tony Rotundo and Kathleen Dalton collected numerical data on the faculty provided by Jane Munroe in the Headmaster's and Dean of Faculty's offices. I gathered information from the College Couseling office, the Office of Academy Resources, and the Business Office.

The committee intended to do a self-study, that is, to conduct all the research, to interpret the data, and to write up the results without outside help. Although the committee included people with expertise in social science, statistics, and data interpretation, the study lacked a sociologist. So Professor Janet Zollinger Giele of Brandeis University was hired as a consultant to the project, along with two graduate assistants, Mary Gilfus and Peter Dunn. In 1984 Dr. Giele helped the committee clarify its goals and was invaluable in constructing a student questionnaire and later the faculty questionnaire that would measure attitudes about coeducation. After the results of the student questionnaire were analyzed on the computer by College Counselor Tim Dempsey, Mary Gilfus and Peter Dunn did further computer work with the data to identify themes and trends. Near the end of the project Janet Giele and Mary Gilfus discussed central findings with us, and they provided useful insights about the meaning of the personality traits and values in the community. Their help was essential to the project.

Our interdisciplinary effort benefited greatly from the help Giele gave us in writing the student questionnaire and posing basic questions about student life. Sociological survey research and computer analysis were used as research tools, rather than as centerpieces of the study. Mary Gilfus' essay explains the data analysis. When Dalton and Rotundo analyzed the survey data, they followed two basic guidelines: first, they took into account the pattern of response and the total number of responses within each sex, and second, they tended to view percentages of male and female responses as significant if at least a 10% difference was evident.

In the second phase of the project new committee members helped us pursue our research further. Henry Wilmer coordinated the writing of the faculty questionnaire, using open meetings and written questionnaires to find out what the faculty wanted to know about itself. Elaine Adams did computer analyses of data on course selection and sex-imbalanced classes (classes in which one sex is greatly outnumbered by the opposite sex). Susan Stott wrote reports on admissions trends, and she interpreted the Brandeis consultants' reports on their multiple regression analyses for us. In addition to coordinating the project, the chairman did a study of faculty attrition rates, student awards and prizes, faculty housing, and other issues, and Nat Smith worked with a graphs sub-committee (Rotundo, Finbury, Dalton, and David Simons) to provide illustrations for the text.

Each committee member received first drafts of the report and the author and chair took every suggestion and criticism to heart and where possible included the changes suggested.

From all across the campus came support from every quarter. Students were indispensable and special assistance was offered by former and current Andover students. In our first year of work, Milisa Galazzi, and Kathryn Baxter (both '84) spearheaded a group of energetic students who took an active role in formulating and pre-testing the student questionnaire. As the year drew to a close, students' support and involvement were central to the success of the ten year anniversary in the spring. Anita Mattedi '84 used her quantitative expertise to transform pounds of computer print-outs to graphs on the faculty questionnaire results and Tim Wright '84 worked on student housing statistics and other studies. Scott Smith '81 analyzed academic data. As a part-time summer job, David Simons '86 translated rough drafted graphs and raw data into intelligible computer graphs, and he worked with the computer graphs subcommittee to decide what information needed to be illustrated with graphs. Dave's technical skill was invaluable to the study, as was his editorial judgment and good humor.

The Coeducation Study had no true home, but hospitality in the form of IBM-PCs were offered by the History Department, Math Department, and the College Counseling office. All the College Counselors, as well as Liz George, Mary Morell, and Gerda Mosca, offered moral support and occasional mechanical advice to the Coeducation Committee Chair and the study's author. Tim Dempsey was invaluable in entering all the data from the student questionnaire onto the computers and giving us pounds of paper to deal with, and Lew Robbins served as the patron saint of computer advice and re-education.

Each department approached gave us full cooperation. From Joy Lauder, who put all the admission statistics together for us with help and support from Meredith Price, to the Headmaster's and Deans' offices, people fit into their already busy schedules our requests for the retrieval of information. Jane Munroe in particular deserves our special appreciation, for she put up with an endless stream of questions and requests and she was so well organized that she invariably had the answers or knew where to get them.

Phyllis Powell turned over her extensive CWIS and WEBS files, and she assisted us in gathering information about gender issues *and* the history of coeducation at Andover. Priscilla Bonney-Smith provided information, assistance in research, and editorial advice. An informal but tremendously useful clipping service (Britta McNemar, Peter Gilbert, Tom Lyons, Mary Minard, Margaret Rotundo and others) provided us with references and articles. Members of the Class of '75 and female *Phillipian* staff members from the Class of '85 and '86 helped us understand the human dimension of coeducation by telling us their stories. School archivist Ruth Quattlebaum knew her history and the available documents so well that she always produced the needed manuscripts from the soggy basement of Oliver Wendell Holmes library. Lynne Robbins, Rachel Penner, and other librarians helped us graciously regardless of hours or vacation schedules. One of the moving spirits behind the founding of the Day Care Center, Jennie Cline, acted as a statistics researcher, and compiled data on college counseling and the infirmary and the extra-curricular involvement of students. Registrar Herb Morton provided some of the most crucial data on course enrollments, test scores and grades out of his records, and the Recorder Joan Schlott patiently plotted the course selections of students over a period of time as well as compiling data on cum laude and AP results.

In addition to editing done by committee members, we asked a variety of people to help us reassure ourselves that our chapters were accurate. Paul Kalkstein and Kathy Henderson read and commented on the athletic chapter, Joe Wennik saved us from one crucial historical mistake, and Jack Richards reviewed the faculty chapter. Trustees Charles Meyer and Stephen Burbank also improved our accuracy on admissions and financial aid data. Doug Crabtree, Natalie Schorr, Jean St. Pierre, Meredith Price, Tom Lyons, Carroll Bailey, Leslie Ballard, Susan Clark, Frank Eccles, Ann Harper, Maggie Jackson, Jonathan Marlowe, Connie LeMaitre, Mary Mulligan, and Francis Taylor also offered much appreciated help to the committee. Derek Williams went out of his way to provide needed support and assistance to committee members. Frederick A. Peterson, former director of the Office of Research and Evaluation, helped us retrieve his files for comparative use.

The Coeducation Study would have been impossible without the skillful people who translated chicken-scratches into text on the word processor: Elizabeth Thompson, Gerda Mosca, Liz George, Becky Egert, Mary Ann Arvai, Cara Mileti, Rhoda Zussman, Dorit Sandorfi, Betty Steinert, and Kathy Lyons. Brenda Lepere must be given special thanks, not only for her expertise and time, but for her unfailing patience and calm particularly near the end of the report which coincided with the opening of school. Her typing and editorial skill made it possible for us to finish the project. Terry Kuhlmann came to the rescue as the deadline for submitting the draft neared, offering copyediting and even emergency word processing help. The author's mother-in-law, Barbara Rotundo, took time out of her busy university teaching schedule to copyedit the text carefully, and her generous gift of her expertise and judgement, added to the revision done by Terry Kuhlmann, greatly improved the study. Director of Publications Ann Parks designed the lay-out of the book.

Educational researchers helped Kathy Dalton as she wrote this study by sharing their work and their insights. In addition to the crucial help of Janet Giele, Mary Gilfus and Peter Dunn, she received assistance from Martha Hennessey, Barbara Finkelstein, Susan Basow, Mary Kay Tetreault, and Roberta Hall. Ted Byers of Cambridge Reports consulted with her on interpreting survey analysis, and Judy Taylor, Roberta Hall,

180

Ralph Neas, John Bachman, Tom Lyons, and Nancy Duff Campbell aided her research on legal sex equity.

We have saved the best for last. Our thanks go to the members of the committee who always did what they could but who never wavered in their support. They investigated, poked, organized, reported, read, edited and criticized. But without the active support and involvement of Donald McNemar and Jeanne Amster, this project would not have flourished. They not only gave us support and wise counsel but the freedom to investigate without limit in order to draw our own conclusions. Without this kind of encouragement from our top administrators, there could have been no substantive work accomplished.

To Kathy Dalton goes our most heartfelt gratitude. What originally may have been seen as a simple report two years ago has grown into an impressive scholarly document. This was due to her own high standards of research and scholarship. To her and her husband Tony Rotundo who gave her the support and encouragement necessary to accomplish this monumental task, our most profound thanks. The fact that they allowed this project to encroach on their sabbatical year is testimony to their interest in and dedication to the project.

Thanks also go to the Abbot Academy Association whose grant enabled us to bring speakers and create a memorable celebration on the tenth anniversary of the co-ed school. They continued their much needed support the following year by subsidizing the cost of the faculty questionnaire; references to their vital support for coeducational programs and creative ideas are scattered through the text.

Of course, the most important people in this project have been the donors. Not only did they come up with the original idea and good money, but as the project flourished and grew, they continued to increase their financial support to meet our burgeoning needs. They also offered invaluable personal support for the investigation and report, and were constantly challenging us to grapple honestly and openly with the important issue at Andover of educating boys and girls together. We have tried to do that.

A Rationale for Research on Coeducation
by Janet Zollinger Giele
Heller School
Brandeis University

In the fall of 1983 I learned of the coeducation study at Phillips Academy when Marion Finbury asked whether I would serve as a consultant. Conversations with Marion and the Coeducation Committee occurred over the next several months. I heard a variety of concerns about how to measure the success of coeducation at Andover. In the spring of 1984 with Mary Gilfus, I helped Marion Finbury to draft the student question- naire that would provide one of the major sources of information for the study.

A year later in the spring of 1985 Marion Finbury and Kathy Dalton called me again to help in the interpretation of results. Mary Gilfus and Peter Dunn, both from the doctoral program at the Heller School, agreed to serve as research assistants. Together we gave technical advice on how to interpret data from the student survey. This appendix de- scribes the general rationale that I followed during formulation of the student questionnaire and in giving subsequent advice about analysis of the data.

The questions that the Ten Year Coeducation Committee posed about the effects of coeducation were myriad: How does the male/female ratio in the faculty affect the education of boys and girls? How does the larger number of boys in the student body affect both sexes? Why are there so many more males in advanced math and science classes and so many more females in advanced language classes? How does the gender of a coach or a player affect interactions on the playing field, or the gender of a house counselor or student affect interpersonal relations in the dormitory?

Clearly the number of possible questions that one could ask of coedu- cation is enormous. A theoretical and methodological framework was needed to give direction and a set of priorities to the survey. As a consul- tant I listened closely to the concerns that were raised and suggested which survey items might lead to the most useful results.

As the Ten Year Coeducation Committee explored the issues involved, and as Kathy Dalton turned the data into a synthetic analysis of coeducation at Andover, I particularly focused on two critical research problems: finding what effect the values and educational environment had on male and female students, and finding what factors in the educational environment encouraged high self-concept. My previous research led me to believe that the optimum environment for learning was one that reinforced all of a student's capacities, some of which might be thought of as more stereotypically masculine (analysis, independence, mastery, competitiveness), and others of which are often characterized as feminine (intuition, interdependence, caring for others, cooperation).[1]

Over the course of my research on changing gender roles, I had developed a theory of gender equality as the result of *crossover*, that is, the potential for both male and female to develop psychological and social capacities that are thought to be characteristic of the other sex. Historically, society has become more complex and roles more specialized in ways that do not necessarily coincide with gender roles. Women must now undertake many roles in the workplace that in an earlier day would have been open only to men. In parenting and family roles, on the other hand, men are expected to do more of what was once called "women's work." Therefore the socialization of future adult men and women must prepare them to combine independence and analysis with caring and feeling.[2] Educational institutions need to consider how to help males and females meet this new developmental challenge. Institutional change is likely to require two types of effort: support for girls who wish to enjoy the same opportunities for individual achievement as boys and support for boys in giving care for others and being attentive to their needs.

The history of feminism itself reveals two different visions of how to attain equality that correspond to these two patterns of educational and developmental change. The first type which I call *universalistic feminism* asks that women be given the same rights and privileges as men. A century ago, pioneers of the women's movement asked for women to be able to enter colleges, medical schools, law schools, to vote, and to serve in public office. Contemporary feminists have asked for coeducation, equal admissions ratios, equal support for women's athletics, and the end of discrimination in pay and promotions. Inclusion and equal access have been the prime goals of universalistic feminism.

A second vision of how to achieve equality between the sexes, which I term *particularistic feminism*, expresses a realization that women and men are usually somewhat different in their tendencies and that the world needs to value more highly that which is distinctively feminine. Nineteenth century women expressed this second type of feminism by reference to the caring qualities of mothers and to the humanistic values of the home. Temperance women, settlement house workers, nurses, and the women's clubs saw it as their duty to raise the standard of public morality, protect the home, clean up the cities, and care for the downtrodden.[3] Contemporary explorations of feminine psychology by Jean

Baker Miller and Carol Gilligan also emphasize the gentle and caring qualities of women.[4] Women more than men take others' feelings into account and try to work out solutions to human problems where everyone wins and no one loses.

While the Ten Year Coeducation Committee put greater emphasis on the universal concern for equal access and inclusion of girls, I urged them to explore gender differences as well as similarities that are at the heart of educational experience. The fact that two types of feminism, one claiming equality and the other claiming difference, existed in the historical as well as the contemporary women's movement suggests that both strategies are necessary to achieve full equality between the sexes.[5] Just as women deserve the same rights and opportunities as men, so men should be able to accept and value in themselves some of the qualities that are associated with women. This is the general set of assumptions that I brought to the coeducation study at Phillips Andover during the initial stage of formulating the questionnaire and again as our Brandeis team advised Kathy Dalton about the analysis and interpretation of portions of the student survey data.

The most direct effect of my two-pronged theory of gender equality was on the choice of items for the self-rating scale by which students described themselves. On a twelve-item scale we placed four "masculine" traits that psychologist Sandra L. Bem found were most often chosen by males, four "feminine" traits most often chosen by females, and four "mixed" traits equally chosen by students of both sexes.[6] Inclusion of this rating scale would later make possible a description of the student population at Andover and enable us to look for links between a student's self-description and that student's gender, attitudes, academic, athletic, and dorm experience, and overall self-confidence.

In looking for connections between educational experience and individual traits we were following a time-worn paradigm in the social sciences that has repeatedly shown how culture and environment can shape personality.[7] Other investigations have shown how experience in a given political or economic system can leave measurable effects on individual outlook. In addition, the socialization experience in family or school can shape self-concept and self-esteem. Satisfaction and self-confidence in turn affect later occupational choices and general adaptation to life.[8] We were expecting that there would be some noticeable effects of coeducation at Andover on the personalities of its students, but we did not know what those effects would be. All we could do at that point was to put elements into the questionnaire that would describe the most relevant aspects of the setting for the shaping of the student's self.

The questionnaire elicits two types of perspective from the students. The first type concerns various aspects of the school—dorm life, extracurricular activities, athletics, social and academic life as the student sees them. The second perspective comes from each student's description of the self. How many hours a week does a particular person give to extracurricular activities? How satisfied, how successful are they? How do they rate themselves according to such traits as being friendly, sympathetic, or competitive?

Such a rich mix of questions obviously lends itself to a search for innumerable connections between students' perceptions of their surroundings and their evaluations of themselves. Some of the findings are interesting just for their *descriptive* value—whether they perceive differences between their male and female teachers, or the fact that males and females evaluate the workload differently.

The real pay off in this student questionnaire, however, was in what social scientists strive to attain—some *explanatory* insight into the connections between educational experience and the nature of the self. The data yielded significant differences among groups that suggested that students who were the ideal "Andover type," competitive, assertive, and independent, were also more likely to be male. This finding demonstrated the culture-and-personality hypothesis that in an Andover culture more heavily weighted toward "male" traits, those males and females with such traits would feel more successful and satisfied because of their congruence with the culture. When our Brandeis team discovered this connection in the data, we felt close to understanding some of the major effects of a coeducational environment on students of each gender.

On the other hand, the finding, despite its importance, was complex and ambiguous. A subtheme of the study is that Type I students represent only about a third of the student body and another two-thirds are the Type II cooperative and sympathetic students with "female" traits and the Mixed type who tend toward neither male nor female pole. We would expect that these Type II and Mixed Type students might suffer low self-esteem simply as a result of not being the classic "Andover type." It turns out, however, that a sizeable sub-group of the Type II and Mixed Type are able to look upon themselves with approval, especially those who have been successful in friendship and service to others. This finding suggests a variation on the culture-and-personality hypothesis. These students who feel satisfaction must be gaining a degree of support and affirmation from the school culture that provides them reinforcement for being acceptable alternative versions of the Andover type. Indeed there is evidence that many of those who feel success in friendship and service to others already do look upon themselves with as much approval and self-confidence as the Type I "ideal Andover" students. This discovery is reassuring for it suggests there is room for several types of students to flourish at Andover, even though the present school culture is still slightly in favor of the independent achiever rather than the friendly student who gains satisfaction from helping others.

To me, however, the most gratifying result of this study is the support that it gives to a crossover theory of sex equality and to a dual strategy for improving the status of female students, faculty, and staff. I find it tremendously reassuring that Phillips Academy has a spread of personality types among its student body, that they are not greatly skewed in the direction of any one type but together represent "male," "female," and "mixed" traits about equally. Moreover, not all the boys exhibit pure "male" trait profiles, nor all girls pure "female" trait profiles. Instead there is healthy evidence that some Andover girls can characterize themselves as assertive and independent and that some Andover boys describe themselves as sympathetic and understanding.

These findings support a dual strategy for realizing sex equality and further improvement in the status of girls and women. One avenue is clearly to continue support and encouragement for girls who follow a more masculine pattern and describe themselves in terms of the Type I traits. But another strategy is to provide extra support and validation for the interdependence, sympathy, sensitivity, and mutual support—the *non sibi* tradition—found in Type II girls and boys, which Kathy Dalton correctly pointed out in chapters five and seven is one avenue for supporting students' affiliative needs. Students of both sexes who exhibit the "mixed" traits of friendliness, and adaptiveness are also deserving of reinforcement and encouragement.

Ultimately, in my view, the fully human adult of either sex combines the best qualities associated with both males and females. Conscious educational policies can help to assure that such persons will emerge, if not themselves exhibiting the whole spectrum of desirable traits, at least respectful of those who represent some other part of it.

Other questions have still to be answered that were outside the boundaries of the P.A. self-study on coeducation; the most elusive of these has to do with the impact of the culture outside the Academy. How much can any one school such as Phillips Andover accomplish in reinforcing a desirable combination of independence and sympathy compared with what a student has already learned at home and through prior experience?[9] How much can conscious educational policy reinforce and raise the status and visibility of women in the faculty compared with the effects of prior socialization, market forces, family obligations, and other factors that are beyond the reach of the school? These questions will continue to provide a challenge to all researchers on coeducation, not just in this historic academy, but also in primary and secondary schools, colleges, and universities for many years to come.

NOTES

[1]Janet Zollinger Giele, "Education for the Future," in *Women and the Future: Changing Sex Roles in Modern America* (New York: Free Press, 1978).

[2]The concept of crossover helps to explain a number of recent changes in both age and sex roles. See Giele, "Crossovers: New Themes in Adult Roles and the Life Cycle," in D.G. McGuigan (Ed.), *Women's Lives: New Theory, Research, and Policy* (Ann Arbor, MI: University of Michigan, Center for Continuing Education of Women, 1980); Giele, "Adulthood as Transcendence of Age and Sex," in N.J. Smelser and E.H. Erikson (Eds.), *Themes of Work and Love in Adulthood* (Cambridge, MA: Harvard University Press, 1980); "Women's Work and Family Roles," in J.Z. Giele (Ed.) *Women in the Middle Years* (New York: Wiley, 1982).

[3]I first distinguished these two types of feminism in my doctoral dissertation. See Giele, *Social Change in the Feminine Role: A Comparison of the Woman's Suffrage and Woman's Temperance Movements, 1870-1920* (Harvard University, unpublished Ph D dissertation, 1961) A similar distinction in types of feminism is made by Aileen S Kraditor in the comparison of suffrage arguments based on natural rights and expediency; see Kraditor, *Ideas of the Woman Suffrage Movement, 1890-1920* (NY: Columbia University Press, 1965)

[4]Jean Baker Miller, *Toward a New Psychology of Women* (Boston: Beacon Press, 1976); Carol Gilligan, *In A Different Voice* (Cambridge, MA: Harvard University Press, 1982)

[5]These two types of feminist strategy are evident in contemporary efforts to achieve sex equality in education, employment, and the family; see Giele, *Women and the Future.*

[6]Sandra L. Bem, "The Measurement of Psychological Androgyny," *Journal of Consulting and Clinical Psychology*, Vol 42 (1974): 155-162 See also "Probing the Promise of Androgyny" in A.G. Kaplan and J.P. Bean (Eds), *Beyond Sex-Role Stereotypes: Readings Toward a Psychology of Androgyny* (Boston: Little, Brown, 1976)

[7]See for example, Alex Inkeles and Daniel J Levinson, "National Character: The Study of Modal Personality and Sociocultural Systems," in G Lindzey (Ed), *The Handbook of Social Psychology* (Reading, MA: Addison-Wesley, 1954); Raymond A Bauer, Alex Inkeles, and Clyde Kluckhohn, *How the Soviet System Works* (Cambridge, MA: Harvard University Press, 1956); Fred Weinstein and Gerald M. Platt, *The Wish To Be Free* (Berkeley, CA: University of California Press, 1969); Alex Inkeles and David Smith, *Becoming Modern: Individual Change in Six Developing Countries* (Cambridge, MA: Harvard University Press, 1974); M L Kohn and C. Schooler, "Job Conditions and Personality: A Longitudinal Assessment of Reciprocal Effects," *American Journal of Sociology*, vol. 87 (1982): 1257-1286.

[8]For a review of the research on the self as a product of the interaction between society and personality, see Morris Rosenberg, "The Self-Concept: Social Product and Social Force," in M. Rosenberg and R H. Turner (Eds), *Social Psychology* (New York: Basic Books, 1981).

[9]I have dealt with the question of prior and outside influence by comparing the adult attainments of women alumnae who graduated from three different colleges between 1934 and 1979 It turns out that family background and mother's role pattern are perhaps as important as educational setting in shaping women's adult life patterns. See Giele, "Coeducation or Women's Education: New Findings on a Perennial Question," in C. Lasser (Ed.), *Coeducation: Past, Present, and Future* (Urbana, IL: University of Illinois Press, 1986)

A Brief Profile of Boys and Girls at Andover
by Kathleen M. Dalton

Because our focus in this study was gender issues, we did not explore in depth other historical and sociological questions such as race, class, or ethnicity at Andover. We examined racial and ethnic cross-tabs of our data to see if different groups had notably different attitudes, and some of the differences have been noted throughout the study.

A few other findings are worth recording here. Andover students enter the school at every grade level from 9 through 12, but there are more 11th and 12th graders on campus than there are 9th and 10th graders.

Andover students come from all over the world, but they are more likely to come from the Northeast U.S. than the South or West. They are most likely to be White or Asian, but about 8 to 10% are Black or Hispanic. They are more likely to be Protestant than Catholic, more likely to be Catholic than Jewish, and they are more likely to be Jewish than the average American. Very little difference in race, religion, geographic origins, or ethnicity existed between the male and female students who answered our student questionnaires except that females had a higher response rate than males, although not enough to skew the results.

No data on Andover students' class backgrounds or economic standing was collected, but we did collect information on their parents' occupations. A brief comparison of our results with nationwide statistics suggests that a smaller proportion of Andover students' fathers are policemen, factory workers, blue collar workers, or unemployed than the average American. A significant portion of P.A. parents work in middle and working class occupations, however. The graph on parents' occupations also shows that a significant segment of Andover parents work in the field of education. P.A. students are more likely than the average teenager to have fathers who are lawyers, doctors, businessmen, managers, or college level educators than the average American teenager, and they are more likely than the average to have a mother who is self-employed or who works in the fields of social science, social work, mental health, or arts.

The contrast in mothers' and fathers' occupations is worth noting, especially because some differences follow the same subject-preference patterns evident in student course selection (arts pursued more often by females, math and engineering by males). One hypothesis we tested in our research was that girls would be more likely to define themselves as strong in math and science if either of their parents worked in math or science related fields. When Mary Gilfus and Peter Dunn tested that hypothesis they found no relationship between parents' occupation and female students' attitudes toward math and science. Instead, gender itself seemed to be the main factor influencing how weak or strong students rated themselves in math or science. However, parental encouragement seems to be one of the central factors in female students' willingness to pursue fields that were formerly defined as male subjects.

Parents' Occupation

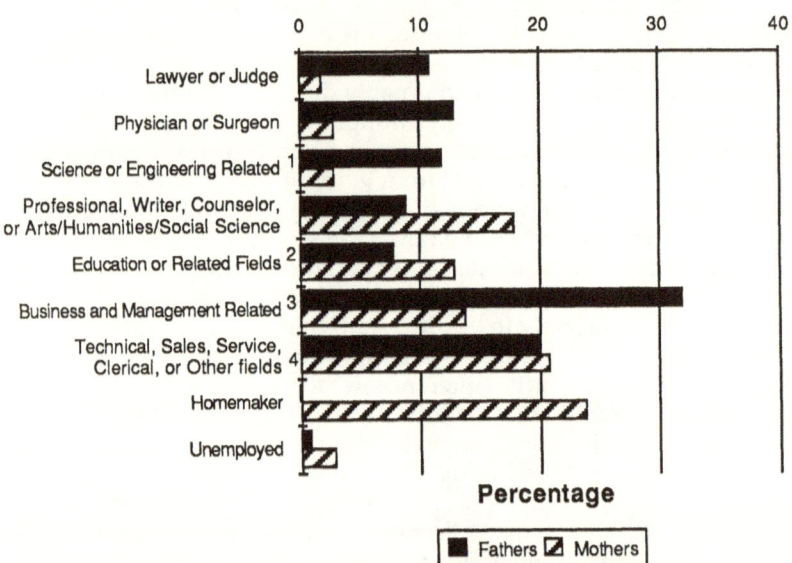

Percentage

■ Fathers ⊿ Mothers

1 Biological scientist, aerospace, chemical, civil, electrical, environmental, sanitary engineer, computer programmer, mathematician, physicist
2 Teacher, administrator in school or university, education specialist
3 Finance, manufacturing, banking, public relations, accountant, owner, manager, government, foreign service, politics
4 Technical fields, therapist, construction, carpenter, electrician, factory worker, skilled and unskilled work, clerical, salesperson, service, law enforcement, firefighter, military, other not classified elsewhere.

Ethnic/Racial/Gender Composition of Students Answering Questionnaire

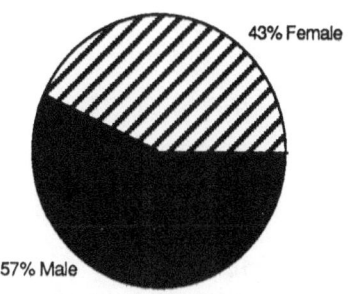

43% Female

57% Male

Students Answering Questionnaire

(Compared to 42% Female, 58% Male Student Body)

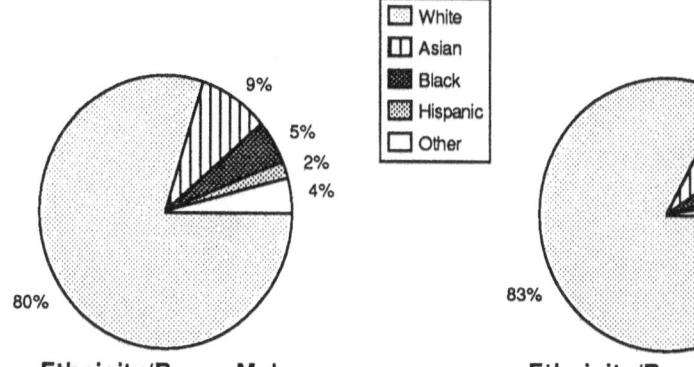

White	
Asian	
Black	
Hispanic	
Other	

9%
5%
2%
4%
80%

Ethnicity/Race: Male

8%
5%
2%
2%
83%

Ethnicity/Race: Female

Regional Composition of Respondents

SQ#46. In what GEOGRAPHIC REGION is your home located?

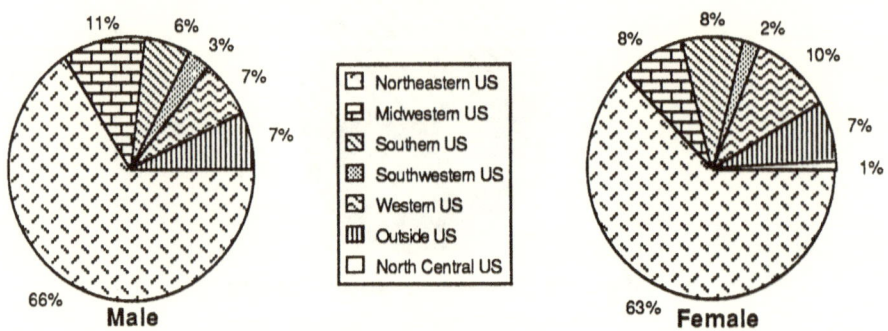

Legend:
- Northeastern US
- Midwestern US
- Southern US
- Southwestern US
- Western US
- Outside US
- North Central US

Male: 66%, 11%, 6%, 3%, 7%, 7%

Female: 63%, 8%, 8%, 2%, 10%, 7%, 1%

Religious Affiliation

SQ#42A. What is your religious affiliation?

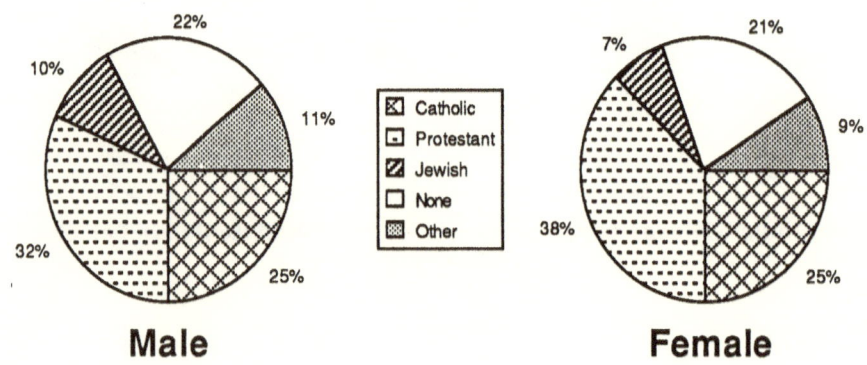

Legend:
- Catholic
- Protestant
- Jewish
- None
- Other

Male: 22%, 10%, 11%, 32%, 25%

Female: 21%, 7%, 9%, 38%, 25%

Phillips Academy Student Survey:
Research Methodology and Summary of Findings
by Mary Gilfus

Some readers will be interested in the methods we used to design, administer and analyze the student survey questionnaire. This report addresses those issues and presents a detailed summary of our findings.

In the spring of 1984 Marion Finbury, chair of the Ten Year Coeducation Committee, met with Dr. Janet Giele, Associate Professor of Sociology at Brandeis University, and me, a doctoral student at the Florence Heller School at Brandeis University. Over the course of several meetings we discussed what dimensions of student life were related to coeducation and drafted the student questionnaire.

Questionnaire Design & Data Collection

We designed the student questionnaire to elicit students' perceptions of themselves and their personal success at Phillips Academy as well as their experiences in the areas of social life, athletics, dormitory life, extra-curricular activities and the classroom.

The questionnaire, which is available from Marion Finbury on request, is an 18-page booklet consisting of 50 sections of closed-choice questions with three open-ended essay questions. This format was selected to allow easy transfer of the data onto computer tapes and to insure easy completion in less than one hour by all students.

We pre-tested the questionnaire with a group of approximately 20 students representing a cross-section of the classes, sexes and racial and ethnic groups in the student population. The pre-test revealed that, with minor revisions, the questionnaire was easily administered and clearly designed to elicit valid responses.

The questionnaire was administered to the entire student body in May, 1984. Students who reside on campus were administered the survey in their dormitories by House Counselors while day students received the questionnaire in their mail boxes. A total of 869 useable questionnaires were returned from a total population of 1200 students, representing a 72% response rate. The student body was composed of 956 boarding students who returned 766 questionnaires at a response rate of 80%. The day student population of 253 students returned 99 questionnaires, which represents a response rate of 39%. The very low rate of returned questionnaires among day students should be kept in mind since this biases all findings toward over-representation of residential students. Those day students who did not respond to the survey may reflect very different perceptions and experiences, thus our findings cannot be generalized to that portion of the student body.

All returned questionnaires were coded and keypunched onto magnetic tape for computer analysis. Preliminary frequencies and percentages of responses on certain questions were computed by Tim Dempsey at Phillips Academy and reported throughout the main body of the report. Scale construction, cross-tabulations, correlations and regression analyses were conducted at Brandeis University by Mary Gilfus and Peter Dunn.

Scales Constructed for Data Analysis

While the majority of findings reported here are straight forward tabulations of student responses to individual questionnaire items, two scales were constructed from multiple questionnaire responses.

Self Concept. The self concept scale is a Likert scale, which is a cumulative scale composed of several questions in which respondents are asked to rank their responses along a 5-point continuum ranging from strongly agree to strongly disagree.

The six questionnaire items which are included in the self-concept scale asked students to rate themselves on a continuum from (1) very positive to (5) very negative on the following dimensions: physical appearance, intelligence, confidence, popularity, health and happiness. Each respondent's scores were summed, resulting in a total self concept score.

The lowest possible self concept score is 30 (six responses in the "very negative" category) while the highest possible score is 6 (six "very positive" responses). The mean self concept score for the entire sample is 13. For cross-tabulation tables, students scoring below the mean are grouped in the "High Self Concept" category, students at the mean are grouped "Average Self Concept" and students scoring above the mean are grouped in the "Low Self Concept" category.

Personality Type. Here we were interested in what personality traits students felt are most characteristic of themselves. The questions used in this scale are derived from the Bem sex-role inventory.[1] Again, using a 5-point Likert rating system, students were asked to rate a series of personality characteristics on a continuum from (1) very characteristic to (5) very uncharacteristic of themselves.

These responses were grouped conceptually into two distinct personality trait clusters. Type I represents the more independent and competitive personality traits while Type II represents the more affiliative, relationship-oriented personality traits. Each student received a separate score on Type I personality traits and on Type II traits.

Type I scores are the sum of individual responses to questions of how characteristic are the following traits: assertiveness, competitiveness, independence, and willingness to take risks. The highest possible score is 4 (four responses of "very characteristic), and the lowest possible score is 20 (four responses of "very uncharacteristic"). For the entire sample, the mean Type I score was 8.71.

Type II scores are the sum of individual responses on the following personality traits: gentleness, sensitivity to the needs of others, sympathy, and understanding. The scoring method is exactly the same as in the Type I scale. The sample mean for the Type II scale is 8.33.

For statistical analyses using correlations and multiple regression, each sub-scale raw score was analyzed independently.

For cross-tabulations, each student was scaled on a ratio of Type I over Type II scores, then grouped according to whether their Type I traits dominate, the Type II traits dominate, or whether they are equally balanced ("Mixed Type").

Data Analysis & Findings

1. *Cross-tabulations.*

The first stage of data analysis consisted of generating cross-tabulation tables which compare male and female students on their perceptions of several dimensions of student life.

Cross-tabulation tables are designed to reveal statistically significant differences between the groups being compared (males and females) by use of the Chi Square statistic and probability tables. A statistically significant difference between groups means that there is less than 5% probability that our findings could have occurred simply by chance.

Tables 1-14 summarize our significant findings. These tables are highly condensed summaries of more complex tables. The Chi Square statistic and degrees of freedom for each table have been omitted, leaving only the probability level and percentage rates of responses. Percentages will not sum to 100% because these are selected highlights from larger tables.

The most striking feature of these findings is that male and female students have expressed very different perceptions of their experiences at Phillips Academy. However, these differences do not lead us to simplistic conclusions about the coeducational experience at P.A.

Female students reported consistently more satisfaction with nearly every aspect of student life at P.A. than male students. The only area where girls are more dissatisfied than boys is in the academic workload. Yet in spite of their satisfaction with P.A., girls find more sexism apparent in the school environment (see Table 1).

Boys outnumber girls in student leadership positions in all areas except the arts (Table 2). Girls overwhelmingly view this as an imbalance, while boys apparently do not (Table 3). Boys more readily rate female leaders as ineffective, while girls rate both sexes about the same in leadership effectiveness.

In the classroom (Table 4), boys see themselves as contributing more to discussions and challenging teachers more while they see their female peers as more silent. On the other hand, girls consider themselves more careful observers and feel that boys have a need to speak on every point. Both sexes agree that boys are more disruptive in the classroom.

When asked how they feel in classes where their sex is in the minority (Table 5), boys tend to feel more comfortable and less inhibited to speak. Neither sex feels ignored or pressured to work harder for a good grade in gender-imbalanced classes.

Male and female students tend to agree that they find male teachers more intimidating and challenging than female teachers (Table 6). Girls are more likely to feel that both male and female teachers show favoritism toward girls but also feel that both male and female teachers call on boys more frequently in class. Both sexes agree that male teachers use more sex stereotypes in class, but girls observe this significantly more than do boys.

Academically, girls feel that their strongest subjects are English and languages and that their weakest subjects are math and science (Table 7), while boys express exactly the opposite academic strengths and weaknesses. Students who are strong in math and science have the highest educational objectives and, not surprisingly, those are more often male students (Tables 8 and 14).

In the other life goals, males place a stronger emphasis on marriage and children while girls place a higher importance on career and self-realization (Table 8).

Although girls expressed greater satisfaction with student life, they consistently rated themselves lower than boys in their personal success at P.A. Boys feel much more successful in athletics, grades, leadership and getting into the right college. The only area where girls feel they excel is in friendships (Table 9).

Girls also rated themselves less favorably on every item in the self concept scale and displayed significantly lower overall self concept scores (Table 10).

In Table 11, both sexes are well-represented among the Type I, Mixed Type, and Type II personality groupings. Yet boys are more likely to see themselves as predominantly Type I (independent, competitive) while girls are more likely to see themselves as predominantly Type II (affiliative and relationship-oriented).

For both sexes, high self concept is more strongly associated with a Type I personality, but this is much more significant for female students (Table 12). It is of interest that for boys a Mixed Type or a Type II personality has little relationship to self concept but for girls these personality types are much more likely to be associated with low self concept.

Finally, high self concept for both sexes is strongly associated with high educational objectives (Table 13). Not surprisingly, the more positively a student feels about him/herself, the higher his or her aspirations will be.

2. *Correlations.*

Correlation matrices were generated in order to determine the degree of association between pairs of variables. The table on correlations included in chapter seven shows the relationship among a select set of variables based on correlation analysis. The number accompanying each arrow represents the Pearson correlation coefficient for that pair of variables and gives the reader a sense of how strong the relationship is. The higher the coefficient, the stronger the relationship between variables. It should be noted that no direction of causation can be inferred from correlation analysis.

In the table on significantly correlated variables in chapter seven we have focused on the correlates of high self concept and Type I and Type II personality traits. We find that a Type I personality is more strongly associated with high self concept than is a Type II personality. Success with athletics, leadership, grades and getting into the right college are strongly related to both the Type I personality and high self concept. Success with friendships and success in service to others correlate highly with the Type II personality and also are associated with high self concept.

3. *Multiple Regression Analysis.*

We were interested in exploring what factors contribute most to high self-concept among the students surveyed. Are male students with Type I personalities the most likely to score high in self concept or are there other, more subtle, attributes which describe those students who achieve a positive sense of themselves?

Multiple regression analysis is a technique by which we were able to test more precisely which variables contribute to increased self concept. We used a step-wise regression method, which allowed us to explore different combinations of variables and select out the most powerful.

In our first regression equation we tested the more simplistic model, hypothesizing that sex of student, personality type, educational objectives and strength in math and science would predict high self concept. This, however, proved to be too simplistic. Sex of student and Type I and Type II personalities all contributed significant increases in self concept, while educational objectives and strength in math and science made no significant difference. Only 26% of the variance in self concept was explained by this model, thus suggesting that we had not discovered the most powerful combination of variables associated with self concept.

In our second model we retained the same set of variables used in the first model and added all of the personal success variables (success with friendships, athletics, grades, knowledge gained, leadership, creativity, service to others, and getting into the right college). Again using the step-wise method, only the most powerful explanatory variables were selected for the final equation.

This model was much more powerful, explaining 45% of the variance in self concept. The configuration of variables which contributed significantly to this variance were: Type I personality, success with friendships, success with athletics, success in service to others, sex of the student, success with teachers' approval and success with personal growth.

A Type I personality is still the best predictor of high self concept and male students are still more likely to score high in self concept, but a more complex picture emerges. Even though the Type II personality disappeared from this equation, a set of variables highly correlated with Type II personality figures strongly in the equation.

We seem to have two alternative, perhaps competing, routes by which students achieve a positive self concept. One route would be that of the Type I personality who is competitive, independent, and risk-taking— more likely a male who is also successful in athletics. The alternative route may be taken by the more affiliative Type II personality who achieves through interpersonal successes with friendships, service to others, teachers' approval, and personal growth. This hypothesis warrants future testing through the use of more sophisticated multivariate techniques, such as factor analysis.

Summary

Our cross-tabulation analyses reveal that boys and girls at Phillips Academy have significantly different perceptions of most aspects of the school environment and also differ significantly in their feelings about themselves. Boys and girls find personal success in different activities, boys rate themselves higher in overall self concept, and girls tend more toward Type II personalities while boys tend more toward Type I personalities.

Our findings suggest that there may be a somewhat better fit between the Type I personality and the school environment, but that this is not the whole picture.

Our findings suggest that certain configurations of personality characteristics and values, more so than sex of the student, determine success and satisfaction at Phillips Academy. The configuration of values and personal attributes which has traditionally been associated with male sex-role behavior, the Type I personality, may still be the most direct route to success in the school environment. But the Type II personality, which values interpersonal relationships over competition, has definitely found avenues toward success within the same environment.

Just as sex-role stereotypes are breaking down in the wider social environment, the boys and girls at Phillips Academy are exhibiting a greater fluidity and flexibility of sex-role behaviors. We have shown that both male and female students are spread fairly evenly among the three personality categories which were devised to measure sex-role stereotyping. We have also shown that the students with less traditional configurations of values and attributes can achieve success in the school environment. This speaks highly of the school environment as it addresses the needs and strengths of a diverse student body.

NOTES

[1]Bem, Sandra L. "Probing the Promise of Androgyny" in *Beyond Sex-Role Stereotypes*, edited by A.G Kaplan & J.P. Bean Boston: Little, Brown & Company. 1976 (46-62)

TABLE 1: SATISFACTION WITH STUDENT LIFE

Category	Rating	% Male	% Female	Significance*
Overall Satisfaction:	satisfied	81.8	86.8	p<.05
Functions:	satisfied	25.4	29.0	p<.05
Friendships:	satisfied	52.0	63 5	p<.05
Rules:	satisfied	26.3	31.0	p<.05
Work program:	satisfied	35.8	41.4	p<.05
Academic Workload	dissatisfied	63.1	75.9	p<.05
Relations between the sexes:	sexist	15.2	27.9	p<.05
	egalitarian	52.2	48.2	
	no opinion	32.6	23.8	

TABLE 2: NUMBER OF OFFICES HELD IN STUDENT ORGANIZATIONS

Category	Rating	% Male	% Female	Significance*
Government	1 or more	13.3	10.6	p<.05
Service	1 or more	25.1	23.2	n.s.
Publications	1 or more	17.6	8.5	p<.05
Clubs	1 or more	29.4	19.4	p<.05
Arts	1 or more	10.3	12.2	n.s.

* Differences are statistically significant when probability (p) is less than .05. No significant difference is indicated by n.s. (not significant).
Note: Tables are summaries of larger tables and therefore totals will not sum to 100%

TABLE 3: STUDENT RATINGS OF STUDENT LEADERS

Category	Rating	% Male	% Female	Significance*
a) Effectiveness				
male leaders	high	29.7	20.2	p<.05
	low	11.3	5.2	p<.05
female leaders	high	13.3	24.7	p<.05
	low	27.0	5.7	p<.05
b) Number of leaders				
male	too many	29.3	58.6	p<.05
female	too many	7.1	0.8	p<.05

TABLE 4: RATINGS OF GENERAL DIFFERENCES IN THE CLASSROOM

Category	% Male	% Female	Significance*
Boys contribute more to discussions	32.8	17.7	p<.05
Girls are more careful observers	25.7	41.6	p<.05
Boys challenge teachers more	56.1	48.9	p<.05
Girls are more silent	31.5	18.5	p<.05
Boys have a need to speak on every point	27.9	33.0	p<.05
Boys are more disruptive	60.2	58.3	n.s.

* Differences are statistically significant when probability (p) is less than .05. No significant difference is indicated by n.s. (not significant)

TABLE 5: SELF-RATING IN GENDER-IMBALANCED CLASSES

Category	% Male	% Female	Significance*
Feels comfortable all of the time	40.8	30 7	p<.05
Never talks less	42.6	29.2	p<.05
Never feels ignored	62.4	56.0	n.s.
Never has to work harder for good grades	66.2	58.8	n.s.

TABLE 6: RATINGS OF TEACHERS' BEHAVIOR IN THE CLASSROOM

Rating	Sex of Teacher	% Male	% Female	Significance*
Intimidating	male	42.3	39.5	n.s.
	female	5.1	7.8	n.s.
Helpful	male	15.7	23.6	p<.05
	female	20.0	11.1	p<.05
Challenging	male	38.3	32.3	n.s.
	female	3.2	4.7	n.s.
Expect too much	male	29.8	19.7	p<.05
	female	14.1	17.2	p<.05
Show favoritism to girls	male	30.3	40.0	p<.05
	female	18.9	4.5	p<.05
Call on boys more	male	12.8	20.0	p<.05
	female	8.0	15.5	p<.05
Use sex stereotypes in class	male	31.7	40.1	p<.05
	female	9.9	3.6	p<.05

* Difference between groups are statistically significant when probability (p) is less than .05. No significant difference is indicated by n.s.

TABLE 7: SEX DIFFERENCES IN ACADEMIC SUBJECTS

Category	% Male	% Female	Significance*
Strongest Subjects:			
Math & Science	44.1	30.1	p<.05
English & Languages	34.9	53.7	p<.05
Weakest Subjects:			
Math & Science	36.3	49.3	p<.05
English & Languages	37.6	24.5	p<.05

TABLE 8: SEX DIFFERENCES IN STUDENTS' GOALS AND OBJECTIVES

Category	% Male	% Female	Significance*
Educational Objectives:			
B.A. or Master's Degree	25.9	36.9	p<.05
Ph.D. or Professional Degree	66.7	54.1	p<.05
Goals in Life:			
Marriage (very important)	63.1	54.0	p<.05
Self-realization	70.8	79.4	p<.05
Career	82.0	88.3	p<.05
Children	54.4	52.1	n.s.

* Differences are statistically significant when probability (p) is less than .05. No significant difference between groups is indicated by n.s.

TABLE 9: STUDENTS' FEELINGS OF PERSONAL SUCCESS AT P.A.

Category	Rating	% Male	% Female	Significance*
Friendships	successful	76.7	85.9	p<.05
Athletics	successful	49.1	36.9	p<.05
Grades	successful	53.0	47.4	n.s.
Leadership	successful	42.8	31.9	p<.05
Getting into the right college	successful	41.6	33.6	p<.05

TABLE 10: STUDENTS' SELF-CONCEPT RATINGS

Category	Rating	% Male	% Female	Significance*
Appearance	positive	66.0	59.9	p<.05
Intelligence	positive	85.9	73.3	p<.05
Confidence	positive	69.3	60.3	p<.05
Popularity	positive	53.4	48.4	p<.05
Health	positive	75.5	67.0	p<.05
Overall Self-Concept:				
	high	37.1	24.8	p<.05
	low	29.5	37.3	p<.05
	average	33.3	37.9	p<.05

* Differences between groups are statistically significant when probability (p) is less than .05. No significant difference is indicated by n.s.

TABLE 11: PERSONALITY TRAIT INVENTORY BY MALES AND FEMALES

Category	% Male	% Female	Significance*
Type I	37.8	27.9	p<.05
Mixed Type	34.0	33.5	p<.05
Type II	28.3	38.5	p<.05

TABLE 12: PERSONALITY TRAIT TYPE BY SELF-CONCEPT BY SEX

	Females* (p<.05) Self-Concept		
	High	Average	Low
Type I	43.3	37.1	19.6
Mixed Type	19.5	37.3	43.2
Type II	15.6	40.0	44.4

	Males* (n.s.) Self-Concept		
	High	Average	Low
Type I	41.5	35.8	22.7
Mixed Type	34.2	34.8	31.0
Type II	33.6	30.5	35.9

* Differences between are statistically significant when probability (p) is less than .05. No significant difference is indicated by n.s.

TABLE 13. SELF-CONCEPT BY EDUCATIONAL OBJECTIVES (ALL STUDENTS)

Self-Concept	Educational Objective			
	No B.A.	B.A.	Master's	Ph.D. or Professional
Low	5.8	16.2	18.9	59.1
Average	7.9	14.9	19.0	58.1
High	6.3	11.3	12.1	70.4

*p<.05

TABLE 14: GIRLS' EDUCATIONAL OBJECTIVE BY MATH & SCIENCE

Math & Science	Educational Objective			
	No B.A.	B.A.	Master's	Ph.D. or Professional
Weakest Subjects	8.8	21.1	15.8	54.8
Strongest Subject	5.5	11.0	15.8	67.8

*p<.05

* Differences between are statistically significant when probability (p) is less than .05. No significant difference is indicated by n.s.

TABLE 15: MULTIPLE REGRESSION ANALYSIS WITH SELF-CONCEPT AS DEPENDENT VARIABLE (STEP-WISE METHOD)[1]

VARIABLE	EQUATION #1	EQUATION #2
Type I Personality	.47*	.32*
	(15.00)	(8.09)
Type II Personality	.15	n.s.
	(4.90)	
Sex of Student	.13	.16*
	(4.07)	(4.25)
Success with Friendships	—	.24*
		(5.89)
Success with Athletics	—	.20*
		(4.99)
Success with Service to Others	—	.14*
		(3.68)
Success with Teachers	—	.12*
		(3.08)
Success with Personal Growth	—	.09**
		(2.13)
Strong in Math & Science	n.s.	n.s.
Weak in Math & Science	n.s.	n.s.
Educational Objective	n.s.	n.s.
Success with Grades	—	n.s.
Success with Knowledge	—	n.s.
Success with Leadership	—	n.s.
Success with Creativity	—	n.s.
Success with Parents	—	n.s.
Success with Independence	—	n.s.
Success Getting into Right College	—	n.s.
	EQUATION #16	EQUATION #2
Adjusted R^2	0.26	0.45
F Ratio	88.64 (3,752)	48.71 (7,396)
Standard Error	2.91	2.45

[1] Standardized Beta weights are reported first for each variable; T scores are reported in parentheses
   * Significant at $p < 01$
  ** Significant at $p < 05$
n.s. Not significant
 — Not in the equation

STUDIES OF OFFICE OF ACADEMY RESOURCES, COLLEGE COUNSELING AND PERSONNEL
by Marion Finbury

OFFICE OF ACADEMY RESOURCES

The figures and reports sent to the Coeducation Committee in response to questions presented to the Office of Academy Resources show that although the alumni structure is predominantly male, the participation of women, both Abbot graduates and Andover graduates, is keenly felt and growing.

The current Alumni Council is made up of 84 members, 57 of whom are male (68% male), and 27 are female. The ratio on the Executive Committee is somewhat more balanced with 13 men (59% male) and 9 women. In the last ten years there have been 2 women presidents of Alumni Council (one is current) who, by virtue of their positions, also serve on the Board of Trustees along with Alumni Trustees, 5 of whom have been women.

The addition of Alumni Trustees on the Board of Trustees helps in some measure to increase the female presence on the Board. At the time of the merger, some Abbot Trustees, both men and women, were included on the Board. Since that transition time two women have been made Charter Trustees. Since there are twelve Charter Trustees only two of whom are women, the Alumni Trustees who have had varying terms (currently four years) do help the imbalance. Currently of the six Alumni Trustees, 3 are men and 3 are women. That brings the total number of male Trustees to 14 and female to 5 and creates a Board that is 74% male (including the headmaster).

It is policy for charter trustees to choose their own replacement and since the inception of the co-ed school although 7 male charter trustees have retired, the number of female charter trustees on the Board has not changed.

Perhaps the greatest percentage of participation is evident both in the Class Agents and the percentage of giving from the co-ed classes since 1974. From the very outset in the class of 1974, the percentage of females in the class who were donors was the same as the males and by 1977 that percentage increased and outstripped male participation. Although a female alumna's average gift tends to be lower than her male counterpart, it could well be a reflection of income in the marketplace and certainly not a measure of loyalty.

A marked increase in the participation of female class agents is also a strong trend. In the ten years since the first class that graduated in 1974 from the co-ed Andover, there have been 76 male class agents and 57 female class agents.

Of the 44 agents that served the first five graduation classes (74–78) only 13 were female. The other 44 served in the last five years which is about the same number as males who served in that period.

ANNUAL GIVING PATTERNS BY ALUMNAE AND ALUMNI

	Sex	Base	Donors	Total Gift ($)	Average Gift ($)	% of Participation
1974	Male	331	120	7824.90	65.21	36.2
	Female	112	41	1923.98	46.92	36.6
1977	Male	270	109	4766.91	43.73	40
	Female	121	57	2239.47	39.29	47
1980	Male	273	94	2672.36	28.43	34
	Female	151	58	1123.50	19.37	38

These figures represent giving for the aforementioned co-ed classes. These figures are not for *one* year, but the class giving over the period July '79 through June '83 clearly shows the percentage of participation of females is vigorous and slightly better than males but the amounts given are smaller.

COLLEGE COUNSELING

From the outset of the "new" coed school the College Counseling Office had a female presence in the top administrative post. For the first years Co-Chairmen were established: Marion Finbury, who had been the Director at Abbot Academy shared the responsibilities with Robert L. Crawford, who had been an assistant to the previous director at the all male school. After that period Mrs. Finbury was named Chairman, a position she held for 4 years until she resigned. Since then the chair has been held by Mr. Crawford.

The first decision made was to allow students to choose their own counselors. Initially, an overwhelmingly large percentage of girls chose the female counselor as well as a few boys who felt the male Andover approach had not met their needs. Mrs. Finbury had come to the combined school with a group of Abbot seniors with whom she had worked as eleventh graders, but as the years progressed the students chose counselors for their "style" rather than their sex.

As the size of the class and the scope of the counseling programs has grown so has the number of counselors, and since 1981 there have been at least two (sometimes three) female counselors and two male counselors.

Class of 1985 breakdown of students and counselors by sex shows that of a total of 393 students who used the College Counseling Office, 57% were boys. Of these students they divided themselves overall in a fairly balanced way with 51% of the girls using female counselors and 52% of the boys using male counselors. There is no indication that the sex of the counselor is paramount in the student's choice.

In order to study the application and admissions statistics from the Classes of 1978, 1980, 1983 and 1985 the College Counseling office chose Brown University, Cornell University, Dartmouth College, Harvard University, the University of Pennsylvania, Princeton University and Yale University. These members of the Ivy League were chosen only because such a large number of Andover students apply to them. It should also be noted that Columbia and Barnard were not used since they were each single sex colleges until Columbia became coed in September, 1983.

The numbers of applications to these colleges reveal that while 72 to 76% of the senior class over these years applied to at least one of these extremely selective institutions, a higher percentage of boys (77–80%) than girls (64–70%) did so.

We can only speculate about the reasons for this pattern and raise more questions:

1. Are boys more ambitious or optimistic?
2. Are girls suffering from comparative lack of self-esteem or are they merely more realistic? (Does the fact that their Board scores are lower discourage them?)
3. Or does it suggest that girls are more amenable to counseling than boys in a climate that has too many students applying to these schools at the outset?
4. Are parental pressures greater on males than on females?

Our study also indicates that a higher percentage of the female than the male applicant pool is admitted to these colleges. There are, of course, exceptions each year at one college or another, but they are never prevalent enough to be considered a trend. There is also a definite trend of girls admitted who have slightly higher averages and lower test scores than their male counterparts.

PERSONNEL

Staff personnel patterns at Phillips Academy are consistent with those we see in the market place. In the school year '83–84 of the 103 office employees only five were male: one was a manager, one was a clerical worker and three were technicians. Most of the offices were run by male administrators overseeing a predominately female staff. The one exception was the library where both the top administrator and staff are female. Among the larger offices that employ five or more staff are the Office of Academy Resources, Admissions, Isham Infirmary, Summer Session and the Treasurer's Office. Until 1984 all of these offices had top male administrators. With the appointment of Phyllis Powell as Dean of the Summer Session, Dr. Joanne Borland as School Physician at Isham and Jeanne Dissette as Dean of Admissions, more gender balance is emerging.

Not surprisingly, the Office of Physical Plant is just the opposite. Of the 100 employees only 12 are female. Of the 12, half are employed in the athletic complex mainly to service girls and the girls locker room—the others do custodial work. This disproportion reflects the small number of women seeking such employment.

Perhaps the most interesting phenomenon is in the Commons. All managers, cooks and bakers are male. Of the twenty dishwashers, only two are female, but all the pantry help who actually do the serving are female. Of course, the physical lifting requirements of the work back in the kitchen may explain why more males hold these jobs.

There is no question that the administration in personnel is very aware of the male/female role stereotyping but is dependent on the applicant pool. They have acted where there has been an opportunity, and small inroads have been made such as the hiring of a male clerical worker and female groundspersons.

SUPPLEMENTARY INFORMATION

ADMISSIONS STATISTICS

	1973	1978	1979	1980	1981	1982	1983	1984
Total Applicants	1653	2545	3285	2853	3165	3167	2999	3106
Girls	509	922	1252	1120	1197	1282	1202	1225
Boys	1144	1623	2033	1733	1968	1885	1797	1881
% girls	30.79%	36.23%	38.11%	39.26%	37.82%	40.48%	40.08%	39.44%
Final Applicants	1195	1884	2747	1999	2228	2208	2181	2207
Girls	397	706	1041	801	861	916	890	883
Boys	798	1178	1706	1198	1367	1292	1291	1324
% girls	33.22%	37.47%	37.90%	40.07%	38.64%	41.49%	40.81%	40.01%
Students Admitted	525	600	643	635	629	638	626	626
Girls	182	216	234	229	246	247	291	247
Boys	343	384	409	406	383	391	335	379
% girls	34.67%	36.00%	36.39%	36.06%	39.11%	38.71%	46.49%	39.46%
Students Matric-ulating	395	441	483	464	474	455	431	469
Girls	144	171	182	174	191	180	197	189
Boys	251	270	301	290	283	275	234	280
% girls	36.46%	38.78%	37.68%	37.50%	40.30%	39.56%	45.71%	40.30%
Students Admitted/ Final Applicants								
Girls	45.84%	30.59%	22.48%	28.59%	28.57%	26.97%	32.70%	27.97%
Boys	42.98%	32.60%	23.97%	33.89%	28.02%	30.26%	25.95%	28.63%

Fall Enrollment						
Girls	457	464	471	492	502	509
Boys	735	737	737	724	707	704
% girls	38.34%	38.63%	38.99%	40.46%	41.52%	41.96%
Boarding						
Girls	366	361	362	373	386	388
Boys	602	607	594	582	570	565
% girls	37.81%	37.29%	37.87%	39.06%	40.38%	40.71%
Day						
Girls	91	103	109	119	116	121
Boys	133	130	143	142	137	139
% girls	40.63%	44.21%	43.25%	45.59%	45.85%	46.54%

Advanced Placement (A.P.)
Exam "SUCCESS" for Classes
of 1978, 1980, 1983

$$\text{Success} = \frac{\text{number of grades of 4 or 5}}{\text{number of exams taken}} = \_\%$$

| | 1978 | | 1980 | | 1983 | |
	male	female	male	female	male	female
English	60%	75%	60%	70%	61%	83%
Math	64%	50%	64%	34%	62%	38%
History	71%	58%	65%	73%	84%	67%
Foreign Languages	81%	87%	54%	80%	64%	73%
Science	84%	90%	81%	56%	80%	78%
Arts	90%	100%	100%	83%	0%	50%
Totals	73%	72%	68%	63%	71%	60%

Number of Advanced Placement (A.P.) Exams
Taken by Classes of 1978, 1980, 1983

| | 1978 | | 1980 | | 1983 | |
	male	female	male	female	male	female
English	27	16	30	23	31	24
Math	75	16	76	35	106	64
History	59	12	52	22	64	36
Foreign Languages	26	23	26	41	28	40
Sciences	77	10	67	18	64	9
Arts	10	4	3	6	2	2
Total	274	81	254	145	295	175
Number of different students taking A.P. exams	121	47	126	71	126	88

"SENIOR HONORS" Awarded at Commencement by Subject Area

Class of

	1978		1980		1983		1985	
	males	females	males	females	males	females	males	females
Arts	9	7	11	6	14	6	12	11
English	7	6	9	5	6	6	2	5
Foreign Languages	16	8	13	17	20	10	20	16
History	7	2	6	3	0	1	3	1
Mathematics	4	0	13	4	25	6	14	10
Sciences	35	7	37	4	15	4	22	12
Religion-Philosophy	0	0	3	4	0	2	5	3
Total Hours	78	30	92	43	80	35	78	58
% of class that is male	64%		64%		57%		56%	
% of "Senior Honors" awarded to Males	70%		68%		70%		57%	

TEACHING AT PHILLIPS ACADEMY
A faculty recruiting flier issued by the Dean of Faculty

It is important for all applicants for a teaching position at Andover to understand that such a position involves more than just classroom teaching. With our very demanding college-preparatory curriculum, which encompasses most of the normal liberal arts disciplines, we are looking for faculty with strong academic backgrounds and teaching experience, but these faculty members must also be prepared to cope with the varying demands that go with a residential secondary school. Because almost 1,000 of our total student population of 1,200 are boarding students, we must ask our faculty to be prepared to reside in and act as house counselors in our dormitories; and because we have a required athletic program, we ask our faculty to be prepared to coach in the program for two terms during the school year.

As a result, the "normal" work load at Andover involves teaching four courses (most of which meet for four 50-minute periods each week), coaching (or supervising an afternoon activity), and supervising a dormitory of anywhere from 6 to 20 students. In addition, the faculty member at Andover is expected to help out with a variety of administrative duties: chaperoning at social functions, dining hall supervision, committee meetings, chauffeuring occasional off-campus trips, etc. At the end of terms, reports must be written on students in the classroom and in the dormitory.

In short, teaching at Phillips Academy is a full-time commitment. While school is in session, it can encompass a good part of every day, and a complete day off is very rare indeed. Faculty are encouraged to be away for at least one weekend per term, but sometimes even this is not feasible. In addition, there is the lack of privacy which necessarily comes from the residential nature of the community.

Because of the very considerable demands on its faculty, Phillips Academy attempts to reward them generously. Starting salaries are at least equal to those of any comparable school, and our median salaries compare roughly with those of associate professors at some of our best small colleges. Andover faculty receive free housing, and may take all meals in the school dining hall at no cost. There are grants for summer study, a generous sabbatical policy, and the chance to send offspring to the Academy at greatly reduced cost.

SELECTED MERGER STUDY FINDINGS
Faculty Attitudes Toward Faculty Roles
(Percentages)
Display IV-15 From Merger Study

	Men	Women	Former Abbot	Old PA	New	All
				Faculty Groups		
1. Concept of multiple faculty roles is beneficial	77	54	45	85	56	69
2. I am expected to take on too many roles	42	32	36	37	50	40
3. I have reasonable choice in my own roles	60	66	64	70	37	62
4. I feel unreasonable pressure to give time to PA	42	47	37	40	58	43
5. I have difficulty in teaching boys and girls together	8	26	21	10	16	14

Faculty Role That I Would First Give Up
Percentages
Display IV-14 From Merger Study

Faculty Groups	Teacher	Adminis-trator	Coach	Extra-Curricu-lar Advisor	House Counselor
Men	6	59	54	60	31
Women	8	44	62	22	36
Abbot 72-73	12	41	62	33	33
PA 72-73	6	58	49	58	29
New	6	59	74	40	42
All faculty	7	55	57	51	33

NOTES

www.ingramcontent.com/pod-product-compliance
Lightning Source LLC
Chambersburg PA
CBHW030434290526
45786CB00001B/288